# RACE AND SECULARISM
# IN AMERICA

Religion, Culture, and Public Life

# RELIGION, CULTURE, AND PUBLIC LIFE

## SERIES EDITOR: KAREN BARKEY

The resurgence of religion calls for careful analysis and constructive criticism of new forms of intolerance, as well as new approaches to tolerance, respect, mutual understanding, and accommodation. In order to promote serious scholarship and informed debate, the Institute for Religion, Culture, and Public Life and Columbia University Press are sponsoring a book series devoted to the investigation of the role of religion in society and culture today. This series includes works by scholars in religious studies, political science, history, cultural anthropology, economics, social psychology, and other allied fields whose work sustains multidisciplinary and comparative as well as transnational analyses of historical and contemporary issues. The series focuses on issues related to questions of difference, identity, and practice within local, national, and international contexts. Special attention is paid to the ways in which religious traditions encourage conflict, violence, and intolerance and also support human rights, ecumenical values, and mutual understanding. By mediating alternative methodologies and different religious, social, and cultural traditions, books published in this series will open channels of communication that facilitate critical analysis.

# RACE AND SECULARISM IN AMERICA

EDITED BY
JONATHON S. KAHN
AND
VINCENT W. LLOYD

Columbia University Press
New York

Columbia University Press
Publishers Since 1893
New York    Chichester, West Sussex
cup.columbia.edu

Library of Congress Cataloging-in-Publication Data
Names: Kahn, Jonathon Samuel, editor.
Title: Race and secularism in America / edited by Jonathon S. Kahn and
    Vincent W. Lloyd.
Description: New York : Columbia University Press, 2016. | Series: Religion,
    culture, and public life | Includes bibliographical references and index.
Identifiers: LCCN 2015022595 | ISBN 9780231174909 (cloth : alk. paper) |
    ISBN 9780231174916 (pbk. : alk. paper) | ISBN 978023154275 (e-book)
Subjects: LCSH: Secularism—United States. | Race.
Classification: LCC BL2760 .R33 2016 | DDC 211/.60973—dc23
LC record available at http://lccn.loc.gov/2015022595

Columbia University Press books are printed on permanent and durable
acid-free paper.

This book is printed on paper with recycled content.
Printed in the United States of America

c 10 9 8 7 6 5 4 3 2 1
p 10 9 8 7 6 5 4 3 2 1

Add cover/jacket credit information

# CONTENTS

# RACE AND SECULARISM
# IN AMERICA

# INTRODUCTION

## MANAGING RACE, MANAGING RELIGION

### Vincent W. Lloyd

T HIRTY FEET high, arms folded, with a steady, piercing gaze, Martin Luther King Jr. now stands on the National Mall in Washington, D.C. Completed in 2011, the King memorial seals the embrace of the once-controversial leader by those across the political spectrum. Barack Obama presided at the memorial's opening, but it was Ronald Reagan who signed into law a bill making Martin Luther King Jr. Day a federal holiday after it passed with bipartisan support in Congress. Ornamenting King's tall figure are fourteen engraved quotations from his sermons, speeches, and writings. Justice, love, and peace are recurring themes. "We shall overcome because the arc of the moral universe is long, but it bends towards justice." "I believe that unarmed truth and unconditional love will have the final word in reality." "True peace is not merely the absence of tension: it is the presence of justice." Amazingly, nowhere among these quotations is there mention of God, sin, Jesus, heaven, or hell. King the Christian preacher is absent. Even more astounding, there is no mention of the plight of the African American community for which King so vehemently fought. The only mention of race is in a quotation suggesting that King advocated forgetting it: "Our loyalties must transcend our race." King's mainstream success, it seems, has come at the cost of his own religious and racial identity. Or, put another way, the careful management of race and religion are the prerequisite for accepting the public significance of a fundamentally raced religious figure. That there is significance to the pairing race and religion, managed together, is the thesis probed in this book.

Martin Luther King Jr. did not speak in secular, race-neutral language. He preached, and he preached from his position as a black American. He preached about the law of God, the damnation of sinners, and divine omnipotence. He preached and spoke from the Bible. In his final speech, delivered on April 3, 1968, in Memphis, Tennessee, King imagines a conversation with God, invokes the classical American form of the jeremiad (troubles today, possibilities tomorrow), cites Amos, describes his miraculous survival from an assassination attempt, prophesies his own death, and concludes, "Mine eyes have seen the glory of the coming of the Lord!" King speaks in the first-person plural about black Americans: "We mean business now, and we are determined to gain our rightful place in God's world. . . . We are saying that we are God's children." In short, from his days as a young preacher coming up in the Baptist church where his father ministered to his last days supporting a public-sector union, King's critical voice was not just a moral voice. It was a theological voice, a black theological voice. This is the voice muted and managed by the secular and postracial regime of America in 2011.

Unveiling the King monument, the first black president also carefully managed his deployment of the language of religion and race. Obama hailed the "slow but certain progress" brought about by King.[1] Because of this progress, "people of all colors and creeds live together, and work together, and fight alongside one another, and learn together, and build together, and love one another." The listener would hardly know that King was particularly concerned about black people or that King was black. Further, race and religion are conjoined, "colors and creeds," in the harmony that is to be America. Of all the activities we people of different races and religions do together, the ultimate is loving—a wonderfully clear marker of the normative Christianity that remains even after any deeper or broader religious vocabulary has been dissolved. The management of race and religion is not administered from some neutral ground. It continues the very specific religious, and racial, heritage of the United States. Indeed, Obama provides his own reconstruction of King's political theology: "It was . . . that belief that God resides in each of us, from the high to the low, in the oppressor and the oppressed, that convinced him that people and systems could change." According to Obama, King's was not a biblical faith or a faith rooted in tradition but a simple humanism, a belief in the inherent worth and dignity of every human being—a secular faith, or a secularist faith, a faith suitable to our secular age. When Obama mentions, once, King's advocacy for African Americans (a race strangely distanced from King, not to mention from Obama, in the speech), it is a story with the moral of perseverance in the face of disappointment and hardship. King moved from a fight for "civil and political equality" to a fight for "economic justice," Obama states, because the former was not achieving enough results for African Americans. Obama adds that, today, he himself is carrying on this fight, enumerating a number of his policy priorities: "world-class education," "health care . . . affordable and accessible to all," and an economy "in which everybody gets a fair shake." In other words, the age of race-based advocacy is over, and even King knew that.

Twenty-eight years before Obama's speech, fifteen years after King's final speech, Ronald Reagan's remarks at the signing ceremony for the Martin Luther King Jr. Day legislation present a quite different articulation of the racial, the religious, the universal, and the American. Reagan focuses on King the black man, and he describes a past (made to sound oddly distant) in which blacks "were separate and unequal," attending segregated schools, taking bad jobs with low wages, and required to use separate facilities.[2] King was committed to nonviolence, Reagan reports, because he believed "that unearned suffering is redemptive." Reagan concludes, "Each year on Martin Luther King Day, let us not only recall Dr. King, but rededicate ourselves to the Commandments he believed in and sought to live every day: Thou shall love thy God with all thy heart, and thou shall love thy neighbor as thyself." In contrast to Obama, whose King was postracial and postreligious, Reagan's King was a black man who believed that the Ten Commandments were the heart of Christian (or American?) faith. For Reagan, people were indeed born with a race, but racial injustice was a thing of the past. And for Reagan, American unity was brought about by a shared Christian moral vision—ultimately a white Christian moral vision—that allowed for national crises to be resolved peacefully. In short, religion was managed by being nationalized while race was managed by being naturalized.

These are but a few recent examples of race and secularism in America. Why race and secularism and not race and religion? Because we are interested in the processes by which race and religion are excluded or managed. We are interested in how these processes are intertwined. And we are interested in how power infects and inflects these processes. In other words, we do not take race and religion to be simply facts about a person, aspects of identity that correspond to boxes on demographic forms. Such a view, we contend, is the product of a specific historical moment, and such a view maintains the power of specific forces. It is a view at home in our world of organized differences, of individuals reduced to arrays of categories for microtargeted marketing not only of products but of politics. It is a view suited to our culture of cultural diversity managed by specialists and administered by state institutions, private companies, and television hosts. It is also a view of religion and race too often projected backward in our historical scholarship. In contrast, we seek to uncover racial and religious formations that are rendered illegible under the current regime and to demonstrate their political potency.

Scholarship on religion and scholarship on race have been moving in the same direction, from different positions. Scholarship on race has turned away from adjudicating the biological or socially constructed nature of race and instead has turned toward an examination of racialization, that is, the sets of ideas, institutions, practices, and technologies that establish and maintain a racial regime—and toward an examination of how that regime has been inhabited or resisted. In the United States, this means that race is not just about black people. It is about the styles of thinking and acting and the legal, political, and social systems that construct a racial line between black and white. This approach further invites reflection on whether those or related mechanisms are in play when other groups are seemingly racialized: Native Americans, immigrants, or Muslims. And it invites reflection on the purportedly postracial that may in fact serve to maintain subterranean racial regimes. Similarly, recent interest in religion has turned from documenting religious beliefs, communities, or practices to exploring the ways that the very possibilities for what religion can be are historically contingent. Secularism names the regime that determines what does and does not count as appropriate religion for a particular sphere—for example, the sort of religious language that can be used by a national politician or the sort of miracles that can be witnessed by a Lutheran pastor in Minnesota. Secularism evokes a religious domain that is managed by power and that is circumscribed by nonreligious forces. The analogy for race: racial-minority communities are managed by power and circumscribed by nonminority, that is, white, forces.

We hypothesize that race and secularism are entwined. Put more starkly, whiteness is secular, and the secular is white. The unmarked racial category and the unmarked religious category jointly mark their others. Or, put another way, the desire to stand outside religion and the desire to stand outside race are complementary delusions, for the seemingly outside is in fact the hegemonic. The chapters that follow test these waters in a number of different places and times, and their authors understand our hypothesis in a variety of ways. They explore various religious and racial regimes, from slavery and segregation to prisons, from African immigrants to black Muslims, from elite postsecular postblackness to black religious quietism. And they explore America from inside and out: from the central mythologies of race and race overcome to the transnational exchanges of racial-religious regimes between the United States and Africa and between the United States and the rest of the Americas. Before embarking, let us first say more about how the study of race and secularism together can productively advance conversations both in the study of religion and race and in American studies. Then, we will map out some historical signposts where race and secularism are coarticulated in U.S. history, recounting the trunk of paradoxes that the chapters to follow will further complicate.

Why has this book not been written before? Why has whiteness characterized not only the secular but also, all too often, critiques of the secular? The seminal works animating conversations about secularism take their starting point from European intellectual history or from complicating that history.[3] Perhaps this is because secularism is approached through secularization, the historical process through which religion recedes from public and, eventually, private presence. Social theories of secularization see it as a process that accompanies modernization: the rise of science and the compartmentalization of social functions reduce the role for religion. This is told as a European story that, at most, echoes in the periphery. But this is not a story about secularism: it does not track the technologies through which religion is managed because management, with its implied agency, is not a part of the story of secularization. A focus on secularism does not imagine a fall from a premodern unified social world to differentiated modernity (a theological narrative itself!).

Rather, it takes the autonomy of the religious to be always contested. While such a contest may spill from center to periphery, from metropole to colony, or vice versa, that is just one of many stories that can be told about it. The contest over the autonomy or management of the religious may also be connected with other technologies of governmentality, such as the management of race.[4]

Scholarship on secularism sometimes accompanies another story about the history of European ideas. With the rise of Protestantism, and with the Wars of Religion, religion comes to be seen as fractious.[5] To avoid violent conflict, secular reasoning is substituted for theological reasoning in conflict-prone arenas, such as international law and public morality. This is told as a European story because of the specifically European Christian history at its core. But secularism as a response to religious strife or, better, as a response to strife attributed to religion has no necessary connection with one place and time. It was on the minds of the American founding fathers as they drafted the Bill of Rights, it was on the minds of the members of the Council of Historians when deciding on the text to be inscribed on the Martin Luther King Jr. memorial, and it was on the minds of Supreme Court justices ruling on sodomy laws. There is no need to take European intellectual history as paradigmatic.

Yet there are more significant problems with the discourse on secularism that has recently flourished in the academy. This discourse often is one of intellectual (or, occasionally, literary) history, and it is at odds with broader currents in religious studies scholarship that privilege religious practice and embodiment. With this in mind, we assert that secularism should be addressed not just as the management of discourse but also as the management of practices and bodies, not just as an elite exercise of power but also as the management of lives of ordinary people. Taking such an approach provides yet another reason to decenter Europe from the secularism conversation, for it discounts the privilege of the supposed intellectual centers. Furthermore, shifting the focus of secularism studies to practice and embodiment makes space for accounts of agency. It is not just that religious ideas are excluded; it is that the way religion is lived is managed by the forces of secularism—and that lived experience often mismatches secularist ideals. In this mismatch are the complex lives and wills of individuals and communities embracing and contesting the construction and management of their religion. Such an approach has been adopted in the study of racialization for at least two decades now, exploring practice, embodiment, and what might collectively be labeled the weapons of the weak; the chapters that follow expand this approach to secularism and to the secularist-racializing knot.

That knot is crucially important and points to an element of secularism drastically understudied. Secularism as an intellectual-historical phenomenon conceals the way secularism and race together manage bodies and lives. The academy and its funders support such a separation. During the Civil Rights Movement the Ford Foundation funded the apparatus of racial liberalism, containing the radical energies of protesters through the prospect of grant money if only they would work within the system, if only they would not demand too much—if only they would accept the meaning of race as given.[6] Today the Ford Foundation funds the Social Science Research Council's Religion and the Public Sphere initiative, curating discussion often explicitly about secularism for an audience of academics and a broader public. With essays commissioned by academic scholars of religion several times a month for its blog, *The Immanent Frame*, this project has magnified the visibility of discussions of religion and secularism across the humanities. Strikingly, these essays feature virtually no discussion of race. We ask whether studying the management or exclusion of religion without also studying the management or exclusion of race captures a symptom and conceals a disease. We ask whether it is ever possible to talk about secularism without talking about whiteness.

America is a prime site to study secularism in practice and to study the intersection of secularism and racialization. As imagined, or fantasized, America is a place of religious and racial diversity, a place where the freedom to be who you want to be has allowed for varied religious and racial communities to call for and achieve recognition of their distinctiveness. Together with the rhetoric of freedom is the reality of management, the subtle technologies of control that create the horizons of possibility for both religious and racialized lives. America presents these technologies both bluntly—in the cases of slavery, segregation, and mass incarceration and in the cases of blasphemy laws and Muslim persecution—and more subtly, in less infamous though no less unjust ways. The racialization of Native Americans, "ethnic" European immigrants, Latinos, and Asians all present variations on the central black-white racial binary. The response to and constitution of such groups as Mormons,

Jehovah's Witnesses, Scientologists, and the Nation of Islam all present fruit-ful sites for investigating secularist inflections always already racialized. The essays that follow begin with the ever-present, ever-powerful black-white bi-nary but also consider less familiar racial and religious sites.

American studies, as a discipline, has pioneered the careful, subtle analysis of the varieties of racialization in the United States and has paid particular attention to the way that racialization enables flows of capital. Furthermore, the last two decades have seen American studies scholarship turn toward the transnational, concerning itself with flows of people, ideas, and capital between America and other parts of the world.[7] American racialization does not happen in isolation but as part of a global network, tracking capital flows that pass easily across national boundaries. Yet American studies scholarship has had relatively little to say about the management of religion or the rela-tionship between secularism and racialization. In tracking the late-capitalist commodification of identity, American studies scholars carefully probe racial, ethnic, gender, and sexual identities but often overlook religious identities. The chapters that follow serve as an antidote, adding religion to the mix.

Race and secularism show up together from the beginning of the Ameri-can story. While the Constitution is a fundamentally secular document, never mentioning God or religion, the Declaration of Independence binds the claim of American autonomy to "the Laws of Nature and of Nature's God" and proclaims "a firm reliance on the protection of divine Providence." In this religiously committed declaration there is no talk of race. Famously and con-foundingly, "all men are created equal." It is in the secular Constitution that the U.S. racial regime is first legally formalized, with Indians and two-fifths of slaves ("other Persons") not counted for the purposes of legislative representa-tion. In this founding moment, so often remembered and mythologized, the racial regime is codified while religion is excluded, and the religious regime is codified while race is excluded. This is not to claim causation, just to note the first in a series of possible entanglements.

Historians have shown that the secularism evinced in the First Amend-ment's religion clauses—"Congress shall make no law respecting an estab-lishment of religion, or prohibiting the free exercise thereof"—was the man-agement of religion by Protestants, for Protestants. For more than a century, the religion clauses applied only to the federal government, not to the states.

Oaths were still sworn on the Bible, blasphemy was criminalized, and many states financially supported churches. Christianity, especially Protestantism, was thought to be important for cultivating civic virtue. In other words, the government was not giving freedom to religion but managing religion by cultivating good religion, that is, religion advantageous to the government. This management of religion by state governments was curtailed by the expansion of federal authority resulting from the Civil War. For example, the Fourteenth Amendment, ratified in 1868, laid the groundwork for the application of the First Amendment's religion clauses to states. This extension of constitutional religious protections to the states was not complete until the middle of the twentieth century—the same time that the Supreme Court began applying the equal protection clause of the Fourteenth Amendment to the legal apparatus that supported segregation, ruling it unconstitutional.[8] A new, ostensibly more just way of managing race was tied to a dramatic shift in the way religion was managed. In short, there are evocative points of intersection between the American disciplining of religion and the American disciplining of race.

Christian-fueled social movements had a complicated relationship with the management of race. While upstate New York was a hotbed both of the Second Great Awakening and the abolitionist movement, the latter only occasionally took on the form or content of religious revival, and it would be an overreach to tell a causal story. But both, we might suggest, are examples of reactions to attempts at managing religion and race, or excluding religion and race, from public life in the mid-nineteenth-century North. They are reactions to secularism and racialization. The same could be said of the Civil Rights Movement a century later.[9] The Cold War consensus had tamed religion, in the democratic faith of a John Dewey and the politically palatable Protestantism of Reinhold Niebuhr, and seemingly tamed racial discord, through the inclusion of African Americans in the military and in wartime industry. But the revivalist mass meetings of the Montgomery Improvement Association and its progeny exposed the nation to novel religious and racial expression and demanded response. Social movements that challenged the secularist, white consensus not only demanded specific rights or religious allegiances but also challenged something more fundamental about the American political project: its envelope for managing difference.

While secularism is often thought of as clearing space for the absence of religion and thereby controlling religion externally, as it were, secularism also affects religion internally, setting the terms in which religion can be spoken and heard. This aspect of secularism, too, can be read together with the dynamics of racialization in the United States. Waves of Catholic immigrants from Ireland and, more recently, Latin America were denied whiteness just as they were denied participation in the secular (that is, Protestant) American consensus. The Catholic Church in the United States responded in a variety of ways, from theology (for example, John Courtney Murray's qualified defense of American religious and racial freedoms) to architecture (for example, the construction of the National Shrine in Washington, D.C., with its ethnic chapels).[10] Black religion, too, exceeded the bounds of acceptability set by white Protestantism and was alternately denigrated and praised for its emotional excesses or authentic spirituality—both highlighting its status outside the norm.[11] Black congregations interested in flaunting their higher class status rejected "uncontrolled" styles of worship, creating religious communities more closely modeled on the respectability of white Protestants.

The possible nexuses of race and secularism vary regionally and with the movements of people. To take one example: the Great Migration of African Americans to urban centers of the North in the first half of the twentieth century disrupted the relatively stable religious landscape of the rural South and opened the door for religious diversity and innovation. In other words, when we reconsider classic secularization narratives—urbanization and industrialization leading to a decline in religiosity and differentiation of social spheres—from the perspective of racialized communities in America, those narratives are intriguingly inflected. African American religious communities in the North provided resources to welcome newcomers from the South, to orient them to their new homes—and to recruit them to new religious communities. From storefront churches to congregations composed largely of West Indian immigrants, to the followers of Daddy Grace, to the early black Muslims and black Israelites, rather than secularizing African American life, the encounter with modernity seems to have broken the secular management of the religious that led white elites to tolerate sleepy Southern churches.[12]

If there ever was a qualitative change in American secularism, it happened in the 1960s and 1970s, contemporaneous with the qualitative change in American race relations. Earlier, secularism primarily entailed the management of religion: the embrace of the liberal Protestant consensus of elites and the marginalization of other religious communities. Starting during those two decades, the discourse and practice of secularism began to shift from management to exclusion. Religious beliefs were excluded from the public sphere, for example, in academic political theory via John Rawls's 1971 *A Theory of Justice*, in public activism by Madelyn Murray O'Hair's American Atheists, and in the muted, hollow religiosity of Richard Nixon (a Quaker). At long last, the Warren and Burger Courts made real the previously nominal wall of separation between church and state, and this notion of a wall extended from church and state to church and society. Christianity itself was transforming: evangelicalism moved from the margins to mainstream, accompanied by a focus on individual relationships with Jesus Christ rather than communal religious experience or social concerns.

Contemporaneously, American racial liberalism was forced to transform as well. The Protestant ethos of the Southern Christian Leadership Conference met competition from the more youthful, more militant, more secular Student Nonviolent Coordinating Committee. As the 1960s advanced, with progress on race issues in the South slow and in the North even slower, black power came to replace colorblind love as the rhetoric of choice among activists. Even though the Black Panthers' social service programs often took place in churches, black nationalists were increasingly suspicious of the power of religious communities to address racial injustice. This suspicion culminated in James Forman's interruption of the Sunday service at Riverside Church in New York City, reading a demand for $500,000,000 in reparations from white churches and synagogues, to be administered by secular black organizations. While these demands were largely rejected, they led to some unexpected alliances, such as the Episcopal Church's funding of the Malcolm X Liberation University in North Carolina (much to the consternation of many lay Episcopalians in North Carolina).[13]

Dovetailing the rise of the black power movement was the development of black theology. Following the organization of a network of black church leaders that supported black power with advertisements in the *New York Times*, James Cone's *Black Theology and Black Power* (1969) and *A Black Theology of Liberation* (1970) proclaimed that African American religious thought affirmed blackness as godliness and affirmed the struggle for black liberation as redemptive—a struggle that was not necessarily nonviolent. Further, Cone proclaimed white churches to be pseudoreligious, to be dispensing a religious message that had no relationship to the gospel of Jesus Christ—a message that thus was essentially secular or, as the secular is sometimes described in theological terms, satanic. What white churches proclaimed as theological was actually the interests of white Americans dressed in religious language. In other words, Cone inverts the common perception of black power: he held that secularism infected everything except the black power movement.

With the end of de jure segregation, combating racial injustice no longer primarily meant opposing unjust laws. Racial liberalism began to mean diversity and inclusivity in universities and corporations and in electoral politics. As the 1970s progressed, the Civil Rights Movement spawned movements for women's liberation (the magazine *Ms.* was founded in 1971), gay liberation (marked by the Stonewall riots, 1969), the American Indian Movement (marked by the 1969 occupation of Alcatraz), and others. Elites had once responded to protest by offering benefits to African Americans. Now the elite response was an embrace of cultural diversity, affirming the value of difference in all its (legible) forms. Jodi Melamed has labeled this phase of American racial management "neoliberal multiculturalism"—neoliberal because it fits so well with the dominant economic regime of the age. Race, gender, and sexuality become identity groups to which one may or may not belong, like an alumni association or bowling league. To this mix we may add religion, reduced to an identity group—another color in the rainbow composing the American nation, another trait of the atomized subject, another niche market for corporate profit.[14]

How have these new techniques of managing religion and race affected religious communities? Mainline liberal Protestantism, overwhelmingly white, continues to decline. Megachurches synthesizing the best, or worst, of white liberal Protestantism, evangelicalism, and African American religion into a hi-tech, postracial goulash have flourished. Such churches represent the careful choreography of religion and race within a sacred space, not just from the outside. At the same time, an antisecularist discourse has flourished among evangelical Christians and Roman Catholics. Richard John Neuhaus, the author of *The Naked Public Square* (1986) and editor of the magazine *First*

*Things*, represented this response. Neuhaus moved from religiously inspired peace and civil rights activism, one form of antisecularist agitation, to a conservative Catholic critique of secularism and multiculturalism, another form of antisecularist agitation. In the 1980s and 1990s, secularism was named explicitly as a problem, one associated with the loss of a moral compass, the loss of traditional values, and, implicitly, the loss of white cultural consensus. Although these antisecularists came in many stripes, they all shared a passion for an imagined America, one in which the "Judeo-Christian" moral fabric went unquestioned. This antisecularism was not limited to whites: Alan Keyes, Clarence Thomas, and T. D. Jakes represent a strand of black moralizing, antisecularist conservatism that, at the same time, is critical of playing "identity politics" with blackness.

As black elites began to be educated in the same classrooms, work for the same organizations, and golf at the same courses as white elites, black political positions came more closely to mirror those of white liberals and white conservatives. The haunting, illegible cries of racial injustice expressed in a theological idiom were muted. The closest analogue to an antisecularist strand in the discourse on race came from the class of black public intellectuals that emerged in the 1990s and 2000s, figures such as Cornel West, Michael Eric Dyson, and, most recently, Melissa Harris-Perry. Each of these figures, perhaps not coincidentally, claims expertise on black religion. Yet because these figures are overdetermined by their media presence, now amplified through social media, this class of black public intellectuals seems less a space from which the multiculturalist consensus is critiqued than an adjunct to that consensus. Moreover, other racialized communities have largely refrained from employing a critique of racialization. Immigrant-rights advocates may employ a language of hospitality and neighborliness, though often divorced from larger religious currents, and Islamophobia has become the banner under which activists decry the persecution of Muslim Americans.

This is the context in which Barack Obama rose to national prominence. Liberals were worried that conservatives had monopolized the use of religious language in American politics, and the "right-wing fundamentalist" support that was seen to propel George W. Bush to the White House needed an antidote. Michael Lerner, with his *Tikkun*, and Jim Wallis, with his *Sojourners*, attempted to provide this liberal religious voice but failed to gain broad traction. What, or rather who, was needed appeared on the stage of the Democratic National Convention in 2004. Barack Obama told his life story, woven around the themes of faith (both in God and in America) and hope (the "politics of hope" compared favorably with the "politics of cynicism"). Obama concluded that "God's greatest gift to us, the bedrock of this nation [is] a belief in things not seen; a belief that there are better days ahead." Liberals had found their own alternative to dogmatic secularism, to a cultural and political wall of separation. They found it in a black man, for racial difference remained the site from which religious difference could speak, seemingly unmanaged.

But religious difference was not really unmanaged in Obama's speech. It is even a stretch to say that there was anything theological about Obama's speech. He did not mention Jesus or talk about sin or commend love of thy neighbor. He did not mention anything specifically Christian. He simply mentioned God, faith, and hope. In other words, even in this seemingly postsecular speech, the theological only appears in a carefully managed form, one entirely legible to a secular audience. In contrast, the power of "right-wing" critiques of secularism and of the Civil Rights Movement critique of secularism was their illegibility from the perspective of the secular, thus implicitly calling into question the legitimacy of a secular framework. Obama's carefully managed remarks on race in his speeches, like his remarks on religion, have drawn much acclaim. Nowhere in his 2004 speech does Obama mention his race or speak of black Americans in the first-person plural. He describes his father as "a foreign student, born and raised in a small village in Kenya." This is part of his narrative of cultural diversity and of America as a nation that embraces many peoples. The only remarks he makes in this speech about African Americans are in lists of the many problems of the many peoples of America. Yet just as Obama's speech was read as deeply religious, it was also read as deeply black. To embrace managed race and managed religion, instead of avoiding both race and religion, is as racial and religious as one is permitted to be in our current secularist, multiculturalist moment.

This background frames how Martin Luther King Jr. is represented today and the context in which the King monument in Washington, D.C., was constructed. Race and religion are carefully controlled; this is precisely the opposite of King's disruptive and transformative appeal to religion and race. The potential that scholarship on race and secularism in America has today is to be disruptive by refusing the naturalness of today's racial and religious formations. Doing so is a threefold task: first, exploring the ways that religion and race are managed at particular places and times; second, exploring how the management of religion and race are entwined; third, exploring the ways that this management is refused. The chapters that follow conduct such exploration both within and beyond the structure of the traditional American historical narrative. As such, the chapters are all critical: they denaturalize the obvious and extol the illegible and so challenge the hold that the powers of the present have on us here, now.

But the chapters that follow do more. The exclusion or management of religion prompts us to remember the potency of what is excluded or managed. Rather than mourn the extent of neoliberal hegemony, as contemporary "critical" scholarship has a habit of doing, remembering the religious—or the theological, as the unmanaged religious is sometimes called—points to traditions of imagining otherwise.[15] Revealing the contingency of the present is not enough. Flagging what is illegible in the terms of the present is not enough. What the recovery of the religious, beyond secularism, offers is a constellation of ideas, practices, and relationships currently illegible but potent and potentially transformative. This lesson gleaned from studying one managed difference can be brought to others. When we turn from religion to race and read it as unmanaged, when we stare blankly at the illegible networks of ideas, practices, and relationships of racialized worlds, we recover something powerful, something potentially transformative. In short, the study of race and secularism does not end with the documentation of managed difference. It begins there and from there strives to unveil worlds apart, worlds of possibility, worlds of justice.

There are three clusters of essays in this volume. The first orients the conversation by reflecting on the nexus of race and secularism through political theory and through the history of religions. George Shulman approaches secularism via the self-conception of the nation-state. Shulman shows how the conception of sovereignty relied on by the nation-state has not only theological roots, as demonstrated by Carl Schmitt and the discourse on political theology, but also racial roots. The state of exception, which Schmitt considers the foundation of sovereignty, is, in the American case, a state of racial terror. Both the theological and racial roots of American sovereignty are often less than visible—potent but repressed. Shulman then identifies a strain of African American thought that resists this racial-religious sovereignty, which he terms the political thought of black insurgency. Josef Sorett examines how, even within black America, racial and religious categories are managed differentially across time, with flows of racial and religious meaning interrupted by incommensurable theoretical frameworks. Moreover, Sorett probes the reflexivity inherent in the study of secularism as theories of secularism change along with the practice of secularism—along with theories of race. Tracking these conceptual movements at the site of African American religious historiography, Sorett pushes theorists of secularism to interrogate their own historical—and racial—presuppositions.

The second cluster of essays examines three case studies in light of the theoretical questions raised by Shulman and Sorett and in light of the scholarly context described in this introduction. These chapters are each readings in the broad sense: close examinations of a text, of media representations, and of religious practice. They demonstrate the critical potential of reading the ostensibly secular with attention to repressed religion and of reading the explicitly religious with attention to how that religion is managed by the secular. They proceed historically, from slavery, to the figure of Martin Luther King Jr., to the contemporary world of Black Muslims in Philadelphia. In telling the story of Henry "Box" Brown, a slave who literally mailed himself to freedom, Edward Blum recovers a historical actor who challenges our assumptions about nineteenth-century secularism. Brown challenges those assumptions, Blum argues, because of his experience as a racialized subject. Offering both historical context and a close reading of Brown's account of his miraculous escape, Blum shows how the heavily policed categories of superstition, religion, and the supernatural are articulated differently, and subversively, by the escaped slave. Erica Edwards tracks the representation of Martin Luther King Jr.'s image in popular culture since his death. Edwards is particularly attentive to the way that media manage identity in our neoliberal era. She tracks how television shows portrayed the unifying and eventually hollow figure of King, demonstrating how media function as contemporary technologies of governance to manage and mute dissent. Dissent in this case names racial and religious difference illegible in our secular, multicultural era. Joel Blecher and Joshua Dubler's chapter examines Salafism's complex relationship with race and secularism in America. In Philadelphia, the location of their case study, Salafism embraces the politics of quietism, discouraging race-based mobilization and direct confrontation with the state. Blecher and Dubler argue that the Philadelphia Salafis subtly but powerfully challenge regnant secularism through their expansive religious-ethical commitments. Moreover, these black Muslims explicitly accuse ostensibly religiously based activists promoting racial justice of buying into the cultural norms of our secular age.

The third and final cluster of chapters inflects the theoretical and historical narratives explored in the previous chapters by approaching the same group of issues from novel perspectives. Cooper Harris posits that invisibility, a key concept (or technology) for American racialization, has a long religious genealogy. Developing this claim in dialogue with Ralph Ellison's *Invisible Man*, the seminal literary exploration of racial invisibility, Harris unveils deep connections between the means through which race and religion are embodied. Tracking Ellison's own varied intellectual resources and expanding to the cultural echoes of invisibility today, including drone strikes, Harris ponders what it might mean to understand race as an unseen but hegemonic theology, making visible and concealing. William Hart's chapter examines the fetish, the frenzy, and voodoo as three sites of racialized resistance to secularism and as three sites of secularist cooptation of race. The story he tells is one of the black Atlantic, tracking these three religious sites in three geographical locales: West Africa, Haiti, and the U.S. South. This chapter thus pushes the volume to consider the American experience in a transnational context, and through this context we can see America anew, see how it is both exceptional and unexceptional. Moreover, it inserts colonialism into the race-and-secularism knot, suggesting that readings "in America" are incomplete without attention to America's own postcolonial status. Willie James Jennings broadens Hart's queries even further. He views the pressing problem for examinations of race and secularism in America not simply as colonialism but as settler colonialism, a distinctive species of colonialism that has recently attracted significant scholarly attention. Settler colonialism does not just manage economic resources but requires the management of bodies and spaces, a management performed almost always by theological discourse. Viewing not only the United States but all of the Americas as subject to settler colonialism, Jennings asks what "secular space" might mean. Probing colonial imaginings of the American landscape, Jennings finds a religious organization of space that, seemingly secondarily but perhaps primarily, serves to also organize race. In other words, Jennings examines the ways in which the management of race and religion both operate through geography, and he shows that geography binds together racial and religious regimes. An ostensibly secular space is in fact a space of whiteness, a space for whites.

The conclusion, by coeditor Jonathon Kahn, ponders the implications for religion of the account of race and secularism that has developed over the preceding chapters. If secularism is the exclusion or management of religion, and if secularism and racialization are entwined, how might religious communities see otherwise, on their own terms, provocatively, and justly? To formulate a response, Kahn takes James Baldwin as a guide. It is by acknowledging impurity and imperfection yet continuing to cultivate the theological imagination that the postsecular can become something more productive than the always already compromised postracial.

Tracy Fessenden's afterword synthesizes themes that emerged in the chapters of the book while locating them in a broader framework of intersectional analysis. If thinking race and secularism together attunes us to pressing questions of justice, how might this nexus be complicated when gender and sexuality are added to the mix? Are they similarly managed by contemporary neoliberalism, and is this management similarly made possible by the repression of religion? Furthermore, how does America's location as superpower, as empire, make the concerns raised by this volume all the more pressing?

## NOTES

1. http://www.whitehouse.gov/the-press-office/2011/10/16/remarks-president-martin -luther-king-jr-memorial-dedication.
2. http://www.reagan.utexas.edu/archives/speeches/1983/110283a.htm.
3. Charles Taylor, *A Secular Age* (Cambridge, Mass.: Belknap Press of Harvard University Press, 2007); Talal Asad, *Formations of the Secular: Christianity, Islam, Modernity* (Stanford, Calif.: Stanford University Press, 2003).
4. For an account of this connection as a story of modernity, see J. Kameron Carter, *Race: A Theological Account* (Oxford: Oxford University Press, 2008).
5. William T. Cavanaugh, *The Myth of Religious Violence: Secular Ideology and the Roots of Modern Conflict* (Oxford: Oxford University Press, 2009).

6. Karen Ferguson, *Top Down: The Ford Foundation, Black Power, and the Reinvention of Racial Liberalism* (Philadelphia: University of Pennsylvania, 2013).

7. See, for example, Winfried Fluck, Donaled E. Pease, and John Carlos Rowe, eds., *Reframing the Transnational Turn in American Studies* (Hanover, N.H.: Dartmouth College Press, 2011).

8. David Sehat, *The Myth of American Religious Freedom* (Oxford: Oxford University Press, 2011); Steven K. Green, *The Second Disestablishment: Church and State in Nineteenth-Century America* (Oxford: Oxford University Press, 2010).

9. David Chappell, *A Stone of Hope: Prophetic Religion and the Death of Jim Crow* (Chapel Hill: University of North Carolina Press, 2004).

10. Thomas A. Tweed, *America's Church: The National Shrine and Catholic Presence in the Nation's Capital* (Oxford: Oxford University Press, 2011).

11. Curtis J. Evans, *The Burden of Black Religion* (Oxford: Oxford University Press, 2008).

12. Milton C. Sernett, *Bound for the Promised Land: African American Religion and the Great Migration* (Durham, N.C.: Duke University Press, 1997); Eddie S. Glaude, "Babel in the North: Black Migration, Moral Community, and the Ethics of Racial Authenticity," in *A Companion to African American Studies*, ed. Lewis Gordon and Jane Anna Gordon (Malden, Mass.: Blackwell, 2006).

13. Devin Fergus, *Liberalism, Black Power, and the Making of American Politics, 1965–1980* (Athens: University of Georgia Press, 2009).

14. Jodi Melamed, *Represent and Destroy: Rationalizing Violence in the New Racial Capitalism* (Minneapolis: University of Minnesota Press, 2011).

15. Cf. John Milbank, *Theology and Social Theory: Beyond Secular Reason* (Oxford: Blackwell, 1993); William T. Cavanaugh, *Theopolitical Imagination* (London: T&T Clark, 2002).

# PART I
## ORIENTATIONS

# 1

# WHITE SUPREMACY
# AND BLACK INSURGENCY
# AS POLITICAL THEOLOGY

George Shulman

HIS ESSAY justifies one big claim by pursuing the implications and then the limits of a specific political theory. The claim is that most versions of the secularization thesis are contradicted both by white supremacy as a historical and political phenomenon and by the terms and forms of black insurgency. The theory at issue is Carl Schmitt's account of political theology as involving sovereignty, decision, and states of exception and, relatedly, his account of "the political" as a kind of intensification of antagonism. I would use his theory to conjure a plausible view of the relationship between race and secularism in the American case but then use black insurgency to show the limits of, to complicate and move beyond, Schmitt's account.

Let me begin by noting the main accounts of secularization. One is the liberal (Lockean) version in which the privatizing of religion is the condition of creating a political community organized around public reason.[1] One is the Weberian view that the demagification of the world proceeds as instrumental reason and worldly asceticism separate from religious origins and, in conjunction with capitalism, creates a bureaucratic iron cage and the dark night of modernity.[2] One is the Marxism that posits a progressive secularization of religion, at first as the democratic state and its double consciousness, then as capitalism melts all that is solid, and finally by a revolutionary process that creates a fully humanized and communist world community.[3]

In each version, secularization can be incomplete, as some people remain wed to the social practices and forms of consciousness associated with religion as an archaic, traditional, ostensibly recessive heritage. The political theorist Wendy Brown thus recently invoked Marx and Freud to call state sovereignty the compensatory heir of theistic expectations and to depict its waning as a religious and thus psychic and political crisis.[4] Other political theorists invoke Nietzsche's depiction of a modernity characterized by the death of god but also by a self-defeating search for what he called theistic substitutes, in truth and reason on the one hand and in the nation-state on the other hand. Christianity persists as the "longing for the unconditional" and "slave morality" driving what he calls "the ascetic ideal."[5] If the legacy of Nietzsche's genealogy is a certain kind of atheism, however, it means endorsing not a liberal, Weberian, or Marxist version of secularization but a kind of postsecularism; after Nietzsche, one sees perspectives at play rather than a final truth revealed, which means that one accepts the ubiquity of faith, which drives every ontology and vision of life, including secularism itself as ideology.[6]

Let me also note the key arguments that contest these dominant stories of secularization. As I've suggested, one is Nietzsche's mythopoetic view that faith is both inescapable and generative. One is Tocqueville's view, updated by Robert Bellah, that American liberal nationalism involves a "civil religion" in which liberal ideals are enframed by a culture of theist faith, Christian moral norms, and providential narrative. In this view, a democratic political community presumes and requires such mythic enframing to posit worthy ends and to exercise self-reflective self-limitation.[7] A third and opposing critique of the secularization thesis is offered by the work of Talal Asad, which argues that secularism bespeaks a disciplinary project wed to state power and colonialism; for Asad, Tocqueville's civil religion is thus a "civilizing" project that authorizes certain individualistic (say liberal or secular) versions of religion and politics by pathologizing other (say liturgical and communal) practices as traditional, nonliberal, and antimodern.[8]

Following Asad and virtually all African American scholars, the following arguments assume that liberal modernity has always been entangled with both slavery and religion and that "secularism" is a discursive formation constituting both religion and race as worldly objects. But by focusing on Carl Schmitt's critique of secularization and bringing it into conversation with critical race theory, my goal is to elaborate this critique by theorizing white supremacy and black insurgency as forms of "political theology" in Schmitt's sense. In turn, though, black insurgency enables me to show the limits and dangers of Schmitt's view of "political theology" and to enlarge what that concept might mean.

We recall that for Schmitt, liberal modernity is antipolitical for two reasons: it devalues sovereignty as decision about exceptions, and it devalues the antagonism of the friend-enemy distinction. Celebrating both "ethics" and markets, both universal moral norms enacted by individuals and contractual (that is, consensual) relations among them, liberalism (in his view) elevates a private realm of interpersonal mediation that purportedly does not involve power or decisions about collective fate. In his view, liberalism also devalues antagonism; that is, in an ontological sense it denies the permanence and depth of difference, and in a political sense it denies how forms of difference generate conflict that cannot be subsumed or resolved. That denial is entailed by liberalism's investment in legal process, parliamentary discussion, and interest-group bargaining, that is, in forms of conflict resolution through procedural and deliberative norms purportedly grounded in consent and reason.[9]

In contrast to what he still calls "politics," Schmitt defines and depicts "the political" in two ways. On the one hand it is the moment of what he calls "decision" that, by declaring an exception to legal norms and institutional routine, at once creates and enacts sovereignty. As moments of "decision" declare a state of exception that breaks or suspends the authority of law or precedent, so the "sovereign" is whoever or whatever power it is that declares and effectively creates this exception. Lincoln displays sovereignty when he suspends habeas corpus, but American revolutionaries at once claim and display the sovereignty of their "constituent power" in their declaration of independence. In turn, such acts of political decision manifest the theological meaning and worldly persistence of what he calls "miracle." Arguing that "every order rests on a decision and not a norm," which is to say that legal structures are founded on faith and will rather than rationality as such, he also depicts acts of decision and so of exception as ways that "the power of real life breaks through the crust of a mechanism that has become torpid by repetition."

In this claim we can hear Jesus—"it is written but I say unto you"—or Luther—"Here I stand; I can do no other"—but also Machiavelli's "armed prophet" or Rousseau's "the people" engaging in revolutionary acts of "founding" or constituent power that establish legal (even moral) order. We can hear the virtually cyclical view of revolutionary (and charismatic) acts of founding, the routinization of authority, and acts of renewal or refounding, a central trope if not the central narrative form in religious and political life in the West. "The political" for Schmitt thus appears only or specifically in speech and action that bears the generative power to break a pattern and thereby to reorder or refound an order, regime, or community. But also, he claims, the capacity to declare and enact an exception is crucial to *save* a norm (or a state) in moments of crisis. (Like Machiavelli, he thus endorses a "constitutional" dictatorship, that is, constitutional authorization for declaring a temporary state of exception to save the law or the state.)[10]

On the other hand, he depicts the political as the declaration of friend and enemy, for in and by this speech act a community constitutes its existential identity and posits a good higher than its members' mere life. Schmitt is insistent both on the inescapability of antagonism, given human plurality, and on its value as a condition of existential self-definition. For by discovering the good that distinguishes a "we" from its "they," human beings are compelled to articulate the terms and meaning of their belonging as a foundational identification. As the articulation of belonging warrants both killing and self-sacrifice, and as mortal commitment gives politics gravitas, so recovering "the political" in this sense might ennoble a liberal modernity that is otherwise bereft of redemptive meaning because it values nothing higher than mere life.[11]

For Schmitt, then, liberalism and secularization work together to devalue "the political" by avoiding the central issues of authority and belonging, and thus they tend to deny or malign—but therefore "manage"—the dimensions of decision and commitment, as well as antagonism and allegiance, in political life. Issues of authority and belonging, and so of both conflict and what once was called "enthusiasm," in turn bear traces of religiosity in the form of the sacred or transcendent, the miraculous, and the affirmation of commitment to a faith valued more than mortal life. As critics have rightly noted, though, Schmitt's political theology uses exception to cement and not only assert sovereignty through the state; his goal is to secure rather than unsettle sovereignty. Likewise, critics rightly see the loss of plurality in his unification of "the friend" as against "the enemy," whereas in politics these categories are more contingent, changeable, and internally differentiated in ways his theory obscures. Despite the efforts of many on the left to appropriate his theory to defend a revolutionary politics, then, it is no surprise that defenders of the national security state have invoked Schmitt since 9/11.[12]

Still, during this era of permanent war some political theorists have used Schmitt's political theology to authorize avowedly democratic projects. For moments of decision and declarations of exception—as the Arab Spring recently demonstrated—can perform the countersovereignty of "the people" against the state acting in their name.[13] Declaring a frontier between the many and the few, antagonism appears as a crucial part of "populist" or oppositional politics. Such an "event," breaking open the continuity and authority of a regime, is readily linked to Jacques Ranciere's idea of the political as "dis-agreement," as the moment, event, or encounter that stages a "dispute" over a sovereign order and the "partition of the sensible" by which it defines who counts as enfranchised and who is "of no (ac)count." For Ranciere, unlike Schmitt, though, any recentering of sovereignty is an instance of what he calls "the police," not of the political, which he defines in wholly ruptural terms.[14]

If for Schmitt secularization means the rule of the ordinary as routine repetition of the same, then moments of decision, exception, and antagonism are the disturbing intervention of the transcendent not in a literal theistic sense but as acts and powers rupturing immanence. "The people" in revolutionary moments can thus be said to enact that role, and in this (Schmittian) sense it is said, "the voice of the people is the voice of God." Even if one argues with Schmitt about where or in whom he lodges the transcendent and miraculous, and even if one rejects his own investment in cementing sovereignty, it is crucial to credit the appeal of his effort to rescue politics from insignificance by depicting the properly political as an extraordinary act, event, or moment that breaks into, opens up, and redeems the ordinary as a routinized or imprisoning iron cage. Thus, even when Hannah Arendt rejects his equation of the political with sovereignty and instead equates the properly political with what she calls "action in concert," she still attributes to it a "natality" (for initiating new beginnings) she calls miraculous and endows with redemptive meaning. The political—whether lodged in state sovereignty by Schmitt or in capacities to initiate by Arendt—thus becomes a fugitive spirit and sacred presence that redeems an otherwise deadened, one could say profane, world. What I would emphasize in Schmitt's concept of political theology, then, is not only decision, sovereignty, and antagonism but also the narrative structure of exceptionality that posits the rule-bound immanence of the ordinary to conjure the political as the extraordinary act that breaks it open. I will dissent from this view later, but my conclusion thus far is that Schmitt's political theology means redemptive investment in the political as a response to a death-in-life equated with secularization under liberalism.

What happens, however, when we think about secularization and the political through the prism of white supremacy and the insurgency of racialized others? Schmitt insisted that "liberalism" was incapable of "the political" in the sense of avowing the centrality of decision, exception, sovereignty, and antagonism, but the history of liberalism in the United States suggests otherwise. Most simply, what Schmitt calls "political theology" is enacted in the United States in racial terms, partly as the metaphysics marking the damned as black to produce a redemptive whiteness, partly as the racial state of exception founding sovereignty, partly as an antagonistic declaration of the constitutive outside and internal other of American liberal nationalism. The declaration of a racialized state of exception can constitute sovereignty in localist, populist, or "Jeffersonian" forms, as in the popular sovereignty of white citizen's councils or the recent Tea Party rhetoric, but also in the "Hamiltonian" form of a national security state authorized by anticommunism and wars on terror. But either way, as blackness is associated with the license that subverts self-mastery, with the dependency that defeats autonomy, or with the irredeemable criminality or violence that threatens order, so "democracy in America" is re-produced by recurrently declaring both a racialized exception to liberal norms and a frontier of antagonism defining the friend by marking the enemy.[15]

What Michael Rogin calls "counter-subversion" is thus Schmittian decision in American drag: liberalism's political theology is revealed as it repeatedly re-constitutes sovereignty, national belonging, and normative citizenship by projecting and enforcing racialized frontiers.[16] But liberalism typically disavows its entanglement with domination, except in extraordinary moments of crisis or hysteria, which in turn are readily forgotten as their legacies are normalized. It is as if Schmitt took "liberalism" at its word rather than looking at its practice, when in fact Schmittian racial politics is the secret that liberalism at once displays and disavows. The racial state of exception in American liberalism is constitutive not anomalous, permanent not temporary, and it remains invisible because it is ordinary; hidden in plain sight, it is a cultural grammar that is unsaid and even denied by those it enfranchises, and it is spatialized in segregated zones of residence, labor, and incarceration. James Baldwin thus called Americans "innocent" not to say they are ignorant of the racialized inequality they endorse or allow but to say that they disavow what they know.[17]

Some of us appreciate Schmitt's Kierkegaardian valuation of the leap of faith (the "decision") in political commitment and of the permanence and value of conflict in human life. But given how the practices that Schmitt calls political theology take racialized forms in European colonialism and American liberalism, it is credible to argue as follows: the "decision" that enacts sovereignty by declaring exception and defining friend and enemy expresses resentment or fear, not commitment; produces violence or tyranny, not nobility; and enacts closure, not faith. As white supremacy reveals, even if his political theology is mobilized on behalf of popular sovereignty, it undermines central democratic values, not only the ethical injunction that would universalize recognition in the name of equality but also appreciation for plurality, participation, and debate. Schmitt's political theology conceives both "the friend" and "the enemy" as a unified or essentialized subject in ways that purify the messy hybridity of a community, demonizing the difference within and beyond it. Moreover, we must ask: can a theory hostile to the quotidian and invested in the heroic or the exceptional be a democratic resource? In turn, a democratic response even to populist versions of Schmitt's political theology might revalue egalitarian universalism and endorse a participatory approach to democratizing (and so ennobling) the practices of ordinary life.

Consider, then, how black political thinkers have addressed white supremacy as (Schmittian) political theology. They have had to pose this question: by what language and action can we take exception to the racial state of exception that constitutes popular sovereignty or "democracy in America?" Working not within a democratic frame but instead to engage the domination and disavowal that at once found and violate it, these critics do not accept the methodological individualism of classic liberalism or the idealization of reason, deliberation, and consensus in modern forms of liberal political thought. They rightly suspect the idealization of plurality and difference in poststructural critiques of classic liberalism or in multicultural adaptations of it. How, then, do figures in the canon of black political thought recast prevailing views of secularization, religion, and the political?

In my own work, I have argued that black political thought has often taken up, used, and revised the biblical genre of prophecy. My reading of prophecy as political theology moves from Schmitt to Martin Buber and thereby to critics of white supremacy such as Douglass, King, Baldwin, and Morrison.[18] On the one hand, they stand with the enemy or alien against which "the people" has constituted itself as a political community, and they thereby invoke a specific countercommunity of the excluded while pointing it toward a violated universality. I stand, Frederick Douglass thus says, with God and the slave against a people constituted by domination.[19] On the other hand, as they take exception to the racial state of exception that violates democratic norms, they revise the dominant form of American civil religion, or move outside it altogether, or try doing both at once. They must revise civil religion because they cannot uncritically endorse American exceptionalism: seeing racial injustice as constitutive not anomalous and doubting progressive narratives that make inclusion a teleological promise, they deny the innocence of the people and the universalism proclaimed by the state. Standing with the slave means standing against the actual nation and standing with captives in exile and conscripts to empire, whose countersovereignty and political subjectivity they would help bring into being by their own speech and action. Black political thinkers typically register a transnational, diasporic, and anticolonial orientation, positioning themselves in Egypt or Babylon, as slaves or exiles within a nation and against an empire.[20]

Black critics using prophecy depart from prevailing ways of theorizing democratic politics. In contrast to liberal norms of toleration and a poststructural ethics of difference, they endorse an adversarial engagement with domination, which entails intensity of judgment rather than (or in tension with) calls for forbearance; critics demand not a pluralism among valid identities or perspectives but a fateful decision to overcome domination and exclusion and thereby to reconstitute a regime. For pluralism as a political and cultural ideal is valid or genuine only on the basis of equality, after the abolition of the color line. They enact a charismatic, extralegal, self-authorizing, and generative political moment—what Schmitt called "decision"—while invoking the countersovereignty of a black subject. Still, many call for reconstituting a national sovereign, a newly, finally unified "American people," though in the canon of black critics of white supremacy there is vigorous, often rancorous debate about the value of national attachment and about whether or how to use and remake the nation-state. But even if critics remain within a "civil rights" perspective, they must take exception to constituted law, and they must declare a frontier of antagonism to the embedded structures that anchor the chimera of whiteness.

It is no surprise, then, that whites typically cast such critics as fanatics opposed to democratic process, but that is because a racial state of exception requires critics to question the authority of law, majority rule, and toleration, as well as idealizations of local self-rule and participation, for each is contaminated by racialized domination. Indeed, they see that overcoming white supremacy remains *the* condition of democratic possibility, period; the alternative is a fraudulent pluralism among those counted as white. For critics in this canon, therefore, politics is not so much a process of deliberation or mediation of plural identities as it is a structure of rule, and a democratic politics must be a struggle against it.[21]

I am suggesting that black political theology resonates with Schmittian ideas of decision, taking exception, and sovereignty in order to contest the sovereignty of white supremacy. What then of the friend-enemy distinction in the formation of a collective black subject? Most of the key figures in this canon do not invert the reified friend-enemy distinction they face in white supremacy, nor do they defuse or diffuse it by a pluralistic ethos. For they see a worldly adversary in constituencies who are invested in domination, formally opposed but disavowing practical complicity, or simply indifferent. During the long Civil Rights Movement critics argued that moral suasion will fail and that whites must be *compelled* (by the nonviolent coercion of boycott or demonstration) to the table, to an engagement, unwilling at first, that over time might change them. Of course, other critics denied the viability of persuasion, decried investment in engagement, and counseled resolute disengagement and nation building by the collective black subject. My point is that these arguments presumed that white supremacy entailed a frontier of antagonism and that even those who endorsed nonviolence knew they were engaging enemies, by forging a countercommunity of friends, though they disagreed about whether enemies could be changed into civic friends. The dangers in the politics of identification and the ethical dilemmas of antagonism cannot be avoided by denouncing Schmitt.

The greatest critics of white supremacy did not idealize, reify, or simplify the categories of friend and enemy but saw them as necessary though fraught political concepts. Indeed, it can be argued that Baldwin, especially, saw "the enemy" not only as those invested in (or indifferent to) white supremacy but as internal to each person, as our capacities for pride, idolatry, disavowal, or rancor, which incline us to deny the reality of the other, to reify the group, to seek supremacy instead of equality, and to revenge injury rather than heal it. He thus stood with the marked against the unmarked, but he also stood in an agonistic relation to every neighbor and citizen.

In sum, the tradition of black political thought has never chastened the judgment of white supremacy as a deranged political theology: this changing-same, which differentiates the damned to produce the saved and which is inseparably linked to practices of sovereignty, remains the constitutive injustice in American life. As Baldwin also insists, however, every accusation contains a plea for community: critics using the genre of prophecy thus remain committed to the idea that overcoming white supremacy would truly benefit those who call themselves white, though they cannot yet (and may never) see how. At the same time, black political theology remains engaged in what Arendt called world building, in the diasporic space between captivity in an empire and citizenship in a nation.

As a mode of insurgency, then, what does black prophecy suggest about secularization? The genre casts secularization as a political project inseparably connected to white supremacy and white supremacy as a deranged political theology linking purifying salvation (from all that blackness signifies) to the sovereignty of "the people" and the state acting in their name. For secularization has feared enthusiasm, privatized congregation, and tried to manage, by containing in forms of propriety, the miscegenating energies that entwine the word and libido in animated bodies acting in concert. Secularization is one face of a biopolitical project seeking to immunize the enfranchised against the infection and impurity signified by racially marked others but carried internally, incipiently, by everyone. The other face of this project is state sovereignty, declaring zones of exception and drawing the frontier to save normative citizens from the racialized impulses, practices, and people in which "terror" is lodged. As Schmitt argued, we see here traces of the conceptual architecture wherein theism was translated into "secular" terms or secularized.

If black prophecy has joined secularization and white supremacy as twinned aspects of the political theology animating modern liberal empire, this genre also has advanced a countertheology that takes exception to the sovereign state of exception, the dark side of a sanitizing secularization. Through this genre, critics have creatively reworked the political and religious themes of decision and exception, of countersovereignty, of antagonism, miracle, and resurrection from a death-in-life. As they bespeak the liturgical traditions and biblical idioms constituting the ordinary life of those living in a racial state of exception, they thus break the image of "religion"—as individual creedal commitment—that has been created by secularization while leaving us with a range of practices that confound the religious-secular dichotomy. Still, there is a generational issue: I am reminded of a question posed after a book talk I gave in 2004: did my argument about prophecy presume the ongoing viability of the black church? If James Baldwin and Toni Morrison are notable partly because of fruitful tensions between their critical (can we say "secular"?) distance and their religiosity, can such creativity continue if black religious practices recede in importance or are captured by neoliberal forms of individualism, as may be the case? Glenn Loury has thus suggested that black radicalism will disappear because the prophetic voice is losing its enabling institutional conditions. At issue, then, is political theology from below, in relation to black insurgency.

Perhaps sociological knowledge can "answer" this question about generational change in religious practices, though I suspect any "empirical" answer remains politically contingent. But the question also suggests another line of theoretical inquiry, to explore other voices, articulating forms of political theology that break with the structure of exceptionality shared by prophetic critics and Schmitt, in which a routine ordinary (as an imprisoning death-in-life) is overcome by the generative acts or popular power that bear resurrection into real life. It is crucial, indeed, to see the forms of religiosity, and of political insurgency, that are rendered invisible or precluded by Schmitt's version of "political theology." How are decision and antagonism, as well as the ordinary and the exceptional, conceived by alternative political theologies?

One possibility is represented in Richard Iton's *The Search for the Black Fantastic*, which rejects what Sacvan Bercovitch calls "the American jeremiad," the narrative form by which critics address the American nation as a collective subject. In Iton's view, this rhetorical idiom can only repeat American exceptionalism and reproduce the limitations of a national framework of "civil rights," which cannot reach the systemic inequality and structural violence characterizing ordinary life in the black diaspora. For Iton, any prophetic figure who bespeaks American civil religion is not critical enough and is readily incorporated into what Bercovitch calls the "rite of assent," whereby examples of dissent prove American progress. This is the meaning of the sanitizing memorialization by which Martin Luther King Jr. is stripped both of blackness and of religiosity. Iton is opposed to prophecy, however, if it only weds black freedom to redemption of the American nation, for if prophecy sees the black diaspora as exile in a Babylon doomed to fall, addresses black people as an exiled, landless nation within an empire, and imagines their redemption across the fictive boundaries of nations, then it advances a political theology bearing radical possibility. Correspondingly, Iton forgoes formal representational politics linked to the nation-state and invests instead in what he calls "the Black Fantastic," which connotes forms of politics, art, and religiosity that are emerging in black popular culture and that address other people of color rather than the state or whites. He thus lodges political redemption in horizontal social relations among peoples of color, in popular cultural productions and idioms, and in the slow building of infrastructure, to sustain a transnational countercommunity in the longue durée, the time that will remain dark until Babylon self-destructs.[22]

What is noteworthy here is, first, the refusal of the state, of formal (electoral and party) politics, and of the entire civil rights ideology that organizes black protest toward recognition and redress by the nation-state and, second, a corresponding embrace of a local-global diasporic circuit that sidesteps the nation-state and that instead emphasizes popular culture, including popular forms of religion as well as other performing arts, as a political site where collective subjectivity is (re)made. Iton locates politics *in* the racial state of exception, in daily life among people of color; ordinary daily life is not a deadening routine to rupture by the intrusion and eruption of revolutionary acts, nor is it the passive object remade by radical regime change at the level of the state, but, rather, habitual practices are the very ground of politics. Redemption, then, is sought not by escaping or transcending the ordinary but by articulating its integrity, richness, and variety, which white culture erases by melodramas of black pathology and by revaluing the daily forms of black agency that white representations render invisible.[23]

If Wittgenstein argued that ordinary-language philosophy enacts a therapy for philosophy by leading words back from metaphysical to ordinary usage, a usage in which habitual rule following entails rather than precludes creative agency, then Iton's version of political theology follows a similar path. If Cavell thus argues that philosophy in modernity abstracts from the adequacy of our ordinary criterial grammar because it disavows human finitude and connection, Iton correspondingly returns to and revalues what might be called the criterial grammar of black popular culture. That culture, viewed as it were horizontally, crosses the divide between church and street posited by secularization theories, by showing the mutual imbrications between the spaces and popular forms of both cultural creation and religiosity as well as their connection to the formation of counterpublics. Rather than identify the miracle with the sovereign decision (by states or a revolutionary subject) that ruptures precedent to create a radical exception, he identifies miracle with the popular agency that continually produces breaks and inflections in local practices. Akin to the natality that Arendt celebrates in political action, this agency is not itself exceptional, as she often suggested, but ordinary. As Bonnie Honig uses Franz Rozensweig to refuse Schmitt's Pauline view of the law, to show how habitual liturgical practices are in fact essential to preparing people to perceive the sacred, so she asks what kind of ordinary practices could prepare people to perceive what Arendt calls miraculous, the unexpected and the new, which life's contingency constantly generates but which we consistently miss. Correspondingly, I am suggesting, Iton's version of political theology shifts our gaze from formal politics, the state, and grand narratives of emancipation to view the vernacular practices of black popular culture as a kind of criteria grammar and liturgical practice that cultivates dispositions essential to freedom.[24]

I would argue that Iton's orientation toward black life is in fact voiced by Baldwin, in tandem and tension with addressing whites about America as a national/democratic project, but Iton separates these elements. He thus moves our attention specifically beyond the territorial American nation to a broader black Atlantic, orients black political identification in diasporic rather than national terms, and so also moves beyond the black church and Christian practices on which Baldwin drew to include both anticolonial histories and other (Rastafarian and Voudou) forms of religiosity. By ignoring sovereignty and the centering of identity that even ideas of countersovereignty seem to entail, Iton's version of political theology also relinquishes the structure of exceptionality by which the sacred and the political are juxtaposed to the ordinary. Rather than tell (or secularize) a Pauline story of death and rebirth, Iton's political theology conceives diasporic culture as a collective practice—both liturgical and congregational—of call and response as well as repetition and revision, which enables deliberation and agency.

Saidiya Hartman has created another version of political theology. Like Iton, she shifts from Schmitt's abstract conceptual architecture to an ethnography of practices in the black diaspora. But unlike Iton, she still emphasizes how sovereignty and exception constitute and structure the ordinary lifeworlds and subjectivity of racialized people. Hartman argues that "slave" should be understood to "designate a relation to law, state, and sovereign power" of those in a condition of "disfigured personhood, civil incapacitation, and bare life" and that this condition "long outlives slavery itself." Building on Orlando Patterson's account of slavery as a condition of social death, she defines slavery and its "after-life" in terms not of exploited labor but of fungibility, as designating those who are a commodity for projection and use, an empty vessel to be occupied, enjoyed, and used up, and an object available not only for sale but for gratuitous violence. As phenotypic and ethnic notions of blackness now recede, she argues, we can see in the foreground "the state of exception and sovereign violence—state of exception not as a temporal suspension of law as Schmitt sees it, but as the achievement of a permanent spatial arrangement that remains continually outside the normal state of law." Racism can dispense with ethnicity or phenotype as it becomes what Ruthie Gilmore calls "the state-sanctioned production and exploitation of group vulnerability toward premature death." These thinkers thus modify our view of slavery: as the production of fungible, dishonored, and disposable lives characterizes the condition of slavery as social death, so "it is sovereignlessness rather than blackness that defines who is vulnerable to enslavement in the early modern period, and that defines who is raced now." By emphasizing vulnerability to violence—regardless of income or prestige—Hartman makes sovereignty and exception sustain ongoing forms of slavery and "race."[25]

Correspondingly, then, how does Hartman's political theology conceive justice and emancipation? Like Iton, Hartman does not follow Schmitt's conceptual architecture to articulate countersovereignty but pursues a phenomenological and ethnographic approach to black life within the state of exception constitutive of modernity, liberalism, and secularization. Her first move is to declare that it is impossible to "repair the injury" of slavery in any of its forms; "justice is beyond the law, and any redress is necessarily inadequate." But while Iton rejects the formal politics that would seek legal redress from the state, Hartman identifies what she calls "fugitive justice," which endorses demands on the state and the law while recognizing their inevitable incompletion. "If what has been done cannot be undone, then the forms of legal and social compensation available are less a matter of wiping the slate clean than of embracing the limited scope of the possible in the face of irreparable."[26]

Accordingly, black subjectivity and politics must live in what she calls the "interval" between "grief and grievance" and also between "the no longer and the not yet." The interval between destruction and "the awaited hour of deliverance . . . of the captive's redemption" is "the master trope of Black political discourse." To inhabit this in-between moment and space is "to live in loss," she insists, but also to imagine and seek "fugitive justice." How so? On the one hand, if that interval is the changing-same imposed by sovereign violence—and its disavowal by those it enfranchises—then inhabiting it means living a negative relation to a law from which we nevertheless seek pragmatic redress. On the other hand, because that interval reflects what Ranciere calls the "partition of the sensible," which designates who and what is counted as real, it is endured and made (more) habitable by creating what Hartman calls "black noise," which "represents the kinds of political aspirations that are inaudible and illegible within prevailing forms of political rationality . . . because they are so wildly utopian." Such "fugitive movement in and out of the frame . . . or enclosure" is "stolen life," declares Fred Moten, a "self-predicating activity" that sustains the idea of an outside to the law by imagining a justice beyond it.[27]

In the face of irredeemable state violence and white incomprehension, if not complicity, in an ordinary life for which "violence and captivity are the grammar and ghosts of our every gesture," black noise represents a stolen natality and bespeaks a dream of redemption at once excessive, impossible, and as necessary as air to breathe.[28] The exception, a figuration of miracle conjured by Hebrews and Christians as an impossible to foreclose but impossible to predict possibility of resurrection from social death into life, is a faith as lodged in the grammar and ghosts of ordinary life as violence and captivity. Black noise is a redemptive dream that takes exception to a state of exception; it imagines a not-yet beyond ordinary practices of life, but in the living interval it transfigures social death into stolen life and subordination into fugitive freedom.

There are significant differences between an insurgent black theology wed to American nationality, as in Baldwin, and one that invests libidinal and identificatory energies across and beyond it, as in Iton and Hartman, but as the contrast between these two show, there is also disagreement about the value of formally political forms of black agency and engagement with law and social policy. If Iton's work matters because it foregrounds varied forms of popular culture and religiosity, the work of Hartman and those clustering under the sign of "Afro-pessimism" matters because it shows how engaging the afterlife of slavery requires reworking and not abandoning the categories of sovereignty and decision as well as the radicality of taking exception as a trope of redemption, even as we embed these in a phenomenology of embodied ordinary practices. Taken together, in their variation and differences, their work exposes how the secularization thesis has sanitized and compartmentalized religious life as part of the process by which sovereign power constitutes a racial state of exception, and in turn their work recovers the circuits of symbolic and libidinal exchanges linking religious forms, creative expression, political energy, and public life. Prevailing forms of secular and liberal rationality reveal their racial constitution by casting this fugitive lifeworld as "noise," not the "white noise" Don De Lillo associated with commodity culture but blackened noise: forms of enthusiasm, congregation, and expression depicted as vulgar, illegible, and archaic—and also incipiently dangerous. Enacting a return of what is repressed by the racial regime of liberal secularity, insurgent forms of political theology, from Baldwin to Iton or Hartman, reverse the gaze of a pathologizing whiteness to disclose a systemic derangement, to place black energy in a life-affirming interval between insurrection and resurrection. Turning our language of analysis from the abstracted to the carnal, from the formal to the embodied, from the categorical to the stained, and from the dichotomous to the miscegenated, the vocation or office of a black political theology remains two-sided: to name every form of idolatry and the willful innocence that sustains it and to bear witness that a contrary power, embodying words and animating bodies, can sustain "life against death."

# NOTES

1. John Locke, *Letter on Toleration* (New York: Oxford University Press, 2010); John Rawls, *A Theory of Justice* (Cambridge, Mass.: Harvard University Press, 1999); John Rawls, *Political Liberalism* (New York: Columbia University Press, 2005).

2. Max Weber, "Science as a Vocation," in *From Max Weber*, ed. Hans Gerth and C. Wright Mills (New York: Oxford University Press, 1958).

3. Karl Marx, "For a Ruthless Criticism of Everything Existing," "Introduction, Contribution to a Critique of Hegel's *Philosophy of Right*," "On the Jewish Question," and "The Communist Manifesto," in *Marx-Engels Reader*, 2nd ed., ed. Robert Tucker (New York: Norton, 1978).

4. Wendy Brown, *Walled States, Waning Sovereignty* (New York: Zone, 2010).

5. Friedrich Nietzsche, *The Gay Science*, trans. Walter Kaufmann (New York: Vintage, 1974), parts 4 and 5; see also *Thus Spoke Zarathustra* and *The Genealogy of Morals*.

6. For the shift from Nietzsche to a postsecular engagement with faith, see William Connolly, *Why I Am Not a Secularist* (Minneapolis: University of Minnesota Press, 2000); William Connolly, *Pluralism* (Durham, N.C.: Duke University Press, 2005); William Connolly, *A World of Becoming* (Durham, N.C.: Duke University Press, 2010). For an incisive critique of the postsecular positions, see Bruce Robbins, "Why I Am Not a Post-Secularist" *boundary 2* 40, no. 1 (2013): 55–76.

7. Alexis de Tocqueville, *Democracy in America* (New York: Vintage, 1990); Robert Bellah, *Broken Covenant* (Chicago: University of Chicago Press, 1992); also see Michael Sandel, *Democracy's Discontent* (Cambridge, Mass.: Harvard University Press, 1998).

8. Talal Assad, *Formations of the Secular: Christianity, Islam, Modernity* (Palo Alto, Calif.: Stanford University Press, 2003); Talal Asad, *Genealogies of Religion: Discipline and Reasons of Power in Christianity and Islam* (Baltimore, Md.: Johns Hopkins University Press, 1993). Also see Saba Mahmood, *Politics of Piety: The Islamic Revival and the Feminist Subject* (Princeton, N.J.: Princeton University Press, 2011).

9. Carl Schmitt, *Political Theology* (Chicago: University of Chicago Press, 2006); Carl Schmitt, *The Concept of the Political* (Chicago: University of Chicago Press, 2007); Carl Schmitt, *Parliamentary Democracy* (Cambridge, Mass.: MIT Press, 1986).

10. Schmitt, *Political Theology*.

11. It is pertinent to note that, despite what we might expect given his notorious anti-Semitism, Schmitt insists that political antagonism does not and should not entail personal

hatred but is rather impersonal or systemic. Proletarian antagonism to capitalism and the bourgeoisie is about interests, not persons. Likewise, he imagines that conflict of national interests does not entail personal animus. A political antagonism is impersonal, or it is not a properly political antagonism. Despite what we expect because of his anti-Semitism, he imagines a class whose assets are expropriated but whose members are not killed off, or a nation defeated in battle but not annihilated. He foregrounds the particularity of each antagonist in a conflict because neither claims a universality that dehumanizes its adversary. He therefore worries that a human-rights regime, purportedly defending the human as such, will create a frontier against those who must be characterized as unhuman, as less than human, as alien, as recent science-fiction movies like *District 19* or *Independence Day* suggest. In his view, it is the pretension to universality (to the human as such) that makes politics more violent or even exterminationist than conflict between "ways of life" that see themselves as one among others, however threatened.

12. One danger in Schmitt's argument about sovereignty is demonstrated by the Patriot Act as a response to 9/11—a permanent state of exception in the name of saving the law and indeed civilization. This state of exception is beyond the law, yet lawful, because it is congressionally authorized and requires reauthorization, but politics now collapses nation/people and state or, better, invests the people in the state as their savior or protector. All the liberal (and democratic) elements Schmitt devalued (rule of law, procedural due process, parliamentary deliberation) are readily sacrificed; as politics is organized around the sovereignty of the state, popular forms of democratic life are subordinated to the plebiscitory and statecentric. A second danger in Schmitt's argument is also demonstrated by those intellectuals who supported the entire paradigm of 9/11 as a moment of exception on the grounds that sacrifice to protect the nation would overcome the corruption of a people otherwise mired in consumer culture and hedonistic or at least self-centered individualism. As once formulated by John F. Kennedy—ask not what your country can do for you but what you can do for your country—the idea of redemptive service here becomes violence and self-sacrifice organized by the state. For a troubling example of this defense of Schmitt in terms of 9/11 see Paul Kahn, *Political Theology: Four New Chapters on the Concept of Sovereignty* (New York: Columbia University Press, 2011); as well as the forum about it on the website "The Immanent Frame," http://blogs.ssrc.org/tif/political-theology-book-blog/.

13. See Anne Norton, "Democracy and the Divine," *Theory & Event* 13, no. 2 (2010).

14. Jacques Ranciere, *Dis-Agreement* (Minneapolis: University of Minnesota Press, 1998).

15. It is noteworthy that James Baldwin called white supremacy a theology in "Everybody's Protest Novel," his great critique of Harriet Beecher Stowe and Richard Wright. For despite opposing slavery, he argues, she still posits the meaning of blackness as sin and damnation, and she makes the condition of redemption whiteness. That theology, a bridge from the Christian split between spirit and flesh to the Cartesian/Enlightenment separation of mind/reason from body/animal, organized the national state, constitutional interpretation, and white abolitionism. For Baldwin, inverting the dichotomy of black and white, as he claims Richard Wright did, was no alternative. A countertheology—and a genuine "pro-

test" novel—must narrate why the discourse of purity was adopted, demonstrate its costs, deconstruct it, and dramatize moving beyond it.

16. Michael Rogin, *Ronald Reagan, the Movie, and Other Episodes in Political Demonology* (Berkeley: University of California Press, 1987).

17. One could say that in the case of Europe, a Schmittian race politics occurred in the colonies, far from the center, and has only appeared postwar, as ex-colonial people of color migrate to the European metropolis. In the American case, the race politics was always near at hand. For the permanence yet changing infrastructure of racialized forms of domination—from slavery to Jim Crow to the postwar "ghetto" and now to hyperincarceration—see Loic Waquant, "From Slavery to Mass Incarceration," *New Left Review* 13 (2002): 41–60. On Baldwin's idea of innocence, see especially "Letter to My Nephew," in *The Fire Next Time* (New York: Dial, 1963).

18. George Shulman, *American Prophecy: Race and Redemption in American Political Culture* (Minneapolis: University of Minnesota Press, 2008).

19. See especially Frederick Douglass, "What to the Slave Is the Fourth of July?" in *Frederick Douglass: Selected Speeches and Writings*, ed. Philip S. Foner (Chicago: Lawrence Hill, 1999), 188–206.

20. I am evoking a range of thinkers, from David Walker to Paul Gilroy, who display a spectrum of attitudes toward seeking racial justice through a specifically national promise and politics.

21. There is a parallel of a sort between critics of white supremacy and critics of class (and gender) inequality because in both cases a structure of inequality must be abolished as the condition of democratic life beginning. The notion of systemic exclusion creates an agonal, adversarial relation to democratic ideals while also presuming that a frontier of antagonism is already in existence and needs to be acknowledged as a condition of political possibility. But as Jared Sexton and Frank Wilderson III argue, workers (and women) are seen as white, that is as human, so that their conflict with bosses (or men) occurs in the register of relative injustice, in terms of exploitation or rights, whereas (as Douglass argued in regard to slavery) those marked black are not registered as human subjects at all. For Sexton and Wilderson, that marking represents the limits of analogy in thinking about subject positions in politics.

22. Richard Iton, *In Search of the Black Fantastic* (New York: Oxford University Press, 2010).

23. "My suggestive reference to a black fantastic, then, is meant to refer to the minor-key sensibilities generated from the experiences of the underground, the vagabond, and those constituencies marked as deviant—notions of being that are inevitably . . . in conversation with, against, and articulated beyond the boundaries of the modern." Anchored in cultural spaces, these sensibilities "struggle to establish and maintain space for substantive, open-ended deliberative activity and the related commitment to nurture potentially subversive forms of interiority. . . . The black fantastic signifies a generic category of under-developed possibilities . . . generated by subaltern populations" (ibid., 16). Insisting on the "impossibility of representing a coherent black subject" (149), Iton also insists that any specific

"place" is a deterritorialized, pluralized "space." "It is worth noting the degree to which Brooklyn and much of the tri-state area has become a hybrid and hyper-articulated diasporic breathing space that was as Afro-Latin as it was Anglophone and Francophone Caribbean, continental African, or African-American. . . . We can think of these sites, and the diaspora itself, as a means of contesting the tendency to erase and collapse locations in which deliberative activity—black thoughts—might occur, analogous to the potentials offered by smaller-scale counter-publics, transgressive interiorities, workshops, collectives, and mechanisms such as the band, live performance, the long-playing record, and the various expatriate festivals. . . . In the illusory but meaningful space between the national and the imperial, where black subjects understood broadly are made . . . cultural actors [are] particularly well-positioned to act, to dis-assemble, re/present, re-imagine. Against this backdrop, the inability or refusal of black artists and their audiences to reproduce national grammars can be interpreted as evidence, at some fundamental level, of anti-colonial labor" (256–257).

24. See Bonnie Honig, "The Miracle of Metaphor: Rethinking the State of Exception with Rosenzweig and Schmitt," *Diacritics* 37, no. 2/3 (2007): 78–102.

25. Saidiyah Hartman and Stephen Best, "Fugitive Justice," *Representations* 92, no. 1 (2005): 1–15.

26. Ibid.

27. Fred Moton, "The Case of Blackness," *Criticism* 50, no. 2 (2008): 177–218.

28. Frank Wilderson III, quoted in Jared Sexton, "The Social Life of Social Death: On Afro-Pessimism and Black Optimism," *InTensions Journal* 5 (2011). http://www.yorku.ca/intent/issue5/articles/pdfs/jaredsextonarticle.pdf.

# 2

# SECULAR COMPARED TO WHAT?

## TOWARD A HISTORY OF THE TROPE OF BLACK SACRED/SECULAR FLUIDITY

### Josef Sorett

One of the themes running through a great deal of the interpretations of Black Theology and Black Religion is the assertion that the Black community did not and does not make distinctions between the secular and the sacred and that it follows from this assertion that the Black church is and has been the locus of the Black community. If this is so, then it means that the church is the locus of the expression of Black cultural life. Politics, art, business, and all other dimensions of the Black community should thus find their expression as aspects of the religious experience of Black folks.

—CHARLES LONG (1981)

N 1981, the historian of religion Charles Long gave an address on the "State of the Field" to the Society for the Study of Black Religion (SSBR), an organization that he had helped found only a decade earlier. The occasion for Long's lecture was, in fact, a celebration of the society's tenth anniversary. Given the persistence of the problem of race in the modern academy, SSBR was founded both to clarify and further intellectual questions related to the study of religion in the African Diaspora but also to provide professional and existential support for black scholars who were an overwhelming minority within a world of religious studies and theological education often experienced as inhospitable if not overtly hostile.[1] Not insignificantly, Long had been elected president of the American Academy of Religion (AAR) seven years earlier, in 1973, making him the society's first African American president. Notably, in 1976 the Christian ethicist Preston Williams—also the first black professor tenured at Harvard Divinity School—became the second African American to hold this office. A decade later Nathan Scott, a scholar of religion and literature, joined Williams and Long as the AAR's third black president.

In contrast to the public prominence of a select few (men), as with the professoriate in general, black scholars of theology and religion remained a small statistical minority. Yet rather than foreground the AAR's racial politics, Long focused his lecture on what he saw as the primary theoretical challenges faced by the members of this young organization. More specifically, Long called attention to what has since been referred to as the "Christian hegemony," as it informed the study of African American religion.[2] To be sure, AAR was itself a relatively new association, and Long was elected its president just ten years after the National Association of Biblical Instructors renamed itself under the more ecumenical (and ostensibly secular) rubric of religious studies. Thus, Charles Long's critique of the centrality of Christian traditions and theological methods within SSBR was part and parcel of a broader conversation concerning the Protestant past and colonial history that had ordered the academic study of religion in North America since the late nineteenth century.

In a lecture that touched upon a variety of topics, Long gave special attention to the question of how theories of secularization were being mobilized in the study of black religion. Long's presence had been central to the SSBR since its inception, even if his core claims largely remained at the margins of the intellectual agenda advanced by most of the association's membership. That is, from the moment of the organization's founding Long was a minority voice insisting that churches not be viewed as the exclusive or primary site for studying religion within African American communities. In fact, Long argued elsewhere that "extra-Christian" sources (literature, folklore, music, etc.) ought to be privileged if scholars were to grasp the "true situation" of black communities in North America.[3] And while what holds as "true" in this account begs for interrogation, his critique of Christianity was well warranted in 1981 and remains so today. Although great strides have since been made to document the religious diversity apparent in black life, churches—the institutional homes of this Christian hegemony—continue to dominate most narratives of African American religious history. A more dramatic extension of Long's critique has taken the form of certain scholars calling for a moratorium on the term "The Black Church."[4]

Most significant for the purposes of this essay, Charles Long's 1981 address connected his standing critique of the privileged narrative of Afro-Protestantism to a series of debates that are an antecedent to the recent surge in secularism studies.[5] More precisely, Long troubled scholarly interpretations that suggested that black communities were somehow immune to the forces of secularization in the West. Indeed, African Americans generally figured as the foil to an otherwise rapidly secularizing Western world, a development that had been hailed as triumphant in the preceding decades.[6] Or, paraphrasing the way Vincent Lloyd puts the matter in this volume's introduction, if this secularizing telos declared that Western modernity had managed to subdue its premodern religious pasts, then black religion confirmed that modernity's racial subjects were not so easily managed. That is, if secularism is a project of managing modern difference, then the frenzied excess associated with African American religion provided proof that racial difference was often unable to be managed, making the prospect of a black secularism implausible.

Charles Long argued that an interpretive insistence that "the Black community did not and does not make distinctions between the secular and the sacred" served the interest of a particular theological position, namely, the social and cultural centrality of "the Black church." To assert that sacred/secular distinctions did not hold in African American communities was both to insist upon an abiding significance of Christian churches for modern black life and to advance the idea of a distinctive black culture. Moreover, it also involved a subtle endorsement of the notion that certain African retentions persisted and thus provided the enduring ethos in which black people in North America practiced Christianity.[7] Long did not elaborate much further to explain or support his claim or these more precise details. Still, his observation invites further discussion on several fronts.

Long alleged that a form of Afro-Protestant apologetics was lurking behind the idea of a denial of (or resistance to) the modern sacred/secular distinction and the oft-assumed narrative of secularization. Such an allegation sets the course for a dialogue about religion and race, respectively. And, more importantly, it highlights how the terms are mutually constitutive as well as often entangled in ways that obscure each other. On one hand, appeals to sacred/secular fluidity are implicated in veiling Christian commitments. Here, Long's critique set the stage for a vision of a nascent black secular, and it decenters Christianity in studies of black religious life. At the same time, by asserting that "extra-church" sources were more exemplary of the "true situation" in which African Americans found themselves, Long also left a notion of authentic blackness as necessarily opposed to Christianity unquestioned. Even if one doesn't cede this assertion of the "extra-church" as the site of what is "true" blackness, Long's argument set the course for a configuration in the study of African American religion wherein the secular and non-Christian forms of religious practice (Hoodoo, Santeria, Vodun, etc.) were conjoined in opposition to the normative position of "the Black Church." In short, the secular conceived as such encompassed all that was not Christian.

To be sure, Charles Long's 1981 address to the Society for the Study of Black Religion captured the confluence of racial discourse and religious difference in ways that perhaps raised more questions than it answered. Still, his remarks anticipated the need for a specific inquiry into the relationship between race and secularism decades before the latter topic became an expansive interdisciplinary field of inquiry unto itself. Though his concern was with black religion, Long called attention to one of the many more subtle distinctions that have since taken shape in recent secularism studies (secularism(s), secularization, the secular, postsecular, etc.). While others have examined the multiple connections between Protestantism and secularism in North America, Long was perhaps the first to invite this line of thinking for the study of African American religion and culture.[8]

However, Charles Long neglected to identify any specific books or scholars to support his assertion concerning the relationship between an Afro-Protestant hegemony and a developing theory of secularism in black culture. As such, assessing the accuracy of his thesis stands as an open question that has yet to be taken up. This chapter takes up this task, yet not in the narrow sense of simply affirming or disavowing a particular idea or author. Rather, Long's 1981 "State of the Field" address here provides a novel entrée into debates about "the secular" (and the complex of related terms) even as it complicates common assumptions about the category of "black religion" and what the term is imagined to represent. More generally, it illustrates how appeals to "the secular" are simultaneously implicated in descriptive and normative projects.

To this end, this chapter attempts to distill a set of more specific arguments that are often up for grabs in what is here identified as *the trope of black sacred/secular fluidity*. To be clear, this trope—as an analytical practice—is as prevalent among scholars of religion as it is in everyday observations about black life and culture. From stereotypes of natural religiosity and myths of magical Negros to accounts of uncritical allegiance to churches, bus tours in search of "authentic" gospel music, and incubators of sexual taboo and intolerance, black communities continue to be imagined as special sites of spiritual virtue and vice. Even when these ideas find empirical support, such appeals still reveal as much about the commitments and concerns of scholars (and lay observers) as they do about any social/cultural or historical fact of black life. That is, they are historiography as much as they are history.

In fact, Long's arguments were illustrative of one particular moment—one historiographic school, if you will—in a longer history in which the trope of black sacred/secular fluidity has been deployed in different ways and to divergent ends. Long's place in this genealogy will be revisited toward the end of this chapter, which more generally attempts to illustrate how race and religion coalesce in the category of black religion, as performed through this trope of black sacred/secular fluidity. In the Americas—and the West, more generally—it is important to keep in mind that black people and cultures in particular have been understood as the hyperreligious foil to a secularizing zeitgeist, as the authentic "antidote" to a modernizing spiritual wasteland, and as the embodiment of a profane affront to the nation's puritanical ethos.[9] Indeed, blackness has figured as both sacred and profane, but rarely has "the black" been conceived of as a secular presence or secularizing force.[10]

The aim of historicizing this particular trope serves, first, to trouble the way sacred/secular configurations have often been imagined as fundamentally different (from the West) when located in relationship to African American culture (in the West). Here the underlying assumption is that the cultural arrangements that hold in black communities can be understood absent broader social and cultural developments in American society in general.

Thus, clarifying the imagined relationship between these two terms (fluid, permeable, but rigidly opposed) is a necessary step toward grasping how entities marked as sacred and secular are entangled in real time. To put the matter another way, the aim here is to interrogate the relationships between the theoretical maps of secularism (the historiographic) and the cultural territories that they claim to apprehend (the historical), in this case, African American religion and culture, specifically.[11] If a certain, and singular, black sacred/secular fluidity is not to be assumed, then how have such distinctions been enacted? In short, how might a black secular be demarcated?

To pursue these concerns, this chapter is organized into two major sections. The first section provides a provisional survey of the literatures on secularism. To be clear, the aim here is by no means to capture the recent explosion of this field in comprehensive terms. Rather, the primary purpose of this section is twofold: to outline some of the primary currents in these debates insofar as they set the context for the discussion of African American religion later in this chapter and to illustrate how the positive ends associated with secularism in general were often constructed in opposition to the negative means that were imaginatively projected onto black culture. The second section delineates a genealogy of *the trope of black sacred/secular fluidity*, highlighting two competing arguments and at least three different moments in which this trope was powerfully reconfigured even as it maintained its single core claim. This genealogy will capture the many fits, starts, and twists that can be observed ultimately to fail to unsettle the very dichotomy (sacred versus secular) that established the trope in the first place, which is also the focus of this essay's conclusion. In sum, the trope of black sacred/secular fluidity maintains a particular understanding of race even as it recasts, reimagines, and critiques African American religion and culture. Ultimately, it also reinscribes the logics of a very familiar Afro-Protestantism that Charles Long sought to push the field beyond in calling attention to appeals to sacred/secular fluidity.

## SECULAR COMPARED TO WHAT?

Today secularism is indeed much more than a popular academic topic. Debates that focus on variations of this theme have risen to prominence in a range of fields, including anthropology, political science, religious studies, sociology, and theology. It has also made inroads into any number of public audiences.[12] On one hand, this renewed debate results from the recognition, in the present, of the limits of the secularization thesis in light of what is often described as a "resurgence of religion" in contemporary society.[13] In this view, a reconsideration of secularism is required in light of religion's very public role in countless current social crises. Yet, on the other hand, from the outset of the modern era it was in opposition to a commitment to "the secular" that the category of religion was constructed as the premodern straw man. That is, the universal category of "religion" emerged as central to a necessarily comparative, academic, and missionary enterprise that posited (for the West) secular reason as the present of a Christian past and attributed (to the rest) a notion of "religion" as grounded in a past governed by outmoded ways of being in the world even as it persisted in ordering their lives in the present.[14] From this perspective, modernity has been a persistent staging ground for a Hegelian master-slave struggle, wherein the secular is parasitically dependent upon religion (and religion upon Christianity), the foil upon which it established its own significance. Indeed, this is one way of rendering what has been referred to as "the Protestant-Secular Continuum."[15] Moreover, whether along a continuum or as a point of contrast/comparison, the effort to mark modern difference—vis-à-vis the secular/religious distinction—was an argument with multiple valences.

Before tracing the evolution of the trope of black sacred/secular fluidity, it is important to offer an entrée into the larger intellectual landscape of recent debates about secularization, secularism, and the secular. To be clear, this glimpse is by no means intended as a comprehensive survey. Rather, my aim here is simply to lay out a few of the central arguments in this robust field of ideas to set the context for my particular concerns with the study of African American religion. As much as this trope of black sacred/secular fluidity has been mobilized specifically in interpretations of African American culture, it is a species of a larger and longer-standing discursive arena that reflects the ways in which the terms race and religion were co-constitutive in the making of the Americas. Moreover, the very category of religion emerged as part of the processes that made the modern West into separate yet interconnected black and white worlds. Those who were deemed to have religion were most often white; nonwhite and especially black people, not so much.[16] Here, religion marked racial difference. Only later did the notion of African Americans as the religious foil to a narrative of secularization take hold. Similarly, the racial binary that has ordered U.S. history is itself, at least in part, a religious practice. And, as much as this binary served to police racial purity, relationships between black and white people have endured. In the Americas, contact and exchange across the lines of race (and the religious and secular) has been a constant.

The history of race contact in the Americas is deeply shaped by asymmetries of power that take their substantive form(s) from a matrix of cultural, economic, political, and racial logics. Christian theology, colonial politics, Enlightenment reason, and racial pseudoscience coalesced in the emergence of the Atlantic world. As such, the politics of black religion are beholden to the theopolitical history of colonialism, which is coterminous with the development of Christianity in the modern era.[17] Thus, contests over the meaning of race in the Americas are not to be understood as a generic "religious" problem. More precisely, contact is necessarily a theological dilemma because of the fundamentally hegemonic position of Christianity in the making of modernity. In the United States, Protestantism has been both the privileged religious discourse and the discursive frame privileged in efforts to define both "religion" and "race," alongside a host of other modern categories.

Such was the case even as race, framed as a secular, modern discourse, was hailed as the principle of social organization that trumped religion—as an umbrella term for a host of "primitive practices" associated with a previous epoch—under the sign of modernity. In short, to be a modern subject was not simply to become secular or to lose one's religion. Rather, it was to acquire "good religion," which meant ascribing to a particular sort of Christianity (read: primarily, ethical, literate, and reasoning). Good religion took on the form of white Protestantism. In contrast, black religion was "bad religion" in that it carried, by definition, evidence of earlier, African ways of being in the world. This reality was not lost on the African Americans (mostly enslaved Africans) who entered into the New World via its underbelly. Such an awareness was noticeable early on, as witnessed in the performance of a distinctive Afro-Protestant repertoire evident in the literature of the slaves. It was also displayed during the early twentieth century, including in the emergence of a rubric of "The Negro Church," as a black Protestant establishment developed amid a broader set of practices associated with the politics of racial uplift.[18] Thus, the articulation of a modern black identity was not so much a story of progress from religion to race, of a secular (white/Euro-American) subjectivity replacing a sacred (black/African) past life. Rather, it entailed a pronounced confirmation that the two—race and religion, colonialism and Christianity—were co-constitutive in the modern world.

The occasion of the arrival of enslaved Africans in the Americas required, in turn, that those who became black in the New World learn to master the dominant scripts—namely, the content (Christianity) and form (literacy) of reason—of their masters as a means of survival. In this view, modernity (whether black or white, in Africa or Europe) is less the radical break from the premodern past than it is often proposed to be. Moreover, the degree to which arguments about a changing relationship between race (as secular present) and religion (as sacred past) were being lent in service to a modern project begins to crystallize. That is, the assertion of the secular over and against religion becomes seen less as disinterested description of a historical shift and more as prescriptive argument in support of a particular vision of modernity. More generally, appeals to any particular configuration of the sacred and secular reveal as much about the normative commitments of the scholar of religion as they do regarding any social, cultural, or empirical fact of modern society. Such appeals, as they are deployed in debates about African American religion and culture, should be understood as varying iterations of what I have identified as the trope of black sacred/secular fluidity.

My concern here, then, is with how African Americans, as New World subjects, have negotiated the logics of colonialism wherein entrance into the modern presupposed (or proposed) the embrace of a secular present over against a religious past. In this view, Afro-Protestantism was a masterful performance of at least two of the primary scripts of modernity, a coming together of race and religion in enactments of a modern black subjectivity—namely, black religion. And what found its earliest form in the literature of the enslaved, as a point of origin for a tradition of black literature and culture in the New World, was simultaneously a sacred and secular performance.[19] Indeed, slave narratives illustrate the disciplining power of the logic of secularism even as they confirm the continued presence of religion, albeit religion in a novel—perhaps secularized—Protestant form. Still, asymmetrical forms of race contact facilitated by colonialism did much more than lead enslaved Africans to reconfigure their identities in light of how they were cast by the colonialists. Rather, modernity itself might be understood as an effort to make sense of this novel, and often brutal, form of contact.

Religion emerged as one of the primary categories constructed anew to achieve this feat—a term that both obscured and revealed much about the emerging social arrangements of the modern era. Yet modernity, as an intellectual enterprise of the West, entailed theorizing the secular as a negative practice. That is, it was in an opposition to an imagined "religion" that the modern was constructed as "secular," even as the secular was articulated as a departure, evolution, extension, or outgrowth from old (primitive, irrational) forms of religion into a new way of being in the world. In this view, the premodern/modern distinction was more a matter of establishing the difference between good and bad religion than it was of the secular replacing religion.[20] At the same time this distinguishing act was also a racial one. Black people entered modernity as a racial anathema, as both religious and void of religion, by definition. And, ultimately, if by virtue of misrecognition, they were taken for granted as the embodied antisecular.

Especially in the context of the United States, two particular strands of thinking predominate. Here, the Enlightenment project of rationalization and specialization translated into the construction of (and effort to partition) two spheres—sacred and secular—as functionally separate, at least in the realm of public life and political deliberation. If not achieved in practice, this was pursued in policy, through legislative efforts to separate the business of church and state. Concretized in the Bill of Rights, it was recorded that "Congress shall make no law respecting an establishment of religion or prohibiting the free exercise thereof." However, the principle of "separation of church and state"—a rather simplistic metaphor taken to define the relationship between two distinct entities—often served to conflate the nation's commitment to securing religious freedom with its desire to prevent the establishment of a state religion.[21] To be sure, protecting free exercise of religion for individual citizens or specific religious communities is quite a different end than attempting to exorcize a theocratic ethos from state politics.

To complicate matters further, at least until the 1960s, federal policies found reinforcement in scholarly theories. Academic orthodoxies endorsed the idea that the United States (and all of "the West," for that matter) was becoming an increasingly secularized society, a belief only strengthened by Enlightenment notions of historical progress. The secularization thesis, in effect, argued that modern societies would be progressively governed by science and reason; religion, as a residue of a primitive past, would gradually give way to these modernizing forces.[22] Ultimately, the story goes, modernity and secularism assumed each other. And this framework still often holds, even as policy commitments to securing secular norms for "public" discourse are confused with projections of religious decline in the "private" lives of citizens.[23] As such, the church/state division and the secularization thesis came together to naturalize an idea of sacred and secular as distinct and opposed arenas of social reality and to enable a historical teleology in which the narrative arc moves progressively toward a secular end. Thus, the secular subject and society figured as the desired (personal) state of being and (collective) social state.

Together, as politics and scholarship, the secular took on the contours of a condition to be achieved. As such, it might be likened (in the inverse) to a doctrine of sanctification—an ongoing process of old things being made new in the image of enlightenment reason—a theological metaphor embraced here, ironically, as a nod to the Christian contours of a history that persists. In this view, however, if the United States had accepted its (secular) saving grace and was in the midst of becoming sanctified, then black Americans were not yet quite saved nor, perhaps, even capable of salvation.

The fervor of religious life in the contemporary United States and around the world has proven the secularization thesis inaccurate, to say the least.[24] However, even when theories of secularization were in vogue in American society, a different view was often held in regards to the significance of religion in black communities. In fact, African Americans were often understood as the exception to the rule of a secularizing modern citizenry. Not only were they considered hyperreligious, but many of the religious practices associated with black folk (most often, what Du Bois referred to as "the frenzy") were viewed as leftovers from a primitive past and anathema to the aims of modern society.[25] Furthermore, such arguments were often advanced in relationship to a claim about African cultural retentions, a recurring question that crystallized most powerfully in the argument between the Howard University sociologist E. Franklin Frazier and Melville Herskovits, an anthropologist at Columbia, during the 1940s and 1950s.[26] In this view, black hyperreligiosity was abetted by the persistence of an African past in which the sacred permeated all of life and in which the corporate arrangements were not subject to the social forces (and attendant categories) that organized/disciplined modern societies in the West. For Herskovits, the religious vitality apparent in African American life was no doubt the product of a cultural disposition that could be traced back to the shores of West Africa before the trauma of enslavement.

Not only were the religious sensibilities shaping black culture perceived to not be receding, but many observed that religion, black churches specifically, played an especially prominent role that pervaded all of black life.[27] Significantly, if not in view of Africa, early academic work described African American religion through a discourse of pathology, as an obstacle preventing blacks from being socialized into productive American citizens.[28] As Frazier and others averred, slavery had severely disfigured black life. In this view, the undue prominence of religion in modern black life was but a residual (and unwanted) product of this not-so-distant past. Though the discourse of pathology has been sufficiently critiqued (although not entirely undone), an exceptionalist account of African American religion has in large part maintained its hold. To be sure, debates about retentions have given way to more nuanced theories of cultural transmission in the context of diaspora.[29] At the same time, the idea of African Americans as inherently or excessively religious should also be understood in relationship to a set of broader discourses on religion in North America (for example, secularization theories, evangelicalism, religious liberalism, etc.) during the twentieth century.

Indeed, a range of complex and seemingly contradictory images has emerged in relationship to social spaces and cultural forms perceived to involve entanglements of sacred and secular in African American culture. Perhaps the most familiar occasion of such an entanglement can be seen in the history of black sacred music. In this case, figures and forms associated directly with a blurring of the boundaries between the religious and secular have also consistently crossed racial lines to find a hearing within mainstream American culture. For instance, many secular black musicians, since the advent of race records, often included one gospel song at the end of otherwise "secular" albums.[30] In other cases, musicians recorded religious and secular albums under entirely different stage names. In general, in the act of crossing over into the "secular" musical world such artists were often understood as having taken the forms (rhythms, cadences, etc.) of black religion with them into the secular realm. Yet the "sacred" content associated with the original lyrics was presumed to have been left behind. At the same time, scholars have also noted that novel forms of "sacred" music often borrowed deeply from innovations in "secular" music. Across the twentieth century, gospel music, specifically, has often been framed as a baptizing of secular rhythms and sounds in the sacred imagery of the Christian Bible, which pervades the black vernacular and is the lingua franca of African American churches.

The most lauded instance of this phenomenon was the founding of the gospel-blues tradition, typically attributed to Thomas Dorsey during the 1920s. Dorsey, himself a former blues musician, brought a southern-inflected blues aesthetic into the sanctuary of Chicago's Pilgrim Baptist Church. In doing so he drew upon his old secular genre to cultivate a new sacred music, which thereby helped revitalize a changing black Protestant culture, first in Chicago and then beyond.[31] Here the seemingly disparate worlds of "sacred" and "secular" music are fluid and mutually informing. While exchanges such as these, which traverse the sacred/secular divide in multiple directions, have certainly been a cause of contention and conflict within religious communities, they have also been a source of cultural creativity, innovation, and inspiration. More germane to the purposes of this essay, whether for reasons of commodification and consumption or those of dogma and doctrine, sacred and secular forms of music have been presented (in scholarship and in the marketplace) largely as belonging to separate and competing cultural spheres.

Black sacred music, as a genre and tradition, is an especially fitting example in that it is understood both as emblematic of African American religious traditions and exemplary in terms of black culture more generally.[32] No cultural form so compellingly brings together matters of religion and race as does the gospel-blues. The coalescence of these two discourses in this musical form helps explain why music figures as such a prominent theme for black artists and intellectuals, who have repeatedly invoked religious music—from the spirituals to contemporary gospel—in their interpretations of black cultural life. It also presents what is perhaps the central irony of (African) American literature and culture during the twentieth century, namely, that a tradition taken for granted as modernist (and therefore secular, if by default) and as modernizing black subjectivities is so deeply tied to—if not dependent upon—a religious repertoire associated with a premodern past.

It should be clear that gospel music, and the history of Afro-Protestantism in which it takes form, is definitively a New World formation. Still, however, African American culture is often assumed to be somehow immune to shifts—such as sacred/secular divisions—in the broader landscape of American religious history. Thus, the vitality of black religion, and especially the frenzy associated with the gospel-blues performance, figures as the powerful foil to a triumphal narrative of secularization. It is received as the repository and renewed presence of an African past in the black American present even as its lyrics enunciate a Protestant theology. This, however, also presents the problem of how best to figure America in African American religious history. And, more precisely, it begs the question of whether it is possible to discern a particular set of ideas or practices that belie an African American (or, "black") way of negotiating, (re)configuring, or resisting the sacred/secular distinction and the related historical teleology of secularization associated with the West. There are, to be sure, a peculiar set of arguments—academic and lay—that have been mobilized to address this very question. Such claims are organized by what I earlier referred to as the trope of black sacred/secular fluidity, and, I argue, they reveal as much about the individuals who make them (and the moments in which they write) as they do about any particular characteristic of black religious life. This trope has been employed toward a range of widely diverging ends. Yet the two most significant arguments embedded within this trope have taken the shape of either a condemnation of the consequences of segregation or a celebration of the significance of African cultural retentions.

Calling attention to the two particular competing visions associated with the trope of sacred and secular in black—which might be described as the deprivation and celebration theories, respectively—helps clarify how this analytical paradigm has persisted even as the attendant arguments evolved. In both cases, a blurring of the sacred and secular distinction and/or refusal of a secularism (whether legal or historical) attributed to the West is taken for granted and understood as distinct to African American life. However, whether to lay blame (white supremacy, slavery) or give credit (Africa, black cultural resilience) figures as the bone of contention. While it is possible to read the historical trajectory of this trope as one of progress from one interpretive school to the next, both arguments can be observed—if as a dissenting position—at the same time that the rival claim was more widely held. Furthermore, although the normative claims attendant to each perspective may no longer hold, the competing logics of the trope continue to shape the more precise ways in which entanglements of sacred and secular are observed in African American religion and culture. Finally, it is worth noting that the trope of black sacred/secular fluidity illustrates as much about the role of religion within black communities as it reveals concerning the significance of race contact in the United States more generally. Better yet, the trope is one iteration of an expansive effort to wrestle with race matters, or to manage race, through the rhetoric of religious difference.

## A GENEALOGY OF THE TROPE OF BLACK SACRED/SECULAR FLUIDITY

The earliest incarnation of the trope can be grouped under the rubric of what I referred to previously as a deprivation theory of African American culture. Here, sacred/secular fluidity is seen as resulting from the wounds of colonialism and enslavement. Such structural interpretations argued that the institution of American slavery did so much damage that black communities lacked the very basic means requisite for social coherence in modern societies. Further, the conditions maintained under Jim Crow segregation continued to deprive African Americans of the resources required to draw such distinctions within an increasingly differentiated social order. In this view, an inability to distinguish, or a lack of differentiation, between things sacred and secular defined black people and communities by deficit. And in the vacuum of social chaos, religion—especially the Negro's church—emerged as paramount.

If for no other reason than that churches were the first (and for many years only) independent institutions within black communities they established a singular presence. That is, churches assumed an all-encompassing role because initially there were no theaters, dance halls, political organizations, fraternal societies, etc. In the face of segregation and a history of enslavement, black churches therefore bore a singular burden. Presumably secular concerns pressed hard on every side. Thus, *The Negro's Church*, to borrow the title of Benjamin May and Joseph Nicholson's seminal study, could not afford the illusion of being concerned solely with sacred matters, whatever those might be. Indeed, sacred/secular fluidity was the forced hand that "The Negro" was dealt.

The renowned sociologist and Howard University professor E. Franklin Frazier was arguably the most prominent African American associated with this perspective. With a series of books about "the Negro family"—focused on Chicago, the United States, and Brazil—*Black Bourgeoisie*, and *The Negro Church in America*, Franklin argued that black people in the New World were without a culture of their own; the middle passage had left a "tabula rasa" in its wake, and "the Negro" had little option other than to embrace "The Ways of White Folks," as Langston Hughes once put it.[33] Frazier's research offered evidence in support of the argument that black people had no alternative other than to adapt to the norms of a presumably white American culture. If black communities made little distinction between sacred and secular, their best bet was to get with the prescriptive program of secularization. Frazier was by no means alone in his views. Similar arguments were advanced by much of what is associated with the Chicago School of sociology and its defining studies of black urban life during the first half of the twentieth century.[34]

Indeed, a deprivation theory of black culture was the dominant perspective for at least the first half of the twentieth century, both on university campuses and beyond. For instance, in his essay "Blueprint for Negro Writing," which was published in *The New Masses* in 1937, Richard Wright put forward a model for black writers that relied upon an appeal to religion in black America as a measure of cultural dysfunction. Wright, himself a product of the Chicago School and Communist Party politics, inveighed that many black people continued to understand themselves and the world through an "archaic morphology of Christian salvation." Slavery and segregation were to blame for this. That is, the centrality of antiquated theologies to modern black life, according to Wright, was "forced upon them from without by lynch mob, bayonet and mob rule."[35] The pervasiveness of religion reflected a particular "way of life," but it was a "warping" one, and it resulted only because "all other channels are closed." For Richard Wright, E. Franklin Frazier, and countless others, sacred/secular fluidity was decidedly bad, and black cultural life required reform. Indeed, a deprivation theory was the racial orthodoxy of the day. Thus, if black people had not yet received baptism in the waters of secularization, then they should at least gather by the river's side.

To be sure, Richard Wright did not set out to offer a theory of black secularism in his "Blueprint for Negro Writing." Rather, the essay issued a critique of the generation of writers before him, many of whom were associated with what had become known as the Harlem Renaissance. Wright likened these artists to "French poodles who do clever tricks," attempting to prove black humanity by producing literature for white readers, critics, and benefactors. Foremost among those whom Wright had in mind was Zora Neale Hurston, who had gained much attention earlier during the 1930s with her folklore writings and novels, including the popular *Their Eyes Were Watching God*.[36] Indeed, Wright and Hurston engaged in a very public argument during the decade, and Wright's "Blueprint" might be understood as a final word in their acerbic exchange.[37] By all accounts, Wright won their war of words at the time, as he went on to become the most prominent black writer for much of the 1940s and 1950s. In contrast, Hurston all but disappeared from the literary scene for roughly thirty years until her novels and legacy were resurrected and her unmarked gravesite discovered by a young Alice Walker.[38]

During the 1930s, Hurston's ethnographic portraits of black life in the southern United States and Caribbean offered an independent, if less accepted, account for the era. A student of the prominent Columbia University anthropologist Franz Boas, Hurston's readings of black culture departed from those offered by Wright, Frazier, and the popular Chicago School of sociology. Like dominant deprivation theories, she observed a certain disinterest among African Americans in the modern sacred/secular distinction. However, for Hurston, this was not the result of slavery's wounds. Nor was it indicative of a failure to meet the norms of modern society. In fact, it revealed the African origins of black cultures in the Americas. Boas's theory of cultural pluralism provided the space for a novel interpretation.[39] In her 1934 essay "Characteristics of Negro Expression," Hurston argued, "the Negro is not a Christian, really." Here sacred/secular fluidity was consistent with a more general disregard for a set of familiar binaries (high/low, good/evil, divine/

human, etc.). In this view, black religious practices were not deviations from a white Protestant norm. Rather, Hurston observed, "The Trickster-Hero of West Africa has been transplanted to America." And this was cause for celebration.[40]

Hurston's identification (and valorization) of a set of independent cultural values within black communities was indeed a dissenting position during the period in which her writings were first published. Only years later, when her work was rediscovered during the 1960s and 1970s, was the trope of black sacred/secular fluidity reconfigured under the cloak of what has here been referred to as a celebration theory. During the 1970s novel sources were claimed, and a wealth of new scholarship was produced that posited the presence of a generative and distinctive black culture in the United States. From this perspective, sacred/secular fluidity revealed the resilience of West African cosmologies and cultural practices that continued to order the lives of the descendants of enslaved Africans on this side of the Atlantic. That black communities drew little distinction between sacred and secular was not evidence of deformity or deprivation. Rather, it was an example of agency and active resistance to the impositions of white supremacy and its secularizing telos. In effect, the debate during the 1940s between E. Franklin Frazier and Melville Herskovits—who like Hurston was a student of Boas—was turned on its head. To be sure, deprivation theories of black culture continued to demand a public hearing, Senator Daniel Patrick Moynihan's 1965 report on "The Black Family" being the most prominent example. At least in part, the new historiography that developed during the 1970s was motivated by the desire to counter Moynihan's argument that a "Tangle of Pathology" defined black communities.[41] Along with other cultural values, black sacred/secular fluidity was to be welcomed as part of an African cultural inheritance. Blackness, as such, rebuffed the narrative of secularization that was being hailed as triumphant at the time. And, now, this black was considered beautiful.

My effort to outline deprivation and celebration theories of black culture serves to illumine the pliability, yet persistence, of the trope of black sacred/secular fluidity. This narrative also reveals how interpretations of religion are always implicated in race matters, and vice versa. Yet the question of whether to attribute cause to black resilience or white oppression is rarely, if ever, a zero-sum game. Entanglements of sacred and secular coalesce with questions of African retentions and American erasures. Black religion is for certain a New World formation even as it carries evidence and imaginings of the old. In many ways this trope, and larger theories of the role of religion in black culture, reached a synthetic culmination with the publication of C. Eric Lincoln and Lawrence Mamiya's *The Black Church in the African American Experience* in 1990. Writing in the *New York Times Book Review*, James Forbes noted, "the whole nation now has at its disposal much information that black communities have always taken for granted," and "liberation and womanist (black feminist) theologians may enter a second phase of engagement and dialogue."[42] Regardless of whether readers took advantage of this new invitation within what W. E. B. Du Bois once called "the veil"—based on ten years of data collection and distilled across five-hundred-plus pages—the authors' collaborative effort remains a defining text in the study of African American religion.

Both sociologists, Lincoln and Mamiya brought many of the field's key theoretical tensions—sacred, secular; Africa, America; social, spiritual—together succinctly with their idea of a "black sacred cosmos." Perhaps as a grand intellectual compromise, descriptively, the authors argued that "the religious worldview of African Americans is related both to their African heritage, which envisaged the whole universe as sacred, and to their conversion to Christianity during slavery and its aftermath."[43] Furthermore, acknowledging religious diversity, they allowed that "different sacred object(s) or figure(s) will be at the center of the black sacred cosmos." If churches were central for African Americans, it was primarily because of Christianity's dominant place in American history, not because they, as social scientists, were engaged in apologetics. Additionally, Lincoln and Mamiya explained, "this cosmos . . . has also erupted in other black militant, nationalistic, and non-Christian movements."[44] "African heritage" was affirmed. And so were Christianity and American slavery. Indeed, the authors' arguments captured the ongoing power of the trope of black sacred/secular fluidity as the end of the twentieth century approached. Yet they also attempted to account for the critical difference provided by their contemporary contexts. In their rendering, black culture and its "sacred cosmos" was always already a composite form. Yet in identifying specific "non-Christian movements," Lincoln and Mamiya also provided an invitation for other scholars to pursue the particular avenues of sacred/secular fluidity.

If the competing claims of celebration and deprivation theories defined deployments of this trope prior to the publication of *The Black Church in the African American Experience*, then scholarship since has pursued the multiple tracks that Lincoln and Mamiya outlined. The trope may persist as a singular explanation in popular discussions. One thinks, as but one contemporary example, of arguments about African American perspectives on same-sex marriage. Here, black people are cast—in fact, empirically measured—as more religious than the general population. And, as the argument goes, they are uncritically loyal to their churches, in particular, and therefore especially homophobic. In this view, a religious (that is, Christian) worldview pervades all of black life and thus shapes black political participation in ways that resist marriage-equality legislation. In short, sacred/secular fluidity figures as the foil to progressive political engagement. To be sure, the sexual politics of black religion (or even of Afro-Protestantism) are more complicated than rendered in this familiar causal account of how religion colors secular deliberations. In this regard, recent scholarship more often than not eschews such essentialist claims concerning the role religion plays in the various spheres of modern black life.

Yet the history of the trope still has not altogether disappeared even as such claims are put forward, across a number of fields, on much more historically contingent terms. For instance, the theologian Dwight Hopkins avers that since the era of slavery black churches "bore more the marks of holistic community . . . than the white Western notion of separating 'sacred' and 'secular.'"[45] Likewise, the ethnomusicologist Theresa Reed argues that the idea of "sacred-secular duality is relatively new" for black people.[46] And, most recently, the historian Wallace Best proffers that African American religion has "historically defied this polarity."[47] Here singular claims, whether in service to narratives of racial deprivation or celebration, are supplanted by descriptive accounts of the work that religion does in different dimensions of black life, as it is revealed in the folklore of the slaves, in the history of black "secular" music, and under the conditions of migration and urbanization.

Sacred and secular are not naturalized terms that are necessarily part of any social order, even if they appear and circulate as such in the history of the trope. As one scholar put it, the sacred is "made so by doing."[48] Indeed, the categories of sacred and secular have helped simultaneously mark matters of time, space, and place, for instance. In this view, the pairing illumines how the sharing of "sacred" space and time at church on Sundays informs the various "secular" worlds that churchgoers occupy during the rest of the week, as Marla Frederick has shown. They are taken up, by Eddie Glaude, to reveal how a specific "sacred" text has shaped racial identities, political organizing, and rhetoric—all of which have been deemed "secular." And the terms also serve as guides for exploring the aesthetic repertoires of religious institutions— what Nick Salvatore has called "sacred performances"—as they circulate via ostensibly "secular" media.[49] In short, black religion is as black religion does.

Black religion, as with religion in general, does what it does in ways that evade easy categorization or rigid boundaries. It involves entanglement of times, spaces, and places that are often marked off or imagined as distinctly sacred or secular. Except, of course, when it does not. Even as sacred and secular are seen as necessarily entangled, sometimes the doing of black religion has involved a clear delineation of the former from the latter and vice versa. Just as the construction of the category of "the secular" is contingent upon a clear distinction from (or drawing of boundaries around) the "religious" or "sacred" other, black religion also resists such permeability. Or, at least, one can find attempts or claims to do so. That is, even if one accepts that fluidity has been the historical norm, there are traditions that have attempted to draw a "definite distinction between the sacred and the secular."[50]

In contrast to the academic orthodoxy of the trope of black sacred/secular fluidity, Cheryl Sanders has noted that black Pentecostal and Holiness traditions, specifically, often demand a clear demarcation. For her, what matters most in marking this difference—more than institutional origins or cultural entanglements—is the issue of "intentionality." Sanders concedes that "all sacred music borrows from corresponding secular music forms."[51] However, in her estimation, sacred/secular difference is less a matter of the actual marking of space, place, or time in a way that is publicly recognized or the appropriate identification of the sources or forms of a particular practice. Rather, the distinction is contingent upon the concerns of a religious actor and how said actor understands the meaning (or purpose) of what they are doing or have done. Thus, gospel music is decidedly not secular because, according to Sanders, the singer privileges such concerns as conversion and Christian edification over entertainment or aesthetic appreciation alone. In this case, the conditions under which a black secular is implicitly acknowledged are in service to a claim for a particular brand—Pentecostal-Holiness—of Christian identity.

As a Christian ethicist, Cheryl Sanders's arguments reject the trope of black sacred/secular fluidity because she sees in it a scholarly disposition that privileges "secular" commitments. Such academic assertions do not correspond to black Pentecostal-Holiness theology and practice. The distinction between sacred and secular matters because, in short, there are black Christians who draw such lines every day. Indeed, (academic) maps should not be confused for (religious) territories. Whereas a concern with race (celebration or deprivation) has clearly animated the history of the trope of black sacred/secular fluidity, for Cheryl Sanders authentic Christian piety was equally at stake in the elision or observation of sacred/secular boundaries. However, the difference in her critique of the trope of black sacred/secular fluidity is not simply about recasting religious motivations over racial matters. Rather, Sanders's argument is indicative of this and more. In fact, it reflects a Christian hermeneutic of the academic enterprise, where the secular categories of modern historical classification (race, place, time, etc.) are subject to explicit theological demands. Indeed, the intentionality that Sanders posits for the "religious" classification of sacred music similarly holds for her understanding of the scholarly task as a student and product of the Pentecostal-Holiness experience.

In her efforts to maintain fidelity to her tradition, in this case, Cheryl Sanders's argument exposed an interpretive fault line—namely, the trope of black sacred/secular fluidity—in the study of African American religion. That is to say, her assertion was historically accurate (with regards to Pentecostal-Holiness traditions) even as it illumined an unstated theological position (tied to mainline Afro-Protestantism) that has ordered the field. To be sure, African Americans, as individuals and in corporate bodies, have engaged in a host of everyday activities as they have constructed and inhabited their religious worlds, and they have done so in ways that reflect the demands and desires of particular social, cultural, political, and historical contexts. In doing so, those aspects of social experience that scholars have marked as sacred and secular, respectively, have often overlapped and become entangled. Yet they have also resisted and repelled one another, refusing easy entanglements and efforts to disentangle. Moreover, within the specific history of the study of religion in the United States, efforts to demarcate sacred and secular in African American culture have borne the marks of a particular liberal Protestant logic. More precisely, the *racial liberalism* that animated early political histories of "the Negro Church" and the *religious modernism* that helped make the academic (secular) study of religion were themselves related species that gained prominence during the same historical moment.[52]

## CONCLUSION

The entangled intellectual and political currents of racial and religious liberalisms coalesced to establish "the Black Church" as the normative locus for the academic study of African American religion. In this regard, the privileging of a politically engaged black church—as the normative locus of inquiry and methodological principle—was itself a peculiar extension of the academic study of religion's Protestant genealogy. Yet when Charles Long gave his 1981 "State of the Field" address before the Society for the Study of Black Religion (SSBR), he lifted up a theme that had yet to garner critical discussion among scholars of African American religion and theology. To recall, Long honed in on a recurring claim that "the Black community did not and does not make distinctions between the secular and the sacred."[53] This essay has referred to this idea as the trope of black sacred/secular fluidity. According to Long, scholars made this claim because they sought to maintain the significance, indeed the centrality, of churches to all of African American life. Perhaps this concern was felt all the more urgently in a historical moment when, according to popular edict, secularization had run its course and Black Power had rendered Afro-Protestantism less relevant, if not impotent.[54]

Yet if black sacred/secular fluidity was the norm, then partitioning off the historic institution of "the Black Church" as no longer relevant was to embrace a bifurcated logic that was foreign to black communities. In this view, claims of black sacred/secular fluidity served to ward off (or counter) the impositions of the larger white society (where a narrative of religious decline was conceded) even as they buttressed support for some black churches. Ironically, in this case notions of racial opposition (or claims for the distinctiveness of black culture) strangely required a concession to Christian privilege. The pairing of racial difference and religious embrace, or the Christian conscription of black difference, appears simultaneously as a distinctive practice of American Protestantism. Moreover, the idea of a black secular figures both as an anomaly and as axiomatic, all the while remaining relatively unquestioned under the banner of liberal (Afro-)Protestantism.

The theoretical implication of Charles Long's observations—the prospects of secularism for the study of African American religion—remains an intervention yet to be had; it is one that this essay has aimed to invite. Here historicizing the trope of black sacred/secular fluidity has served as one move toward engendering the prospect of an implausible black secular. In this regard, Charles Long's singling out the trope of black sacred/secular fluidity was itself illustrative of a particular historical intervention in a longer historiography.[55] To be sure, much has since been done to call attention to the more precise ways in which sacred and secular have been produced—as distinct and entangled—in African American history. Still, the presumptive logic often remains the same, assuming a fluidity that begins with the "sacred" (churches, doctrines, theologies, etc.) and tracks these phenomena as they travel outward into the realm of the "secular." More precisely, the historical trajectory of secularization (from sacred to secular) reinforces a Protestant past and point of origin. That is, this directional logic begins with the "sacred" and moves outward—across time, space, place, and tradition—to a variety of corresponding seculars. Long's own language of "extra-church traditions" concedes as much, simultaneously moving the field to its margins and maintaining its Christian center.

In ways quite different from Charles Long, Cheryl Sanders confirmed the stakes at play in the trope of black sacred/secular fluidity. Long's critique was animated by a post-Christian racial ecumenism that embraced a diverse set of religious traditions and sources, along with (and owing to) the insights of the social sciences. In contrast, Sanders's rejection of this trope was informed by allegiance to a specific strand of Christian orthodoxy. As much as the study of African American religion has not eschewed its preoccupation with and privileging of "the Black Church," despite the provocations of Long and others, the Pentecostal-Holiness experience to which Sanders appeals has similarly long remained at the margins of the field. Ironically, it may be that the recent increased interest in black Pentecostal and Holiness traditions in the United States is the development that helped occasion the conditions of possibility for the apprehension, if by way of critique, of a black secularism.[56] That is, whether American Pentecostalism is rightly defined by a revival of the premodern (that is, biblical charismata) or a rejection of the modern (science, reason, etc.), it certainly represents a challenge to the racial and religious liberalisms that instantiated the privileged loci of institutional Afro-Protestantism.

The competing claims proffered by Charles Long and Cheryl Sanders bring to the fore a liberal Protestantism that has long held the center in studies of African American religion and has determined the discourse on sacred and secular entanglements more generally. Christian institutions (especially Protestant churches) remain as the primary sites from which various forms of religious power, meaning, or authority originate. Protestantism also helped produce the very categories and methods that created the discursive terms, vis-à-vis religious studies, for deciphering all of the above. Thus, when discussions of African American religion extend beyond black churches, the trope of black sacred/secular fluidity maintains its analytical appeal, and a peculiar Protestant logic persists. The Christian hegemony (that is, "the Black Church") so often the target of a strident critique continues subtly to hold sway.

Moreover, race and religion coalesced in the production and maintenance of a particular "politics of respectability" within the context of an Afro-Protestant establishment that was pivotal in determining the discursive terms for the study of black religion.[57] This brand of modernist Christianity allows openness to "extra-Christian" traditions on distinctly Protestant terms even as it has excluded those Protestant practices (for example, Pentecostal-Holiness) that are deemed, on one hand, theologically exclusive and, on the other, culturally "primitive." Yet such a formulation bears its own bifurcations. It also obscures the ways Protestantism and secularism are entangled and

how competing sacred/secular imaginings are themselves Protestant productions. Moreover, it illustrates how the relationship between theory (or theology) and practice is often obscured in the study of religion, and thus reveals
how scholars of African American religion—with or without stated Christian
commitments—participate in a form of racial politics that conforms to the
logics of a Protestant hegemony in the United States.[58]

# NOTES

1. Editorial, "Black Faculty in Religion Departments at the Nation's Highest-Ranking Universities," *Journal of Blacks in Higher Education* 7 (1995): 28–31.

2. Eliza McAlister and Henry Goldschmidt, eds., *Race, Nation, and Religion in the Americas*
(New York: Oxford University Press, 2004), 17.

3. Charles Long, *Significations: Signs, Symbols, and Images in the Interpretation of Religion*
(Aurora, Colo.: The Davies Group, 2004), 7.

4. Quoting Curtis Evans, "The History of the Black Church," on National Public Radio
(November 27, 2008), http://www.npr.org/templates/story/story.php?storyId=97572839.
For academic work that has been key in troubling the idea of "the Black Church," see Cur-
tis Evans, *The Burden of Black Religion* (New York: Oxford University Press, 2009); Barbara
Savage, *Your Spirits Walk Beside Us: The Politics of Black Religion* (Cambridge, Mass.: The
Belknap Press of Harvard University Press, 2008); and Eddie S. Glaude Jr., "Pragmatic
Historicism and 'The Problem of History' in Black Theology," *American Journal of Theology
and Philosophy* 19, no. 2 (1998): 173–190.

5. Janet Jakobsen and Ann Pelligrini put forward the idea of a "Protestant secular" in the
introduction to their edited volume *Secularisms* (Durham, N.C.: Duke University Press,
2008), 6.

6. On April 8, 1966, *Time* featured the cover story, "Is God Dead?," which popularized debates concerning the challenges that scientific gains posed to traditional ideas about God.
For a signal work that hailed the secularization thesis, see Peter Berger, *The Heretical Imperative: Contemporary Possibilities of Religious Affirmation* (Garden City, N.Y.: Anchor, 1979).

7. See the discussion of E. Franklin Frazier's debate with Melville Herskovits in Albert
Raboteau, *Slave Religion: The "Invisible Institution" in the Antebellum South*, updated ed.
(New York: Oxford University Press, 2004), 48, 55. A similar argument is posed for the
contemporary era in the definition of a "black sacred cosmos" by C. Eric Lincoln and
Lawrence Mamiya, *The Black Church in the African American Experience* (Durham, N.C.:
Duke University Press, 1990).

8. Jakobsen and Pelligrini, *Secularisms*. Also see Tracy Fessenden, *Culture and Redemption:
Religion, the Secular, and American Literature* (Princeton, N.J.: Princeton University Press,
2006); and John Lardas Modern, *Secularism in Antebellum America* (Chicago: University of
Chicago Press, 2011).

9. See Evans's discussion of the idea of black people as "naturally religious" in *The Burden of Black Religion*, 3–16. For a discussion of African Americans as the "antidote" to modernism, see Ann Douglass, *Terrible Honesty: Mongrel Manhattan in the 1920s* (New York: Farrar, Straus and Giroux, 1996), 94.

10. Here I mean to signal Stuart Hall's appeal to "the black" in theorizing black culture without appealing to racial essentialism. Stuart Hall, "What Is This Black in Black Popular Culture?" in *Black Popular Culture*, ed. Gina Dent (Seattle, Wash.: Bay Press, 1992), 21–33.

11. My aim here, in referencing Jonathan Z. Smith's seminal essay and, now, edited volume (Jonathan Z. Smith, *Map Is Not Territory: Studies in the History of Religions* [Chicago: University of Chicago Press, 1998]) is to call attention to the distance between the academic terms invented/utilized by scholars of (African American) religion and empirical realities of what those terms are invoked to describe and analyze.

12. It is beyond the scope of this essay to detail fully recent academic debates about secularism. Seminal works in this regard include Charles Taylor, *A Secular Age* (Cambridge, Mass.: Belknap Press of Harvard University Press, 2007); Jakobsen and Pellegrini, *Secularisms*; Michael Warner et al., eds., *Varieties of Secularism in a Secular Age* (Cambridge, Mass.: Harvard University Press, 2013); Philip Gorski et al., eds., *The Post-Secular in Question: Religion in Contemporary Society* (New York: NYU Press, 2012). For an example of its popular salience, see David Brooks, "The Secular Society," *New York Times* (July 8, 2013).

13. For an insightful discussion and critique of the recent surge in secularism studies, see Fenella Cannell, "The Anthropology of Secularism," *Annual Review of Anthropology* 39 (2010): 85–100.

14. For a book-length discussion of the idea of religion as central to marking modernity, see Talal Asad, *Genealogies of Religion: Discipline and Reasons of Power in Christianity and Islam* (Baltimore, Md.: Johns Hopkins University Press, 1993); Talal Asad, *Formations of the Secular: Christianity, Islam, Modernity* (Palo Alto, Calif.: Stanford University Press, 2003). Gil Anidjar, "The Idea of an Anthropology of Christianity," *Interventions: International Journal of Postcolonial Studies* 11, no. 3 (2009): 367–393, provides a helpful discussion of the Christian history of the category of religion.

15. For a discussion of the "Protestant-Secular Continuum," see Fessenden, *Culture and Redemption*.

16. For an extended treatment of how the category of religion mediated colonial relationships, see David Chidester, *Savage Systems: Colonialism and Comparative Religion in Southern Africa* (Charlottesville: University of Virginia Press, 1996).

17. Anidjar, "The Idea of an Anthropology of Christianity"; Chidester, *Savage Systems*.

18. For a helpful analysis and critique of uplift ideologies, see Kevin Gaines, *Uplifting the Race: Black Leadership, Politics, and Culture in the Twentieth Century* (Chapel Hill: University of North Carolina Press, 1996).

19. For an extended discussion about the literary rites that enabled black entrée into modernity, see Henry Louis Gates Jr.'s argument about the slave narratives and the "trope of the talking book" in *The Signifying Monkey: A Theory of African-American Literary Criticism* (New York: Oxford University Press, 1989).

20. By this I mean to suggest that the normative logic at work in the secular/religious differentiation is similar to what Robert Orsi argues concerning the distinction made between good and bad religion. Robert Orsi, *Between Heaven and Earth: The Religious Worlds People Make and the Scholars Who Study Them* (Princeton, N.J.: Princeton University Press, 2006).

21. Ronald F. Thiemann, *Religion in Public Life: A Dilemma for Democracy* (Washington, D.C.: Georgetown University Press, 1996), 42–71. Thiemann is referencing the Establishment Clause of the First Amendment.

22. For a few works that capture and critique the secularization thesis, see Jose Casanova, *Public Religions in the Modern World* (Chicago: University of Chicago Press, 1994); Christian Smith, ed., *The Secular Revolution: Power, Interests, and Conflict in the Secularization of American Public Life* (Berkeley: University of California Press, 2003); Jon Butler, "Jack-in-the-Box Faith: The Religion Problem in Modern American History," *Journal of American History* 90, no. 4 (2004): 1357–1378.

23. I do not mean to draw an overly simplistic distinction between public and private life. Rather, my intention is to indicate that the principle of "the separation of church and state" served to create norms for public discourse and to protect the rights of citizens to practice religion as they please in their families and religious communities. The principle reveals that different norms are meant to govern the shared national political community and the various religious communities that exist therein.

24. Butler, "Jack-in-the-Box Faith," 1360–1364.

25. African Americans are included as one case of "primitivism" in the early study that adopted the term: Frederick Morgan Davenport, *Primitive Traits in Religious Revivals: A Study in Mental and Social Evolution* (New York: MacMillan, 1905), 45–59. For a more recent critical treatment of this term, see Jacob Olupona, ed., *Beyond Primitivism: Indigenous Religious Traditions and Modernity* (New York: Routledge, 2003).

26. For a recent examination of this debate's import for the study of African American religion, see Evans, *The Burden of Black Religion.*

27. W. E. B. Du Bois, *The Negro Church: A Report of a Social Study Made Under the Direction of Atlanta University* (Walnut Creek, Calif.: Altamira, 1903); Benjamin E. Mays and Joseph Nicholson, *The Negro's Church* (New York: Institute of Social and Religious Research, 1933); Carter G. Woodson, *The History of the Negro Church* (1921; Ann Arbor, Mich.: University Microforms, 1974).

28. Wallace Best connects this analysis to the Chicago School of sociology of the early twentieth century. In particular Best cites Nicholson, *The Negro's Church.* Wallace D. Best, *Passionately Human, No Less Divine: Religion and Culture in Black Chicago, 1915–1952* (Princeton, N.J.: Princeton University Press, 2005), 3–4, 197. Of course, this analysis was not made solely regarding African American religion. As Tracy Fessenden and others have shown, similar arguments were made during earlier periods regarding the Roman Catholicism of European immigrant communities. Fessenden, *Culture and Redemption*, 111–136.

29. See, for instance, Paul Christopher Johnson, *Diasporic Conversions: Black Carib Religion and the Recovery of Africa* (Berkeley: University of California Press, 2007); Jacob Dorman,

*Chosen People: The Rise of Black American Israelite Religion* (New York: Oxford University Press, 2013).

30. Evelyn Brooks Higginbotham, "Rethinking Vernacular Culture: Black Religion and Race Records in the 1920s and 1930s," in *The House That Race Built: Black Americans, U.S. Terrain*, ed. Wahneema Lubiano (New York: Random House, 1997), 157–177.

31. For an introduction to the history of gospel music, see Michael Harris, *The Rise of Gospel Blues: The Music of Thomas Andrew Dorsey in the Urban Church* (New York: Oxford University Press, 1994); Horace Boyer, *How Sweet the Sound: The Golden Age of Gospel* (Montgomery, Ala.: Elliot and Clarke, 1995); Guthrie Ramsey, *Race Music: Black Cultures from Bebop to Hip Hop* (Berkeley: University of California Press, 2003); Jerma Jackson, *Singing in My Soul: Black Gospel Music in a Secular Age* (Chapel Hill: University of North Carolina Press, 2003).

32. Stuart Hall turns to spirituals as the primary example of the "deep structures" of black life in his classic essay "What Is This Black in Black Popular Culture?" in Dent, ed., *Black Popular Culture*.

33. E. Franklin Frazier, *The Negro Family in Chicago* (Chicago: University of Chicago Press, 1932); E. Franklin Frazier, *The Negro Family in the United States* (Chicago: University of Chicago Press, 1939); E. Franklin Frazier, "The Negro Family in Bahia," *American Sociology Review* 7, no. 4 (1942): 465–478; E. Franklin Frazier, *Black Bourgeoisie* (Glencoe, Ill.: Free Press, 1957); Langston Hughes, *The Ways of White Folks: Stories* (New York: Vintage, 1990). Hughes used his series of short stories under this title, at least in part, to illustrate that black people had no monopoly on the problems of cultural pathology.

34. For an overview of the Chicago School of Sociology, see Martin Bulmer, *The Chicago School of Sociology* (Chicago: University of Chicago Press, 1986).

35. Richard Wright, "Blueprint for Negro Writing," in *The Norton Anthology of African American Literature*, 2nd ed., ed. Henry Louis Gates and Nellie McKay (New York: Norton, 2004), 1403–1410.

36. Zora Neale Hurston, *Their Eyes Were Watching God* (1937; New York: Harper, 2006).

37. Glenda Carpio and Werner Sollors, "The Newly Complicated Zora Neale Hurston," *Chronicle of Higher Education* (January 2, 2011).

38. Alice Walker, "In Search of Zora Neale Hurston," *Ms.* (March 1975).

39. For a discussion of the influence of Franz Boas's ideas about cultural pluralism on African American writers, see George Hutchinson, *The Harlem Renaissance in Black and White* (Cambridge, Mass.: Harvard University Press, 1995), 29–124.

40. Zora Neale Hurston, "Characteristics of Negro Expression," in *The Norton Anthology of African American Literature*, 2nd ed., ed. Henry Louis Gates and Nellie McKay (New York: Norton, 2004), 1041–1053.

41. For examples, see John W. Blassingame, *The Slave Community: Plantation Life in the Antebellum South* (New York: Oxford University Press, 1972); Eugene Genovese, *Roll, Jordan, Roll: The World the Slaves Made* (New York: Vintage, 1976); Lawrence W. Levine, *Black Culture and Black Consciousness: Afro-American Folk Thought from Slavery to Freedom* (New York: Oxford University Press, 1977); Raboteau, *Slave Religion*.

42. James A. Forbes, "Up from Invisibility," *New York Times Book Review* (December 23, 1990).

43. Lincoln and Mamiya, *The Black Church in the African American Experience*, 2.

44. Ibid., 7.

45. Dwight Hopkins, *Shoes That Fit Our Feet: Sources for a Constructive Black Theology* (Maryknoll, N.Y.: Orbis, 1993), 1.

46. Theresa Reed, *The Holy Profane: Religion in Black Popular Music* (Lexington: The University Press of Kentucky, 2003), ix–39.

47. Best, *Passionately Human, No Less Divine*, 2.

48. Karen E. Fields, "Translator's Introduction: Religion as an Eminently Social Thing," in Emile Durkheim, *Elementary Forms of Religious Life*, trans. Karen E. Fields (1915; New York: Free Press, 1995), xlvi.

49. For further discussion, see Marla F. Frederick, *Between Sundays: Black Women and Everyday Struggles of Faith* (Berkeley: University of California Press, 2003); Eddie S. Glaude, *Exodus: Religion, Race, and Nation in Early Nineteenth-Century Black America* (Chicago: University of Chicago Press, 2000); Nick Salvatore, *Singing in a Strange Land: C. L. Franklin, the Black Church, and the Transformation of America* (Urbana: University of Illinois Press, 2005).

50. Cheryl J. Sanders, *Saints in Exile: The Holiness-Pentecostal Experience in African American Religion and Culture* (New York: Oxford University Press, 2000), 89.

51. Ibid., 89. Sanders advances a similar critique of Womanism, alleging a dependence on nonbiblical (i.e., secular) literature as reflecting its identity as non-Christian. See Sanders's contribution to "Christian Ethics and Theology in Womanist Perspective," *Journal of Feminist Studies in Religion* 5, no. 2 (Summer 1989): 83–112.

52. Savage, *Your Spirits Walk Beside Us*; Evans, *The Burden of Black Religion*; Orsi, *Between Heaven and Earth*; William Hutchison, *The Modernist Impulse in American Protestantism* (Durham, N.C.: Duke University Press, 1992). As can be seen here, this is just as much the case for interpretations of African American religion and culture. As I have argued elsewhere, racial ecumenism and religious liberalism are of a kind. See Josef Sorett, "We Build Our Temples for Tomorrow: Racial Ecumenism and Religious Liberalism in the Harlem Renaissance," in *American Religious Liberalism*, ed. Leigh Schmidt and Sally Promey (Bloomington: Indiana University Press, 2012).

53. Charles Long, address on the "State of the Field." James Evans quotes from Long's speech in *Spiritual Empowerment in Afro-American Literature: Frederick Douglass, Rebecca Jackson, Booker T. Washington, Richard Wright, and Toni Morrison* (Lewiston, N.Y.: Edwin Mellen, 1987), 1. A full copy of this speech, held within the archives of the Society for the Study of Black Religion (SSBR), was generously made available to me by Dr. Larry Murphy, SSBR's archivist and historian.

54. In the preface to his first book, *Black Theology and Black Power*, James Cone states that various iterations of the claims of Black Power (e.g., Malcolm X, "Christianity is the white man's religion!") motivated to him to begin a black theology, at least in part, as a defense of his parent's faith, which was then considered untenable by many of his peers. James Cone, *Black Theology and Black Power* (New York: Harper and Row, 1969), xiii.

55. In his 1981 "State of the Field" address to the Society for the Study of Black Religion, Charles Long explicitly elevated several of these new historical works as resources for developing a "black cultural methodology" in the study of religion. Black theology would be more sound if it gleaned from the gains of the "empirical disciplines." The study of religion in black America would be best served, he argued, by an engagement with allegedly secular sources and methodologies. See also Forbes, "Up from Invisibility." Work by historians such as John Blassingame, Eugene Genovese, and Lawrence Levine helped define a new historiography that posited a culture in the slave quarters. Raboteau's *Slave Religion* (1978) extended such arguments more squarely into the field of American religious history. James Cone's black liberation theology was animated by a similar impulse to take seriously the black cultural context in which Afro-Protestantism took shape. Like Cone, Charles Long came of age intellectually amid these developments. Whereas Cone interpreted black life—and Black Power, precisely—through the categories of Christian theology, Long more directly drew upon this new historical research in his efforts theorize "the religion of blacks in the United States." For Long, the sources that were central to the current historiographic moment demanded a "secular" method of inquiry (i.e., social scientific rather than theological) and required sources that were necessarily more expansive than the context of Christian churches.

56. Here I mean to suggest that Cheryl Sanders's critiques in *Saints in Exile* anticipate what has more recently been described as the "New Black Theology," which includes a critique of what it identifies as the secular in previous generations of Black Theology. As I understand it, an effort to mark more explicitly the lines between sacred and secular is understood as serving the purpose of delineating a more "authentic" (or orthodox) Christian black theology. For a review of these developments, see Jonathan Tran's 2012 cover story, "The New Black Theology," *The Christian Century* (January 26, 2012).

57. For an extended discussion of "religious respectability" in the study of African American religion, see Jonathan L. Walton's discussion in *Watch This! The Ethics and Aesthetics of Black Televangelism* (New York: NYU Press, 2009).

58. For a discussion of the "politics of respectability" and also an example of uplift ideology in a religious context, see Evelyn Brooks Higginbotham, *Righteous Discontent: The Women's Movement in the Black Baptist Church, 1880–1920* (Cambridge, Mass.: Harvard University Press, 1993).

# PART II
## READINGS

# 3

## SLAVES, SLAVERY, AND THE SECULAR AGE

### OR, TALES OF HAUNTED SCHOLARS, LIBERATING PRISONS, EXORCISED DIVINITIES, AND IMMANENT DEVILS

Edward J. Blum

**W**HAT DID it mean and how did it feel to live as a slave within a secular age? What could the insights, experiences, and actions of women and men who were legally owned by other women and men reveal about the place of race amid the swirl of the secular? How might the spectacular new scholarship on the rise of secularism look differently if it placed race and slavery at its center rather than on its periphery? Trafficking with one slave who freed himself over the roads and waterways of America circa 1851 allows us to map some avenues that cut into and through the circuits of secularism, race, and religion during the nineteenth century. Henry Brown not only ruminated on the multiple meanings of religion, religions, and the religious in American society in his writings. He also performatively enacted the life of one living through the material artifacts, ideological structures, and group dynamics of slavery and freedom, secularism and faithfulness.

To gain his liberty, Henry Brown purchased and placed himself within a prison. He had been a slave in Virginia for some thirty years when he hatched perhaps the most creative escape plan in American history. He contorted his five-foot, eight-inch, two-hundred-pound body into a wooden box that was three feet long, two feet wide, and two feet deep. For air, he drilled several small holes into the wood, and to keep cool, he carried a pouch of water to wet his face. A friend mailed him the 250 miles from Richmond to Philadelphia. After twenty-seven hours, he arrived and heard a voice say, "let us rap upon the box and see if he is alive." Brown responded audibly to the rapping, and what followed was, as he put it, his "resurrection from the grave of slavery."

As a fugitive, Brown embarked on a new career as an innovative abolitionist stage performer. Once again framed by wood (stages), he reenacted his boxed entombment and subsequent "resurrection." The box even became a part of Brown's identity. While many slaves renamed themselves as fugitives to obscure their pasts or to proclaim their new autonomy, Henry Brown kept his first name and surname. He added, though, a middle one that forever linked the object of his escape to his identity: "Box."[1]

The physical box was not the only one Brown encountered in and out of slavery. In his personal narrative published in 1851, the same year Herman Melville released his story of a crew held captive within another wooden box in *Moby-Dick*, Brown presented the religious and moral education of his youth as a series of mazes. There were enclosed corridors that left him bewildered at times, angry at others, and inspired to enact the death-defying at yet others. "My mother used to instruct me in the principles of morality, as much as she was able," Brown explained, "but I was deplorably ignorant on religious subjects, for what ideas can a slave have of religion . . . ?" His mother told him "not to steal" and not "to lie." He was "to behave himself properly in other respects." When it came to his masters, Brown endeavored to speak for himself and other enslaved children when he acknowledged: "I really believed my old master was Almighty God, and that his son, my young master, was Jesus Christ."[2]

How did Brown conflate his master with "The Master"? Why did he perceive one son to be quite another one? The first explanation Brown offered was his master's supposed control over nature. "When it was about to thunder, my old master would approach us, if we were in the yard, and say, 'All you children run into the house now, for it is going to thunder.'" Beyond the master's accurate meteorological prophecies, the second evidence of his godliness was his goodness. "Our master was uncommonly kind, and as he moved about in his dignity, he seemed like a god to us." Brown recalled that it was not until he reached the age of eight that he abandoned such "childish superstition."[3]

Brown had to unlearn these original viewpoints, which he called superstitions, so he could come to know "religious" subjects and "religion" itself. His youthful reflections crashed into other approaches to God and Jesus when he overheard his mother talking about a church baptism. Unlike Charles Grandison Finney, a powerful evangelical revivalist, or Joseph Smith, the leader of the new Church of Jesus Christ of Latter-day Saints, who went alone into the wilderness to experience God and Jesus in new forms, Brown learned his lessons as part of a family discussion.[4] A woman at church was asked if she knew that Jesus had died for her sins. She responded that she "knew he had come into the world . . . but . . . had not heard he was dead." She explained her lack of knowledge by appealing to her geographical, residential, and communication limitations. Since "she lived so far from the road, she did not learn much that was going on in the world." A worried Brown also understood the sacred to be immanently and materially part of this world and asked his mother "if young master was dead." She explained that they were talking about "our Saviour in heaven" and not the young master. Brown asked "if there were two Saviours." Then his mother "filled" him with "astonishment" when she explained that the "young master was not 'our Saviour.'"[5]

This correction led to a flood of startling questions and revelations. Since God and his master were not one and the same, then who or what was God, and where was God? Who was this Jesus who had come into the world, had died, but could no longer be seen? Moreover, as Brown came to learn more about slavery through experiences and stories of whippings, sexual abuse, food deprivation, family dismemberment, and imprisonments, his perspective on slave masters changed dramatically. The so-called followers of Christ "evinced more of the disposition of demons than of men." If readers wanted to know how far Brown had come after his escape—not just physically but religiously as well—they could hear his "opinion of the slaveholding religion of this land. I believe in a hell, where the wicked will forever dwell, and knowing the character of slaveholders and slavery, it is my settled belief, as it was while I was a slave, even though I was treated kindly, that every slaveholder will infallibly go to hell, unless he repents."[6]

The more Brown observed the religion of slaveholders and what they wanted for their slaves, the more he rejected them. As an adult, Brown considered the great "wonder" to be that he "did not imbibe a strong and lasting hatred of everything pertaining to the religion of Christ."[7] In time, Brown began to view God as transcendent and disembodied; God was a distant and all-seeing friend who spoke to and aided the oppressed like himself. He explained the origins of his escape plan this way:

> I felt my soul called out to heaven to breathe a prayer to Almighty God. I prayed fervently that he who seeth in secret and knew the inmost desires of my heart, would lend me his aid in bursting my fetters asunder, and in restoring me to the possession of those rights, of which men had robbed me; when the idea suddenly flashed across my mind of shutting myself up in a box, and getting myself conveyed as dry goods to a free state.[8]

A free fugitive, Brown then dedicated his life to the "sacred duty" that was "the redemption of my fellow men."[9]

For Henry Box Brown, slavery was the central element in his perceptions of the human and suprahuman, of this world, ones before, and ones beyond. Slavery colored his recognitions of and reckonings with "superstition" and "religion," the "Almighty" and the demonic, the material and the immaterial. His childhood beliefs were not simply naïve enchantments of youth; they were lived experiences with fleshy, embodied men and women like himself. His view of the master and master's son as God and Jesus respectively was not a mix-up. He believed that gods walked the earth, interacted with him, told him where to go, when, and how. When his questioning led his mother to indicate that these were only men, Brown had to locate new senses of being, beings, and the relationships between. He did not reject religion or religiosity. Rather, as he described it, he became free to have "a religion." His particular Christianity became one choice among various options, which included the faiths of the slavemasters, the faiths of the slaves, and hatred for Christianity in general. Brown discovered for himself a moving faith, one that drove him to box himself for and to freedom and one that reevaluated his former god to be the devil.

Tarrying with Henry Box Brown suggests some new ways to think about what it meant to live during the supposedly secular age that was the nineteenth century. According to Charles Taylor and several other historians, sociologists, and political philosophers, this century in Europe and North America was part of the emerging "secular age." It was near the end of a more than five-hundred-year march from societies where "belief in God" was "unchallenged and unproblematic" to a time when religion was "understood to be one option among others." The secular age, as Taylor envisions it, was defined by tectonic shifts. The porous self was closed or at least could be closed. No more was it assumed that sacred forces could penetrate the physical world and its bodies. This now "buffered self" became aware of "the possibility of disengagement." Moreover, Brown's time was one where nationalistic revolutions, biblical higher criticism, and the emergence of Darwinian evolutionary theory were upsetting the bulwarks of traditional faith experiences.[10]

The work that has most substantively applied Taylor's insights to the age of Henry Box Brown has been John Lardas Modern's provocative *Secularism in Antebellum America*. With Taylor, Modern asks what it meant to "live in a secular age." Through innovative readings of everything from the American Tract Society to spiritualist séances to constructions of mechanical contraptions, Modern showcases how the "range of choices" was patterned by circumstance, institutions, machines, and media. As distant forces such as the "invisible hand" of markets, print producers, and machines acted upon humans, the authority that had once been handed only to the supernatural was now brought into the natural world. God seemed to come down to earth but be hidden amid a cloud of humanity and a whirlwind of technology. According to Modern, American modernity and its secularism were built upon supernatural encounters where ghosts were created, subjected to new explanations, and then cast away or controlled and harnessed.[11]

Brown's narrative calls for recognition both of how these seismic shifts were racialized and also that the arcs of history and cultural expressions that Taylor and Modern detail were contingent upon racial subjugation and mastery. At a most elemental level, Brown's autobiography and his performances address Taylor's and Modern's emphasis upon the "conditions of belief, experience and search" as "lived experiences" where religious matters were an "immediate reality, like stones, rivers, and mountains."[12] Just as Taylor and Modern are obsessed with the issue of living amid a secular age, Brown was fixated on how to live within and beyond a slave age. Even more, Brown's narrative suggests that considerations of God, superstition, religion, religions, the religious, supernatural power, and the links among the material and immaterial were profoundly shaped by racial experiences.

At another level, the bodies and persons of slaves were both an immediate reality and a distant influence for the white Europeans and Americans discussed by both Taylor and Modern—highlighting and haunting their worldviews. Brown's actions, words, and performances endeavored to destabilize the world the slaveholders had made, and in so doing, they revealed how people on the underside of modernity influenced the trajectory of modernity.[13]

Slaves, slavery, and race haunt and trouble the stories crafted by Taylor and Modern. When these scholars endeavor to explain who they study, they stumble. Taylor begins by claiming he studied "The change which mattered to people in our (North Atlantic, or 'Western') civilization." Then later, he declares, "I shall be concerned, as I said above, with the West, or the North Atlantic world; . . . the civilization whose principal roots lie in what used to be called 'Latin Christendom.'"[14] As at the beginning, Taylor then employs the possessive "our" when speaking of this history. Time and again he refers to "our civilization" or "our western civilization."[15] One offhand aside recognizes trouble in this conflated "our" of the past and the present. When discussing the shift from an age when the supranatural could intervene at any time to an era when the supranatural was only felt at particular holy times and seen as distant or removed at most other times, Taylor turns to a racial analogy. Consider, he writes, the time when a "race riot at home" broke out. It "may disturb our equanimity, but we rapidly revert." The "we" in this case are whites who are only affected by race when it comes in the form of a riot, and then "we" can return to our raceless lives. The causes of the race riot are inconsequential to Taylor, and there is no sense that the "equanimity" felt by one community could be contingent upon the frustrations of the rioters.[16]

Modern, for all his concern over language, hidden meanings, and unspoken assumptions, rarely acknowledges that his America is white, middle class, and northern. His "Protestants" include white spiritualists but not black Methodists. Rather than confront his exclusion of people of color explicitly, Modern hides behind the language of "others" and buries black people and their words in footnotes. Modern includes a quotation from Frederick Douglass, for instance, but in a footnote at the bottom of a page.[17]

By "burying" and running from blackness, Modern, probably unbeknownst to himself, follows the lead of his inspiration, Herman Melville's *Moby-Dick*. Early in the novel, a lead character of *Moby-Dick*, Ishmael, enters a "negro church" where he beholds "a black Angel of Doom" preaching about "the blackness of darkness." Ishmael mutters "Ha" and backs out. It appears to be a "Trap" to him.[18] Modern never excavates the meaning of this impression and this choice. He never wonders why Ishmael avoids this "trap" but not Ahab's. What was it about the "blackness of darkness" that compelled Ishmael to leave? If society had deemed Ishmael to be a "negro" or a legal "slave," how would the story have been different?[19]

But Modern cannot avoid slaves or slavery; they frame his book far more than he may realize. While it may be easy to become lost in the verbosity of the book's subtitle, the main title provides a chronological and geographical marker: "Antebellum America." Of course, "antebellum" here refers to the decades that preceded the Civil War. Since there would have been no war without slaves, a point President Abraham Lincoln made clear in his Second Inaugural Address, they also then were crucial to the title's name: "antebellum." The title sets readers into a world that was somehow, someway, made by slaves and slavery.

In moving slaves and issues of race from analogies, footnotes, or titles to the center of the conversation, we can view the troubling ways in which Taylor and Modern use universal claims to cloak their particularisms. In *Secularism in Antebellum America*, Modern contends that he deals with the "inscriptions made by a relatively privileged subculture upon themselves and others." The "others" here are acted upon but never actors themselves. At no point do they manipulate the materiality around them, such as transforming a box into a vessel of liberation. Taylor goes much further. He explains that his study of "our civilization" provides answers to "universal human concerns."[20] In both cases, Modern and Taylor claim that their limited sights have broader implications, and it appears that in both cases the unseen, unheard, unremembered slaves of the United States are figures either acted upon by other forces or simply inconsequential elements of their societies.

By ignoring race and people of color, this new scholarship on "the secular" and "secularism" repeats a fundamental flaw of the older work on "secularization." That work, which sought to explain how and why the Western modern world turned away from religion, tended to ignore people of color entirely. When it did include African Americans, for instance, and try to make some sense of their high churchgoing rates, secularization scholarship fumbled for explanations.[21] Taylor, Modern, and others who have been critical of the secularization thesis and have turned to notions of the secular have duplicated their omission and have once again hidden what race has to say to and about issues of secularization, the secular, and secularism.

Henry Box Brown, however, knew a thing or two about how to make meaning from absence. He figured out how to use hiddenness to make presence, to turn boxes into bridges, to worship God by warring against others, and to exorcise evil by incarnating it. Brown and slaves like him suggest that studies of the secular may want to tread lightly and attentively around the crates and spaces they do. For, who knows, a human may be there, hidden, transforming the environment and remaking the cosmos.

## HOL(E)Y BOXES

Before we read the narrative of Henry Box Brown, we behold the box. In his published narrative of 1851, an illustration of his "resurrection" from it preceded the written portion. A white man and a black man hold the box top, which reads, "Philadelphia / This Side Up / With Care." To the side, one white man appears shocked; another stares stoically at the emerging Brown. On the box top, we see five holes. Brown had drilled these small "crevices" before and during the journey. It was from them he received the precious air he needed to remain alive, follow God's direction, and begin his sacred calling. The box was so vital to Brown that it became a part of his name.[22]

In the years before Brown's narrative, evangelical Christians and antislavery activists had turned to visual displays as another form of moral suasion. The American Tract Society, for instance, was one of a number of new evangelical organizations that flooded the nation with printed ephemera and didactic dramas. Their short tracts typically included a few images, and the organization was quite aware that the visuals were essential to their morals. In 1824, the ATS declared that tracts "*should be entertaining. . . .* There must be something to allure the listless to read, and this can only be done by blending entertainment with instruction." Pictures were central to this "allure."[23]

Antislavery activists too rushed into the world of the visual. They agreed that visual culture could be a powerful tool for influencing sentiment and political choice. From stereotypes of kneeling slaves asking "Am I Not a Man and a Brother?" to illustrated versions of *Uncle Tom's Cabin*, antislavery activists deployed the visual for emotional and political effect. Visual technologies and presentations were drawn into their religious and moral crusades.[24]

Boxes—literal and figurative—were essential to the ideological structures of Brown's age. Intellectually, the Enlightenment was a boxing endeavor. The rage to categorize drove Europeans to define, categorize, and reduce to boxes everything from the diversity of the animal kingdom to the flora and fauna that covered the ground. The modern concept of "race" was also part of this boxing trajectory. Seeking to differentiate and create hierarchies of humans, Europeans and Americans invented racial thinking by boxing humans into categories and seeking to affix meaning to the various groups.[25] The physical and the spiritual were tied together. Phrenologists of the nineteenth century believed they could locate moral and intellectual qualities of a person on her or his head, and they developed boxed grids of the cranium to show where moral meaning resided.[26]

Brown's box was not only on display in his narrative. A children's book from 1849 contained a chapter about "Henry Box Brown" that detailed his story. The chapter in *Cousin Ann's Stories for Children* featured Brown standing within his box, shaking hands with a white man who had opened it. According to the chapter, Brown's idea came from "a lucky thought," and Brown was a hero. Sadly, since his family in North Carolina were illiterate, they would never have the chance to read his story, and they would never be able to write to him.[27]

Although "Cousin Ann" referenced the box idea as "lucky," Brown viewed it as inspired by God. Even more, in his narrative, to act upon the box was to participate in God's movement in this world. Unknowingly, humans who touched it were actually conduits of God's activity in the world. As Brown recalled in the narrative, at one point while within the box, it was set on its side. Facing head down, Brown feared he would die as the blood rushed toward his brain. At the same moment, a white passenger on the vessel had tired of standing and was searching for a place to sit. He saw Brown's box and pushed it over so it rested lengthwise, forming a bench to sit upon. This man's desire for comfort saved Brown's life, yet when Brown remembered it he exclaimed, "I lifted up my soul in prayer to God, who alone, was able to deliver me."

In this case, acting upon the box—even when failing to recognize there was anyone in it—became an act of God. The box, which enclosed Brown but then which he enclosed within his name, was present not simply for the ways it contained this fugitive. It was there for the ways he transformed it into a mechanism of uncontainment.

The presence of the box also mattered for what it lacked. Holes bored into it were essential as well. Holes mattered to Brown, and they matter intensely to Charles Taylor and John Lardas Modern, too. One of the key points in *A Secular Age* is the closing of the porous self. Before modernity could disenchant the world or romantics could try to reenchant it, a fundamental shift had to take place whereby many people became convinced either that purposeful suprahuman forces did not act in this world or that humans could stop them from entering one's body and soul. The creation of a buffered self in place of the porous self was essential to a later anthropocentric shift. The buffered self had the power to resist angels or demons. The self could recognize itself as a self; it could determine where it ended and where others began. This buffered self, moreover, could close itself to other forces.[28]

Before modernity, porousness had left many Europeans and Americans terrified of possession. They feared devils and demons bewitching them and their loved ones. Their anxiety manifested itself in witchcraft trials, rituals, and executions. By the mid-nineteenth century, however, the enlightened and buffered self had so disenchanted the world that many modern men felt themselves invulnerable and self-possessed. Taylor sums it up this way: "In general, we relate to the world as more disembodied figures than our ancestors."[29]

The buffered self, however, was also a boring self, at least for some. The anthropocentric shift that Taylor discusses led some Americans and Europeans to pine for an enchanted world. Some romantics found it in art, beauty, and nature. Others, as Modern and other scholars have shown, moved toward spirit rapping and spiritualism. They longed to be possessed or at least for spirits to speak to them through rapping on tables or speaking through mediums. One individual even created a machine with which to copulate to make the spirit world manifest in the material realm. Possession became an obsession, Modern finds, but one that humans thought they could at least manipulate and at best control.[30]

Slaves like Henry Brown understood categories, boxes, porosity, and possession in registers quite distinct from the ones described by Modern and

Taylor. While white Europeans and Americans fretted over and then desired spiritual possession, African Americans in the antebellum South experienced embodied possession. Their enslavement was legal, physical, sexual, spiritual, and communal. They were the literal possessions of slave masters, and the totality of American society was geared to justify and defend their bondage. Moreover, their bodies were anything but buffered. With the cat-of-nine-tails or the cow skins, masters could make slave bodies porous: the proof was in the flowing, dripping blood. Modernity's buffering of the self—whether spiritual or physical—simply did not apply to the bodies of slaves.[31]

In Brown's narrative and many others from slaves, violence against bodies was described in spiritual terms. Samuel Northrop remembered how he prayed while being whipped, but God failed to answer. "I was all on fire," he wrote of his physical sensations. "My sufferings I can compare to nothing else than the burning agonies of hell!"[32] Brown detailed one particular occasion where an overseer actually used a Bible to beat a slave. "This professing christian proceeded to try the effects of the bible on the slaves' body, and actually dealt him a heavy blow in the face with the sacred book!" In this case, the good book was unable to do the trick, so the overseer turned to a stick instead.[33]

Male slave owners, furthermore, could use their penises to penetrate the bodies of slave women and men. Regarding slave women, Brown wrote, masters could "violate her person at any moment, and there is no law to punish him for what he has done. . . . [It] is my candid opinion, that one of the strongest motives which operate upon the slaveholders in inducing them to maintain their iron grasp upon the unfortunate slaves, is because it gives them such unlimited control over the person of their female slaves."[34] William Anderson discussed how at the New Orleans slave auction, the women "were stripped and whipped." These women were beaten "until they yielded; then by debauchery and incest" raped by the white men. Anderson could only conclude, "If there is anything like a hell on earth, New Orleans must be the place."[35]

Of course, Taylor and Modern may respond that they are discussing different forms of porosity and possession. They may suggest that they were dealing with perceptions of suprahuman or immaterial forces acting upon the human and material. Yet how do we differentiate between human and suprahuman forces in the context of enslavement? Brown described a time when he believed his master and master's son to be God and God's son. Sojourner Truth's first biographer wrote that early in her enslavement "she looked upon her master as a *God*; and believed that he knew of and could see her at all times, even as God himself."[36] John Jea, who lived as a slave in New York and in freedom became a preacher who traveled throughout the Americas and Europe, disdained Southern whites for failing to teach slaves the Christian faith. In his 1811 autobiography, he explained, "We were often led away with the idea that our masters were our gods."[37] Repeated use of the word "master" in social and religious circles made the line between human and divine awfully blurry. Slave spirituals used the phrase "Massa Jesus" on many occasions, and in catechisms for slaves, whites routinely referred to themselves as "master."[38] Moreover, if we take Taylor and Modern seriously that they want to understand how religion and secularism are "lived," then the distinctions may fall apart. What is the difference between Satan or God demanding sexual favors and a master doing the same? In both cases, possessed individuals were compelled by stronger agents to be and remain porous.

What is striking about Henry Brown, however, is that he put porosity to work for self-possession and that he made it tangible in the actual box and his representations of it. He bore holes not because being buffered was boring but because being buffered was impossible. He made a box not to confine but to confuse the men who would be masters. The box and the holes were necessary. To take ownership of himself, he created pores in his box. The holes were necessary so he could breathe and survive. The holes provided some measure of light. The holey box became so holy to Brown that he made sure to represent it during his displays and boxed it within his own name. The box and its holes became part of the evidence of his resurrection. Sounding like the doubting disciples of Christ's age, those who now saw the box saw it as proof of his resurrection: "if I had not myself been present at the opening of the box on its arrival," wrote J. McKim later, "and had not witnessed with my own eyes, your resurrection from your living tomb, I should have been strongly disposed to question the truth of the story."[39]

## EXORCISING GOD, RAISING THE DEVIL, AND THE METAPHYSICAL MASTERY OF FORMER SLAVES

The creation of a boxed and porous prison for self-possession and self-definition was performative, visual, and religious magic unlike anything

Americans had seen before. Little wonder that Brown became a celebrity performer and highly sought speaker. But two other of Brown's amazing feats were the exorcising of God and the immanentizing of the devil. Within his slave family, he found a way to transform God from corporeally immanent to disembodiedly transcendent. At the same time, Brown resurrected demons from hell and placed them in the human landscape and structures. In these ways, Brown's metaphysics may have been more complicated than the theorist Michel Foucault's definition of metaphysics. Reviewing a work, Foucault offhandedly suggested that metaphysics dealt primarily with the "materiality of incorporeal things." For Brown, the flow was not simply one to another. His metaphysics was about banishing certain incorporeal entities from this world's material realm and then finding ways to materialize other incorporeal beings. In the flows up and down—earth to heaven and hell to earth—Brown redrew the material and spiritual map of the realm supposedly possessed by white men.[40]

Understanding how and why Brown exorcised God Almighty from the body of slaveholders and then transfigured masters into demons is important for a number of reasons that speak to issues of living amid a secular age. First, as Brown understood it, these maneuvers allowed him to have "religion" and be "religious." Second, they helped explain systematically and theologically the power and place of slavery in his life and culture. Third, at a time when evaluative and comparative religion was becoming all the rage, they allowed Brown a way to render, critique, and ultimately judge among various "religions" in America.

According to Taylor, the age of the Enlightenment problematized the presence and power of god and devils. The Protestant Reformation and the emergence of Providential Deism were critical in this story. By challenging Catholic "mysteries" and by focusing less on God's interactive powers and more on anthropocentric capabilities, they shackled the once-omnipotent God and provided humans with a sense of invulnerability.[41]

Both Taylor and Modern find that some kind of malaise followed the banishment (or at least handcuffing) of God and the devil. Many people felt that the overarching significance of their lives seemed gone. They now experienced disconcerting ordinariness. The resulting romantic period, as discussed by Taylor, was an effort to reenchant the world through beauty, nature, and art. According to Modern this moment was a time when new technologies and bureaucracies took the place of God's immanent power, and the result was a fetishizing of machines, statistics, and organizations.[42]

In contrast, nature did not necessarily reveal the handiwork of God for Brown and his family. One of the first lessons he remembered from his mother was one where she would place him on her knee and point to the forest trees, "which were then being stripped of their foliage by the winds of autumn." She would "say to me, my son, as yonder leaves are stripped from off the trees of the forest, so are the children of the slaves swept away from them by the hands of cruel tyrants." Brown recalled that her voice "would tremble." She "would seem almost choked with her deep emotion."[43]

Of course, his mother also taught him a key lesson: that his master was not "the master." Although it came as a shock to Brown, his master's lack of divine immanence was certainly not met by malaise or a feeling of ordinariness. In fact, since his master was not "the master," this fired Brown not only to search for new links to the divine but also to act in concert with that suprahuman power.

While "nature's God" failed to offer Brown the awe and wonder it did for romantics, darkness from the confines of the material box provided the light for Brown to experience and participate in God's blessings. Once again, lessons from family life were central. This time, it was the sale of his wife and children. After he witnessed them sent away, his "soul called out to heaven to breathe a prayer to Almighty God." He looked to a God who "seeth in secret" and one who "knew the inmost desires of my heart." It was this immaterial God who inspired Brown's material salvation. During his prayers, "the idea suddenly flashed across my mind of shutting myself up in a box, and getting myself conveyed as dry goods to a free state."[44]

There was no malaise from this immaterial God. There was inspiration to board a box. During the hours trapped in the box, when Brown "tumbled along drays, railroad cars, steam-boat, and horse carts," he prayed. Then, reaching Philadelphia and being removed, he experienced his "resurrection from the grave of slavery." In the narrative, Brown recalled bursting out in scriptural song. Psalm 40 was now a lived reality for him:

I waited patiently for the Lord;
And he inclined unto me, and heard my cry.

He brought me up also out of an horrible pit,
Out of the miry clay, and set my feet upon a rock, and established my goings.

But exorcising God from one set of material beings and worshipping an immaterial sacred being instead was only one part of the metaphysical equation.
The other was immanentizing what white European and American culture
had long attacked: radical evil. Brown and other slaves brought back to life a
moribund concept for many whites of the Enlightenment and characterized
it as very much at work in this world: supernatural evil. In their hands, hell
and the demonic were operationalized not simply to damn slavery and slaveholders but to create a notion of slaveholders' religion and then evaluate it and
declare it to be false.[45]

Brown was not alone in locating radical evil in the lives, structures, and
bodies of slaveholders. As slaveholders continued to hold slaves, justify it
based upon Christianity, and inflict physical, emotional, and spiritual wounds
on the enslaved, a conviction arose among some slaves that slaveholders were
not genuine Christians. One slave named Aaron explained that slaveholders
could not truly "see" the Bible, because their evil hearts and deeds kept them
from being able to hear God's word. "The slaveholders can't see to read the
bible," he explained in 1845, "because their hearts are shut up with sin and
iniquity, and is stained with the African's blood." The only explanation Aaron
had for this was "the devil that blessed them with that wicked bad deed."[46]
Another former slave, Boyrereau Brinch, was convinced that slaveholders
would never make it to heaven because they failed to follow the injunction
of the Lord's Prayer, "Forgive us our trespass, as we forgive those that trespass
against us." The slave power, Brinch concluded, was nothing more than what
"the arch fiend of hell, attempted to gain over this creator."[47]

Frederick Douglass described this kind of belief as an evolving one. Before
he was ten years old, he came to the conviction that "in due time" God "would
punish the bad slaveholders; that he would, when they died, send them to the
bad place, where they would be 'burnt up.'" Several years later, though, after
feeling, seeing, and hearing more of the horrors of slavery, Douglass claimed
that slaveholders "*cant go to heaven with our blood in his skirts*." Douglass concluded, "Slaves know enough of the rudiments of theology to believe that
those go to hell who die slaveholders."[48]

It appeared a widespread conviction that slaveholders were not true Christians and that they would not go to heaven. After Mary Reynolds recounted the beating she took from her white overseer Solomon, she exclaimed, "I know that Solomon is burning in hell today, and it pleasures me to know it."[49] During the Civil War, one black soldier in Missouri wrote to his still-enslaved daughter that he intended to free her. Even though her mistress claimed that slavery was God's will, this soldier rejected it. "And as for her cristianantty I expect the Devil has Such in hell. You tell her from me that She is the frist Christian that I ever hard say that aman could Steal his own child especially out of human bondage."[50]

All of this added up to a position for some that slaveholders were worse than hypocrites or heathens. They were not Christians at all but the children of the devil who lacked any "religion" or potentially lost religion by holding onto slaves. Francis Federic described how after a particularly bad whipping of one slave woman, a group of slaves had a meeting and "decided by two-thirds of the company that 'the debil was but a debil,' but that their masters professed to be Christians, and yet their acts made them worse than the devil."[51] Leonard Black rested his claim on the Bible. "I can prove by the scriptures that slave-holders are worse than the devil," he wrote, "for it is written in St. James, 'Resist the devil, and he will flee from you;' but if you undertake to resist the slave-holder, he will hold you the tighter."[52] Harriet Jacobs described one master who "boasted the name and standing of a Christian, though Satan never had a truer follower."[53]

As slaves and fugitives like Brown cast slaveholders and slavery as demonic, they participated in the formation and judgment of comparative religions. As various scholars have shown, the middle of the nineteenth century was a robust era in evaluative religiosity. Protestants accused Catholics of being frauds and blasphemous. The new Church of Jesus Christ of Latter-day Saints was attacked as a fraudulent faith spread by the con artist Joseph Smith. From court cases to printed tracts, Americans were widely and wildly creating "religions," evaluating "religions," and determining which was what. Slaves and fugitives did the same, and slavery was the core element of their faith renderings and judgments. While some slaves certainly juxtaposed their new or emerging Protestant Christianity against other fashions of faith, such as hoodoo and conjure, Brown and many others positioned their Christianity against the Christianity of Southern whites.[54]

Once believing his master and master's son to be God and Jesus, Brown in time came to identify "the religion of the slave-holder" as something quite different. "But the religion of the slave-holder is everywhere a system of mere delusion," Brown claimed in his narrative, and it was "got up expressly for the purpose of deceiving the poor slaves."[55]

Frederick Douglass as well refused the right of slaveholders to claim Christianity. He rhetorically deployed separable categories for "the religion of the South" and "the religion of Christianity" and often discussed how the two had nothing in common. The "religion of the south is a mere covering for the most horrid crimes," he fumed in his first narrative, "a dark shelter under, which the darkest, foulest, grossest, and most infernal deeds of slaveholders find the strongest protection." He concluded that in slavery "we have religion and robbery the allies of each other—devils dressed in angels' robes, and hell presenting the semblance of paradise."[56]

At their most extreme in these questions of religious authenticity, a few slaves maintained that masters had no religion. This was, perhaps, a counter to whites' descriptions of African peoples as having "no religion." Advocating slavery as a positive good, for example, Charles Colcock Jones explained that as the original African slaves died out, their children were "better looking, more intelligent, more civilized," and "more susceptible of religious impressions." Since they had "no religion to renounce," they "grew up in the belief of that of their masters."[57] The former slave Charles Ball recounted his grandfather's counteropinions. "He entertained strange and peculiar notions of religion," Ball explained, "and prayed every night, though he said he ought to pray oftener." Ball's grandfather "never went to church or meeting," and he maintained "that the religion of this country was altogether false, and indeed, no religion at all."[58] After watching a revival meeting where some masters sang and prayed, one former slave asked another, "if there is any religion in that noise?" The friend shot back, "Pshaw, no . . . Religion is willing and doing good to others—this is only bawling."[59]

# CONCLUSIONS

Frederick Douglass was frustrated with Henry Box Brown. When Brown and other former slaves revealed their escapes through writing, speaking, and performance, they gave slave catchers too much information. Douglass wanted silence and absence to be weaponized. If runaways could keep their travel paths and plans mysterious, they could bring emotional terror to the whites who hunted them. "I would leave him to imagine himself surrounded by myriads of invisible tormentors, ever ready to snatch from his infernal grasp his trembling prey," Douglass wrote in 1845. He wanted slaveholders to feel the overwhelming power of darkness and lack of sight. "Let him be left to feel his way in the dark; let darkness commensurate with his crime hover over him; and let him feel that at every step he takes, in pursuit of the flying bondman, he is running the frightful risk of having his hot brains dashed out by an invisible agency."[60]

Douglass wanted absence and silence to act upon slave owners. Henry Brown acted upon a box to free himself. When we spend time with them and other former slaves, the words of Charles Taylor sound almost absurd: "In general, we relate to the world as more disembodied beings than our ancestors; the center of gravity of the person each one of us is, as we interact with others, has moved out of the body."[61] This certainly was not the case for Brown. Moreover, his relationship to the box, and Douglass's hope that slaveholders would fear "an invisible agency" wielded by runaway slaves, complicates John Modern's emphasis on the external forces that seemed to exert influence over humans. With Brown, it was what he did to the box (and what others did to it—either pushing it over or representing it visually) that showcased the power of God in this world. With Douglass, it was by runaway slaves *not* describing their actions that they could impact whites.

If Henry Box Brown and his friends had the power to subvert the laws of slavery with a holey box or strike terror into the minds and hearts of whites simply by not saying anything at all, then he and they certainly can upend current works on the emergence of the secular age in America and beyond. Slaves did not necessarily live "less embodied lives." Their selves were not buffered, and the law made sure of that. They did not necessarily search for enchantment in the wilderness where barren trees seemed to reflect their weathered family lives.

But it is not simply that the lives of slaves or people of color did not fit within the scope of Taylor's or Modern's universes. They haunted them, and they did so with physical contraptions like boxes and ideological maneuvers like exorcising the corporeal God and materializing the cast-off devil. Fugitive slaves like Brown took the ability to select religions, and they not only made faiths for themselves but also created categories by which to damn their former masters.

At perhaps the deepest level, narratives and stories like Brown's reveal that to live is not simply to think or be circumscribed. To write about what it meant to "live" during Brown's age means to get close to the nitty-gritty of whippings and human trafficking. It is to sit on the knee of a mother who may have to see what was once her body sent away from her. It is to understand how a human would find light in a prison, resurrection via riverboat, and take the box that had enclosed him and enclose it within his own name.

## NOTES

1. For more on Brown, see Daphne Brooks, *Bodies in Dissent: Spectacular Performances of Race and Freedom, 1850–1910* (Durham, N.C.: Duke University Press, 2006), 66–130; Jeffrey Ruggles, *The Unboxing of Henry Brown* (Richmond: Library of Virginia, 2003).

2. Henry Box Brown, *Narrative of the Life of Henry Box Brown, Written by Himself* (Manchester: Lee and Glynn, 1851), 3–4.

3. Ibid., 4–5.

4. Charles Grandison Finney, *Memoirs of Reverend Charles G. Finney Written by Himself* (New York: A. S. Barnes, 1876), 13–23; Richard Lyman Bushman with Jed Woodworth, *Joseph Smith: Rough Stone Rolling* (New York: Knopf, 2006), chap. 1.

5. Brown, *Narrative of the Life of Henry Box Brown*, 5–7.

6. Charles Stearns, *Narrative of Henry Box Brown, Who Escaped from Slavery in a Box 3 Feet Long and 2 Wide* (Boston: Brown and Stearns, 1849), 47, 55, 91.

7. Brown, *Narrative of the Life of Henry Box Brown*, 3.

8. Ibid., 51.

9. Ibid., i.

10. Charles Taylor, *A Secular Age* (Cambridge, Mass.: Belknap Press of Harvard University Press, 2007), 3, 42. James Turner, *Without God, Without Creed: The Origins of Unbelief in America* (Baltimore, Md.: Johns Hopkins University Press, 1985). Charles Mathewes and Christopher McKnight Nichols, eds., *Prophecies of Godlessness: Predictions of America's Imminent Secularization from the Puritans to the Present Day* (New York: Oxford University Press, 2008).

11. John Lardas Modern, *Secularism in Antebellum America: With Reference to Ghosts, Protestant Subcultures, Machines, and Their Metaphors . . .* (Chicago: University of Chicago Press, 2011), 7.

12. Taylor, *A Secular Age*, 12.

13. Walter D. Mignolo, *The Darker Side of the Renaissance: Literacy, Territoriality, and Colonization* (Ann Arbor: University of Michigan Press, 2003); Paul Gilroy, *The Black Atlantic: Modernity and Double-Consciousness* (Cambridge, Mass.: Harvard University Press, 1993).

14. Taylor, *A Secular Age*, 21.

15. Ibid., 12, 15.

16. Ibid., 100.

17. Modern, *Secularism in Antebellum America*, xxiv, n. 11.

18. Ibid., 15.

19. There is a large literature on race and *Moby-Dick*. See, for instance, Sterling Stuckey, *African Culture and Melville's Art: The Creative Process in "Benito Cereno" and* Moby-Dick (New York: Oxford University Press, 2008).

20. Taylor, *A Secular Age*, 22.

21. I am indebted to the work of Stephen Tuck for this point. See, for example, Steve Bruce and Roy Wallis, "Secularization: The Orthodox Model," in *Religion and Modernization: Sociologists and Historians Debate the Secularization Thesis*, ed. Steve Bruce (Oxford: Oxford University Press, 1992), 8–30.

22. Brown, *Narrative of the Life of Henry Box Brown*, frontispiece, iii.

23. David Paul Nord, *Faith in Reading: Religious Publishing and the Birth of Mass Media in America* (New York: Oxford University Press, 2004); Candy Gunther Brown, *The Word in the World: Evangelical Writing, Publishing, and Reading in America, 1789–1880* (Chapel Hill: University of North Carolina Press, 2004); *Proceedings of the First Ten Years of the American Tract Society* (Boston: American Tract Society, 1824), 10.

24. Jo-Ann Morgan, *Uncle Tom's Cabin as Visual Culture* (Columbia: University of Missouri Press, 2007); Radiclani Clytus, "'Keep It Before the People': The Pictorialization of American Abolitionism," in *Early African American Print Culture*, ed. Lara Langer Cohen and Jordan Alexander Stein (Philadelphia: University of Pennsylvania Press, 2012), 290–317.

25. Andrew S. Curran, *The Anatomy of Blackness: Science and Slavery in an Age of Enlightenment* (Baltimore, Md.: Johns Hopkins University Press, 2011); Kenan Malik, *The Meaning of Race: Race, History, and Culture in Western Society* (New York: NYU Press, 1996), chap. 2; Charles H. Long, *Significations, Symbols, and Images in the Interpretation of Religion* (Philadelphia: Fortress, 1986).

26. Stephen Tomlinson, *Head Masters: Phrenology, Secular Education, and Nineteenth-Century Social Thought* (Tuscaloosa: University of Alabama Press, 2005).

27. *Cousin Ann's Stories for Children* (Philadelphia: J. M. McKim, 1849), 22–26.

28. Taylor, *A Secular Age*, 35–42. See also Charles Taylor, *Sources of the Self: The Making of the Modern Identity* (New York: Cambridge University Press, 1992).

29. Taylor, *A Secular Age*, 141.

30. Modern, *Secularism in Antebellum America*, chap. 2 and epilogue. Ann Braude, *Radical Spirits: Spiritualism and Women's Rights in Nineteenth-Century America* (Boston: Beacon, 1989); Catherine L. Albenese, *A Republic of Mind and Spirit: A Cultural History of American Metaphysical Religion* (New Haven, Conn.: Yale University Press, 2007).

31. Walter Johnson, *Soul by Soul: Life Inside the Antebellum Slave Market* (Cambridge, Mass.: Harvard University Press, 1999).

32. Gilbert Osofsky, ed., *Puttin' on Ole Massa: The Slave Narratives of Henry Bibb, William Wells Brown, and Solomon Northup* (New York: Harper and Row, 1969), 243.

33. Brown, *Narrative of the Life of Henry Box Brown*, 26–27.

34. Ibid., 9.

35. William J. Anderson, *Life and Narrative of William J. Anderson, Twenty-four Years a Slave; Sold Eight Times! In Jail Sixty Times!! Whipped Three Hundred Times!!! or The Dark Deeds of American Slavery Revealed. Containing Scriptural Views of the Origin of the Black and of the White Man. Also, a Simple and Easy Plan to Abolish Slavery in the United States. Together with an Account of the Services of Colored Men in the Revolutionary War—Day and Date, and Interesting Facts* (Chicago: Daily Tribune Book and Job Printing Office, 1857), 17, 22, 50.

36. *Narrative of Sojourner Truth* (1878; New York: Arno, 1968), 33.

37. Graham Russell Hodges, ed., *Black Itinerants of the Gospel: The Narratives of John Jea and George White* (Madison, Wis.: Madison House, 1993), 90, 94. For more on Jea, see Yolanda Pierce, *Hell Without Fires: Slavery, Christianity, and the Antebellum Spiritual Narrative* (Gainesville: University Press of Florida, 2005), chap. 2.

38. See Edward J. Blum and Paul Harvey, *The Color of Christ: The Son of God and the Saga of Race in America* (Chapel Hill: University of North Carolina Press, 2012), 95–98.

39. Brown, *Narrative of the Life of Henry Box Brown*, iv.

40. Michel Foucault, "Theatrum Philosophicum," in *Aesthetics, Method, and Epistemology* (New York: New Press, 1998), 347. Modern, *Secularism in Antebellum America*, 10.

41. Taylor, *A Secular Age*, esp. chap. 2.

42. Ibid., esp. chap. 10; Modern, *Secularism in Antebellum America*, esp. chap. 3.

43. Brown, *Narrative of the Life of Henry Box Brown*, 2.

44. Ibid., 51.

45. Jeffrey Burton Russell, *Mephistopheles: The Devil in the Modern World* (Ithaca, N.Y.: Cornell University Press, 1986); Andrew Delbanco, *The Death of Satan: How Americans Have Lost the Sense of Evil* (New York: Farrar, Straus and Giroux, 1995); Robert Muchembled, *A History of the Devil: From the Middle Ages to the Present*, trans. Jean Birrell (Cambridge: Polity, 2003); D. P. Walker, *The Decline of Hell: Seventeenth-Century Discussions of Eternal Torment* (Chicago: University of Chicago Press, 1964). For new work on the importance of hell and damnation, see Pierce, *Hell Without Fires*, 129; W. Scott Poole, *Satan in America: The Devil We Know* (Lanham, Md.: Rowman and Littlefield, 2009); Kathryn Gin, "Damned Nation? The Concept of Hell in American Life, 1775–1865," Ph.D. diss., Yale University, 2010; Jennifer Hildebrand, "'Dere Were No Place in Heaven for Him, an' He Were Not Desired in Hell': Igbo Cultural Beliefs in African American Folk Expressions," *Journal of African American History* 92, no. 2 (Spring 2006): 127–152.

46. *The Light and Truth of Slavery: Aaron's History* (Worcester, Mass., 1845), 25–26.

47. Benjamin F. Prentiss, *The Blind African Slave, or Memoirs of Boyrereau Brinch, Nick-Named Jeffrey Brace* (St. Albans, Vt.: Harry Whitney, 1810), 147–148.

48. Frederick Douglass, *My Bondage and My Freedom* (1855; New York: Arno, 1968), 68, 90, 195.

49. Quoted in Lawrence W. Levine, *Black Culture and Black Consciousness: Afro-American Folk Thought from Slavery to Freedom* (New York: Oxford University Press, 1977), 35.

50. "Missouri Black Soldier to His Daughters, and to the Owner of One of the Daughters" (September 3, 1864), Freedmen and Southern Society Project, http://www.history.umd .edu/Freedmen/rice.htm.

51. Francis Fedric, *Slave Life in Virginia and Kentucky* (London: Wertheim, Macintosh, and Hunt, 1863), 67.

52. Leonard Black, *The Life and Sufferings of Leonard Black, a Fugitive from Slavery* (New Bedford, Mass.: Benjamin Lindsey, 1847), 19–20.

53. Linda Brent [Harriet Ann Jacobs], *Incidents in the Life of a Slave Girl* (Boston: Published for the Author, 1861), 76–77.

54. Jonathan Z. Smith, "Religion, Religions, Religious," in *Critical Terms for Religious Studies*, ed. Mark C. Taylor (Chicago: University of Chicago Press, 1998): 269–284; J. Spencer Fluhman, *"A Peculiar People": Anti-Mormonism and the Making of Religion in Nineteenth-Century America* (Chapel Hill: University of North Carolina Press, 2012); Yvonne P. Chireau, *Black Magic: Religion and the African American Conjuring Tradition* (Berkeley: University of California Press, 2003).

55. Brown, *Narrative of the Life of Henry Box Brown*, 29.

56. Frederick Douglass, *Narrative of the Life of Frederick Douglass, An American Slave*, ed. Benjamin Quarles (Cambridge, Mass.: Belknap Press of Harvard University Press, 1980), 110, 157. For more on Douglass and definitions of religion, see Jon Pahl, *Empire of Sacrifice: The Religious Origins of American Violence* (New York: New York University Press, 2010), 76–84.

57. Charles C. Jones, *The Religious Instruction of the Negroes in the United States* (Savannah, Ga.: Thomas Purse, 1842), 64.

58. Charles Ball, *Slavery in the United States, a Narrative of the Life and Adventures of Charles Ball* (New York: John S. Taylor, 1837), 21–22.

59. Quoted in Mark M. Smith, *Listening to Nineteenth-Century America* (Chapel Hill: University of North Carolina Press, 2001), 78; Reverend J. W. Loguen, *The Rev. J. W. Loguen, as a Slave and as a Freeman* (Syracuse, N.Y.: J. G. K. Truair and Co., 1859), 262–263. A white minister in Ohio echoed this assertion. In an 1845 debate over whether slavery was sinful, he made a claim that certainly Frederick Douglass, Harriet Jacobs, and Henry Box Brown would have applauded: "where there is no every-day justice among men, there can be no religion." See *A Debate on Slavery: Held in the City of Cincinnati* (Cincinnati, Ohio: William H. Moore and Co., 1846), 172.

60. Douglass, *Narrative of the Life of Frederick Douglass*, 136–137.

61. Taylor, *A Secular Age*, 141.

# 4

# "WELCOME BACK TO THE LIVING"

## RESURRECTIONS OF MARTIN LUTHER KING JR.
## IN A SECULAR AGE

Erica R. Edwards

## TWILIGHT MEMORIES, SECULAR RESURRECTIONS

**W**HILE CHARLES Taylor's influential *A Secular Age* defines the shift to secularity in Western modernity as "a move from a society where belief in God is unchallenged and indeed, unproblematic, to one in which it is understood to be one option among others, and frequently not the easiest to embrace," secularism might better be understood as a political rationality than as a period.[1] According to Saba Mahmood, secularism doesn't prescribe the separation of state and religion so much as it remakes "certain kinds of religious subjectivities (even if this requires the use of violence) so as to render them compliant with liberal political rule."[2] Given the entanglement of charismatic leadership and the black freedom struggle in public understandings of the U.S. Civil Rights Movement, understanding the representation of civil rights history in U.S. popular culture as it intersects with the history of secularism helps us understand how this political rationality has shaped our understanding of the black freedom struggle, contemporary U.S. political culture, and normative family values. In this essay, I read the resurrections of Martin Luther King Jr. in contemporary television series as indices of anxieties about temporality, contemporary black politics, and charismatic black leadership in our secular age. Reading a 2003 episode of *The Twilight Zone* through a black feminist analytic and in the context of a post-2000 public culture of mourning for slain black leaders, I argue that the resurrections of King in contemporary American television series reinforce normative notions of black nationhood based in inheritance and masculine authority.

The secularization of black churches in the wake of emancipation in the nineteenth century corresponded to blacks' displays of bourgeois decorum, the adoption of Methodist formalism, and the migration out of the rural South. In this context, "emotive expression yielded to the cerebral serenity of northern, cosmopolitan African American church life."[3] As I argue elsewhere, the charismatic leader in African American culture emerged in public culture and print media as a figure who mediated the shift to modern urban culture in the late nineteenth and early twentieth centuries.[4] The charismatic leader—in both religious and secular contexts—was to be both instructed by sacred scripture and by the spirit, and he alone could effect the proper mix of emotionality and literate, secularist poise. If, as I argue, the charismatic leader emerged in U.S. culture after Reconstruction both to compel and contain black movements for freedom, the nostalgia for black leadership that circulates in post-1960s American culture reveals the connections between the secularization of black religion and politics and the secularization of U.S. public culture. As Vincent Lloyd astutely notes in the introduction to this volume, "the careful management of race and religion is the prerequisite for accepting the public significance of a fundamentally raced and religious figure." If the histories of progressive black theological thought and activism are "muted and managed by the secularist and racial regime" of the contemporary United States, as Lloyd argues, the funneling of radical black theologies into a "faith suitable to our secular age" demands that the progressive black theological labor of charismatic leaders such as Martin Luther King Jr. be rearticulated in the languages of secularism.[5]

This relationship between nostalgia for charismatic leadership and the secularization of U.S. public culture accordingly comes into view most clearly when we consider the ways that memories of King circulate in U.S. politics and popular culture. In a 1986 episode of *The Cosby Show* airing in January, days before the Martin Luther King Jr. holiday, the characters of the show gather before the living-room television, transfixed by a broadcast of King's 1963 "I Have a Dream" speech.[6] As King moves from the "Let freedom ring" refrain to the speech's closing words, "Free at last, free at last, thank God Almighty, we are free at last!" the youngest child, Rudy, lies across her parents' lap, clutching her teddy bear until she falls asleep; the teenage sisters Denise and Vanessa reconcile after an episode-long conflict over a sweater; and the Huxtables' only son, Theo, sits on the arm of the sofa, leaning forward as he stares into the black-and-white image of King instructing the nation in nonviolent social change. The flashback to the March on Washington grounds, centers, and unites the family at 10 Statewood Avenue in Brooklyn, King's voice reverberating some twenty-three years after its original recording in the Reagan-era, urban, middle-class enclave of the Cosby world and transforming what would otherwise be a lighthearted sitcom into an earnest lesson in the black protest tradition.

Twenty-six years later, the memory that once inspired awe and reverence on the TV-within-the-TV at the Huxtable home has become a joke. A 2006 episode of the Cartoon Network's *The Boondocks*, "The Return of the King," features a bumbling cartoon version of King, who awakes after a thirty-two-year coma to the postmodern world, the assassination attempt of 1968 having only "critically injured" him. An anachronistic King finds an apathetic populace that commercially worships him while eschewing the very ethic of nonviolence that characterized his radical vision: King's poster hangs in the Apple store, but King is called anti-American by a conservative talk-show host; his image graces a fast-food restaurant's paper tray liners, but he struggles to gain support for his political movement.

The militant *Boondocks* protagonist, Huey Freeman, escorts Dr. King through the Freemans' Chicago suburb, convincing King to lead a new "revolutionary black political party." The campaign reaches its tortured climax when an exasperated King finally lambastes his constituents at a fête he had intended to be the first meeting for his new political party:

> Will you ignorant niggers *please* shut the hell up?! Is this it?! This is what I got all those ass-whoopings for? I had a dream once. . . . But lo and behold, some four decades later, what have I found but a bunch of trifling, shiftless, good-for-nothing niggers? And I know some of you don't want to hear me say that word. It's the ugliest word in the English language. But that's what I see now: niggers. And you don't want to be a nigger.

King announces to his now-captive audience, "I know I won't get there with you; I'm going to Canada." Afterward, King's speech and subsequent disappearance anger the people and spark the revolution Huey has hoped for: "And the revolution finally came," Huey's voiceover announces. A black mob descends on the White House, NBA players go on strike, BET's founder Robert Johnson "apologizes to Black America for the network he founded," and Huey's reverie ends as the episode draws to a close, his voiceover announcing, "It's fun to dream."

What might be read as an isolated episode of irreverence in *The Boondocks* is actually part of a larger phenomenon in African American culture, a collection of texts and spectacles that articulates a deep-seated ambivalence toward the legacy of civil rights in general and toward King in particular. *The Boondocks*'s "The Return of the King" and *The Cosby Show*'s "Vanessa's Bad Grade" express two different manifestations of a nostalgic longing for King's charismatic leadership, as the fantasy of King's return provides the narrative bedrock of the televisual spectacle around King's body and sermonic oratory. Where *The Cosby Show* resurrects King to congratulate the Huxtable family on its upward mobility and bourgeois values, *The Boondocks* brings him back to mount a scathing critique of contemporary black culture that, ironically enough, echoes Bill Cosby's controversial rant against black cultural pathology in his May 2004 speech about black youth killing each other "over pound cake."[7]

Representations of civil rights in contemporary African American narratives betray both a hauntological longing—"a desire for dead things to come alive"—and a yearning to exorcise the political past from contemporary politics.[8] Even as charismatic 1960s leadership asserts itself as a memory that meddles in the lives of young black characters like Huey Freeman, eager to leave what Todd Boyd has glibly called "that civil rights shit"[9] behind and get on with the business of post–civil rights progressive politics, it haunts the heuristic mise-en-scène of contemporary narrative to teach, to aid, to instruct, and to change. That is to say, black cultural discourse on politics after civil rights is in the midst of a generational tug-of-war that has yet to be won. Houston A. Baker has defined a generational shift—after Thomas Kuhn's *paradigm shift*—as "an ideologically motivated movement overseen by young or newly emergent intellectuals who are dedicated to refuting the work of their intellectual predecessors and to establishing a new framework of intellectual inquiry."[10] If the young "postsoul" and hip-hop generations reject the political style of their civil rights–era elders, the story of its coming of age and attempted break with its forbears is often reflected in literature and film. The result is a cultural milieu rooted in contradictions: contemporary black popular culture, Mark Anthony Neal writes, "considers issues like deindustrialization, desegregation, the corporate annexation of black popular expression . . . the globalization of finance and communication, etc. . . . while collapsing on *modern* concepts of blackness."[11] Neal argues that the postsoul aesthetic "renders many 'traditional' tropes of blackness dated and even meaningless in its borrowing from black modern traditions" and that "the post-soul aesthetic is so consumed with its contemporary existential concerns that such [soul-era] traditions are not just called into question but obliterated."[12] This assertion quietly echoes the theory that Adolph L. Reed advances in *Race, Class, and Politics* about the "loss of historicity" or "social amnesia" that characterizes post–civil rights American culture:

> The past . . . is reduced to positive (as similarity) or negative (as deviation) affirmation of whatever currently exists. To the social amnesiacs past and present appear as discontinuous, and thus practically irrelevant to each other, or the past flounces around as a Mardi-Gras image: this week's banalities adorned by replicas of obsolete artifacts; in either case only a reified present seems to organize life.[13]

Yet the relationship between black popular culture and the past cannot be defined simply by a positive view of the "golden age" of black American life or by a negative attitude toward it; rather, the past functions as both a mythical ideal of past glory days *and* a "Mardi Gras" token to be consumed and later discarded. Contemporary black cultural production, according to Neal, appropriates black modern cultural and political projects in order to "derive meanings more in tune with contemporary experiences."[14] The complicated relationship between black postmodernism and history is one, as Neal suggests, rooted in contradictions.

Any understanding of contemporary black cultural production must make sense of the cultural logics of the post–civil rights era, which has been characterized by the competing desires to return and to move forward. This backward-forward impulse may indeed be endemic to the postmodern condition. The philosopher Andreas Huyssen contends that while "modern societies have put ever more weight on thinking the secular future as dynamic and superior to the past," postmodern societies have transformed temporality itself through time-and-space-compressing technologies like the Internet and the bullet train, such that the "future seems to fold itself back into the past," and utopian impulses are projected not forward but backward.[15] The explosion of civil rights iconography in black televisual and film culture since the late 1980s may be read, in Huyssen's words, as a potential "reaction . . . of mortal bodies that want to hold on to their temporality"—their experience of time as progressive and "real"—against a world of simulation.[16]

Extending Huyssen's notion of "twilight memories"—"generational memories" that fade into the horizon as the lights of a modernizing urban landscape push them out of view—I argue that postmodern, or postsoul, African American culture is driven to a large extent by the twilight memories of civil rights–era charismatic leadership, which surface as secular resurrections in contemporary television. Twilight memories are recollections "that reflect the twilight status of memory itself," twilight being the time of day that precedes what Huyssen calls "the night of forgetting," the time of day that "seems to slow time itself, an in-between state in which the last light of the day may still play out its ultimate marvels. It is memory's privileged time."[17] Twilight, then, might be imagined as a site of loss *and* possibility, where memory stages a final battle against oblivion, when time threatens either to swallow the past or reveal its mysteries before the arrival of darkness. "Twilight" is the best name for the kind of memory that conjures King in contemporary black popular culture: King resurrections hold out the promise of ultimate marvels while keeping in sober view the darkness of the present, wrought by the devastating effects of global capital on black enclaves in the urban United States.

## POSTMORTEM CHARISMA

To understand the cultural work of twilight memories in the popular cultural resurrections of King requires that we analyze the uses of charisma in contemporary American culture. The cultural lore surrounding King's leadership draws on a larger myth of charisma, the idea that social or political change on a mass scale is best produced by a happy marriage between a dynamic leader and a willing band of followers.

*Charisma* names a political ideal, a set of assumptions about authority and identity that structures how political mobilization is conceived and enacted. More than a static form of authority, charisma names a figural process of authoring and authorizing. In Max Weber's political sociology, informed by church history and by Paul's New Testament epistles, in which the *charismata* are gifts or manifestations of the Holy Spirit, charismatic authority is held by leaders who are "neither appointed officeholders nor 'professionals' . . . but rather [are] the bearers of specific gifts of the body and mind that are considered 'supernatural.'"[18] Charisma, a mixture of sacred and secular impulses—at once mystical and practical—is a group structure in which authority, or the right to rule, is centered around one exceptional figure perceived to be gifted with a privileged connection to the divine, evidenced by some form of miraculous "proof": spectacular oratory, a death-defying stunt, the conversion of water into wine, and so on. The charismatic leader is, from this perspective, both gifted and a gift: he is given divine authority and power, given *to* the people, and given *for* the sake of historical change.

Social scientists writing since Weber have suggested that charisma functions largely as a system of mutual need-fulfillment. The group satisfies the leader's narcissistic need for approval, perhaps compensating for some childhood trauma or lack, while the leader, in exchange, gives voice to the group's repressed political desires. The charismatic leader "shows [the group] how all the accumulated stuff of repression and frustration can be lit up into a magnificent fireworks, how the refuse of daily drudgery can be converted into a high explosive of pervasive destruction."[19] The charismatic leader promises excitement and then stability as alternatives to meaningless chaos and lack: "He becomes the indispensable guide in a confused world, the center around which the faithful can gather and find safety. He comforts sufferers . . . takes over the responsibility of history and becomes the exterior replacement of their disintegrated individuality. They live through him."[20]

For black Americans, charisma has become an organizing myth for ideas of political mobilization. While social historians have distanced their scholarship from "great man" theories of history, the history of black social movements *as* the byproduct of charismatic leadership continues to circulate widely in popular culture. Clayborne Carson's essay on King's charisma, for example, suggests that in popular civil rights history, "a Great Man is seen as the decisive factor in the process of social change, and the unique qualities of a leader are used to explain major historical events."[21] The leader is history's indispensable protagonist: without him, history (what is believed to have happened) *and* historical narrative (what is said to have happened) are impossible. Carson goes on to suggest that King has functioned as the necessary protagonist in the public narrative of civil rights and is seen as the movement's exemplary political spokesperson and miraculous history maker. He embodies, for post–civil rights black culture, the quintessential charismatic leader and great man—the king, as it were, of black history and black politics.[22]

King can be said to have garnered what Ann Ruth Willner calls "postmortem" charisma, the mythology surrounding a charismatic leader after his or her untimely demise. Willner explains that after the leader's death, "he and his works take on . . . a mythical quality and become part of the reservoir of myths and symbols of his society and perhaps even for others. . . . Even those for whom he was not charismatic and those for whom he ceased being so share in the drama he enacted. And they too transmit its awe and aura to their descendants."[23] The charismatic leader assumes a second rise to power after death, becoming "the Prometheus of politics who . . . steals from the gods by stretching political reality beyond the bounds of belief and prediction."[24]

While King's position at the center of the civil rights cultural-historical imaginary makes for good television drama, it obscures the role of everyday activism in black freedom movements and does not question the masculinist foundations of black leadership ideology.[25] Even as King's leadership is decentered by recent scholarship and by contemporary black expressive culture, his memory is often resurrected to buttress the very flaws of democracy that his philosophy and organizing worked to combat.[26] King's visage graces advertising billboards, his name is announced on street signs,[27] and he is brought back to life on prime-time television. But these resurrections often serve only the very conservative use that charisma serves: the restoration of the hierarchies on which market society stands.[28]

## MEMPHIS; OR, DISNEYLAND, TENNESSEE

In their 1992 hit song "Tennessee," the southern hip-hop group Arrested Development pleads to the Almighty, "Take me to another place / Take me to another land / Make me forget all that hurts me / Let me understand your plan." The song could have served as a fitting score for a *Twilight Zone* episode that aired eleven years later about a man who goes to Memphis in search of life's meaning. In April 2003, the United Paramount Network revival of *The Twilight Zone*—itself an act of resurrection of the 1960s series—featured an episode titled "Memphis," a historical melodrama starring Eriq La Salle and directed by Forest Whitaker. The episode's climax is a restaging of King's tragic 1968 assassination, but the show weaves a story that mediates the millennial present and the utopian past in the tale of Ray Ellison, a young law clerk who is struck by a car and is transported from Memphis in 2003 to Memphis in 1968 just in time to save a single mother and her son from bank foreclosure and homelessness and to attempt to save King from the ultimately successful attempt on his life. In this episode, the history of civil rights is both laid to rest and resurrected, mourned and conjured, in a post–civil rights televisual séance in which King plays the central character, the ghost of civil rights past.

Ironically, if the Beale Street neighborhood site of the "Memphis" episode is any indication, Memphis itself may be understood as a kind of twilight zone that architecturally gestures to the generational shift in zeitgeist and the shift in the mode of production from industrial to casino capital.[29] Memphis was one of the South's early stars of the twentieth century: after surviving the two yellow fever epidemics after the Civil War, city developers gained prosperity by discovering "millions of gallons of the purest water in the world,"[30] and with the construction of the Frisco Bridge in 1892—then, the only Mississippi River bridge south of St. Louis—the city would become a major port. By the Depression era, the city had experienced exponential population growth and modernization and even managed to outgrow many other cities through the 1930s: the architectural historians Eugene Johnson and Robert Russell point out that by "the time of Pearl Harbor, the population had risen from 250,000 to nearly 300,000, and many Memphians were living in much better houses than they ever had before."[31]

When Lyndon Johnson's Great Society plan promised capital to the city for what was benignly called "urban renewal" in the 1960s, Beale Street, one of the "principal streets of black America," found itself being bulldozed to make way for what would ultimately become, in the late-capitalist moment, a kind of historical amusement park. Johnson and Russell argue that city planners tried to "dupe tourists by substituting fake . . . new buildings for the actuality of the old ones. They wanted Main Street, Disneyland, instead of Beale Street, Memphis."[32]

The tragedy of the Beale Street neighborhood in Memphis history underscores its value as a site in which time and space are compressed so that it functions as an amusement park or museum in the present. To return to Huyssen, it is "a site of possible resurrections, however mediated and contaminated, in the eyes of the beholder."[33] Thus, Memphis is a fitting case study for investigating the ways that twilight memories function in the resurrected urban spaces of the contemporary United States. Memphis, where King was assassinated, is a city where the Civil Rights Movement's legacy is often contested. Across from the city's National Civil Rights Museum, the activist Jacqueline Smith has staged a protest against the Lorraine Motel memorial site. "Her protest has been literally street politics in that she has lived, eaten, and slept on the sidewalk across the street from the museum," Derek Alderman writes. "She advertises the museum as the 'National Civil Wrong Museum,' distributes protest literature, and provides museum visitors with an alternative vision of how to commemorate King."[34]

At stake in Memphis is the question that Renee C. Romano and Leigh Raiford ask in their foundational volume on public memory and the Civil Rights Movement: "How should civil rights figures, events, and accomplishments be memorialized in contemporary American life and what is at stake in how they are portrayed in the arena of popular culture?"[35] Thomas Kane's argument about the National Civil Rights Museum in Memphis is that while it risks locking the civil rights legacy into a simple and remote past, it does not leave viewers with a history of the black freedom movement that is "ultimately untouchable, sealed in the crypt" of the museum.[36] Rather, he argues, "the recreation of the rooms encourages a kind of temporal openness, where the visitor can imagine the contingency of history and fantasize about his or her participation in altering events."[37]

If Kane is correct that the creation of "temporal openness"—historical contingency—allows viewers to participate in King's "unfinished project" of rehabilitating U.S. democracy, the same might be said of *The Twilight Zone*'s "Memphis" episode. But whereas the museum re-creates the scene of King's assassination in order to, like "The Return of the King" episode of *The Boon-*

*docks*, remind viewers that King's vision of nonviolent social change cannot be easily domesticated in the present, "Memphis" relies on King's postmortem charisma as its narrative foundation. As such, it offers closure by transferring King's power onto a protagonist who takes King's place as patriarch and savior of the race. The episode, that is, leaves King at home with the patriarchal agenda that his image is often called to serve in today's political marketplace. The ideology that comfort is offered by the restoration of the black father figure to his rightful place in the post–civil rights landscape, I argue, thwarts the radical political possibility of twilight memory, eschewing temporal openness in favor of an easy closure around patriarchal notions of house and home.

## REENTERING THE TWILIGHT ZONE

*The Twilight Zone*, in its original incarnation of 159 episodes between 1959 and 1964, was, according to Marc Zicree, "the first . . . TV series to deal on a regular basis with the theme of alienation—particularly urban alienation," and it was a show that confronted alienation by encouraging viewers to "reach out to others" and to trust in "their common humanity."[38] Premiering at the height of the Civil Rights Movement and during what is often regarded as television's "golden age"—the age that gave viewers *I Love Lucy* as the first successful network series and formulaic sitcom—*The Twilight Zone* appeared precisely at the moment when black social movements went "live"[39] and when television was giving consumers a choice between the drama of the news and the banality of the sitcom.[40] Anthology shows of the post–World War II years, like *The Twilight Zone* and *Alfred Hitchcock Presents*, drew on the conventions of live theater to "present audiences with something not quite like anything they had seen before."[41] Keith Booker argues that *The Twilight Zone* in particular used representations of "ontological confusion" to confront both alienation in the Marxian sense and routinization in the Weberian sense, combating, he says, the feeling "that every aspect of life, even the most 'private,' [was] being regimented to meet the . . . needs of capitalist economic expression."[42]

Efforts to suppress the mystical dimensions of life were, for Weber, at the heart of routinization under capitalist conditions but could be remedied by the rise of a charismatic leader gifted with a privileged connection to the divine that could mediate between an oppressed people and the God who would deliver them. It seems uncanny, in that case, that the 2003 "Memphis" episode of *The Twilight Zone* represents both ontological confusion—the blurring of lines between animate and inanimate, living and dead, past and present—and a resurrected charismatic leader, to confront the protagonist's crisis of meaning.

"Memphis" begins with a law clerk named Ray Ellison (played by La Salle) being treated by a doctor after having traveled to Memphis from New York to see a medical specialist about his cancerous brain tumor. The aging doctor informs him that he has "five months, maybe six" to live, and a sullen Ray leaves the medical center pondering his own mortality after he realizes that a younger Memphis doctor's experimental brain cancer treatment will not be covered by his insurance policy. The story, then, is framed by Ray's mortal anxiety and his lament that he "is not leaving much of a life"—an heir—"behind." Just before Ray is hit by a car at a busy Memphis intersection, a voiceover comforts viewers by saying, "[On] the worst day of his life, Ray Ellison's luck is about to change. He's gonna have a chance to save his future by altering the past." An injured Ray wakes up in 1968 and is nursed by single mother Adelaide Tyler, whose son, Lucas, immediately latches onto Ray as a father figure.

Ray uses his legal expertise to save Adelaide's home from impending bank foreclosure and, in his attempts to reenact the car accident that landed him thirty-five years in the past, discovers that he has arrived in history in time to save Dr. King from his April 3, 1968, assassination. Ray then hurries to the Mason Temple Church of God, where he can hear the prophetic moments of King's final "I've Been to the Mountaintop" sermon, what Thomas Kane has called King's "automortography," or telling of his own death. "I would like to live a long life," King says. "Longevity has its place. But I'm not concerned about that now." The *Twilight Zone* audience misses King's telling the congregation, "I may not get there with you," as Ray's attempts to get into the church and repeated protestations of "They're gonna kill Dr. King!" drown out the audio recording. But King can be heard saying, "And I'm happy, tonight. I'm not worried about anything. I'm not fearing any man. Mine eyes have seen the glory of the coming of the Lord." The omission here is not insignificant: if Kane is correct that King's automortographic final speech "provides grounds for a more active form of citizenship" by gesturing to his own unfinished project—"I may not get there with you"—and centering the people in the project of democracy by saying that they will "as a *people* . . . get to the promised land," the *Twilight Zone* episode stifles the democratic impulse of King's message and leaves the viewer with only a mournful hagiography.[43] This is a melancholia that only lasts moments, quickly giving way to a rush of excitement as Ray hobbles, in the next scene, through the Beale Street neighborhood to the Lorraine Motel, where he will again attempt and again fail to save Dr. King from assassination. The ontological confusion that *The Twilight Zone* achieves is perhaps best captured by the myriad collisions in this scene as Lucas speeds toward Ray, Ray runs toward Dr. King, and the assassin's bullet accomplishes its mission in spite of the multiple salvation efforts at work.

Booker explains that in the original *Twilight Zone*, ghosts surface to do the work of eschatology, confronting the reality of death and questioning the final destination of souls. Ghosts trouble the very questions of existence: What does it mean to live, and what does it mean to die? "In *The Twilight Zone*," Booker writes, "even seemingly straightforward ghost stories . . . were based primarily on the difficulty of making an unequivocal distinction between the living and the dead. . . . It turns out to be possible . . . to cross the boundary between life and death."[44] I would argue that the same is true of the "Memphis" episode, which features King as a ghost who returns to the present to force viewers to confront what the "death of civil rights"[45] might mean in the contemporary urban landscape.

King's sole responsibility here is to the heirs of civil rights—his mission, in effect, belongs *only* to the present and not to the past. King's appearance in "Memphis" *out of history* is emphasized by the puzzling omission of King's objective in 1968 Memphis: the striking sanitation workers and protesters are made invisible, their challenges to the Memphis government and claims to citizenship are silenced, and saving Dr. King is all that matters. For Ray, the ghost of King surfaces to help deal with the alienation and routinization that ensues not *only* because of the waning of affect that Jameson argues is an essential effect of late capitalism but also because of the fading out of the spectacle of civil rights that was featured, as Sasha Torres suggests,[46] as a live televisual presence throughout the 1960s. Ray is left only with a mediated memory of the telegenic charismatic leader and the intense desire to resurrect or to save the dead Dr. King. As his attempt to change history here fails, he must confront King's death anew.

Ray meets King's death with a refusal to mourn characteristic of the melancholic subject. As Alice Rayner's work on ghosts in theater explains, there are two responses to the melancholy that accompanies the loss of an object of desire: there is introjection, or mourning, in which the subject "reorganiz[es] libidinal energies" and diverts them away from the lost object, essentially "letting it go"; and there is incorporation, or the refusal to mourn, in which the subject unconsciously "puts the lost object in a place, as though it were actually kept 'in' the body . . . as though it were a monument and memorial that preexisted every corporeal memory."[47] "The concept of incorporation," Rayner explains, is "a form of magic," as "desire . . . is both maintained and excluded from consciousness, sealed off against any kind of knowledge other than phantasmic" or ghostly.[48] Incorporation functions as "a kind of theft to reappropriate the pleasure object" by sealing it away in the recesses of the unconscious.[49] Here, then, Ray internalizes King; he *incorporates* the lost object such that King no longer inhabits the "sealed crypt of history"[50] but rather the living tomb of Ray's own body. The ghost, however, is the symbol of the inevitable failure of incorporation as a psychic technique, the inability to seal memory away in the recesses of the imagination. The ghost exists precisely because memory defeats the melancholic subject's best attempts at repression.

When Ray awakes from his three-day slumber, the old Memphis doctor greets him, "Welcome back to the living," and Ray finds himself saved by the gifted hands of a now adult Lucas Tyler. Lucas reminds Ray to fight from his head and his heart and points to the latter, which the episode has constructed as the figurative final resting place of King. The coma narrative here is one that is reversed by the "Return of the King" episode of *The Boondocks* that aired two years later. In both cases, Dr. King is revived in an Oedipal drama in which the ghost—the father who haunts—must be not exorcised but incorporated, the present made a living tomb for the past. Ray is possessed by King and can now face his own mortality "not fearing any man"; rather, having seen the glory of King resurrected and incorporated, he can complete the real mission of his time travel: saving Lucas.

## PAPA'S BABY: "REIGNITING THE LEGACY"

The story of the "Memphis" episode involves two significant attempts at salvation: the first, which fails, is to save Dr. King; the second, which succeeds, is to save the pathological black family symbolized by Adelaide Tyler and her son, Lucas. The episode finally reveals itself as a patriarchal romance cloaked in nostalgia for King's charismatic leadership. The linking of *charisma* as a sociopolitical ideal to the patriarchal romance is performed often in contemporary black public and popular cultures in general and in the dramas of the post–civil rights black urban South in particular.

In a central scene of "Memphis," Lucas interrupts an exchange between Ray and a white Memphis police officer by telling the officer that he is his uncle from New York and not schooled in the laws of Jim Crow. Ray then uses his faith in neoliberal colorblindness to convince Lucas that he doesn't have to be afraid of police officers: "Where I'm from, things are different from the way they are here," he tells Lucas. "Police aren't supposed to talk to you like that. . . . When you know you're right, you don't need to be scared." He goes on to tell the young man he "can't be a man without fighting" when Lucas tells him that he often has to defend himself when he is teased about the large birthmark on his face. In this scene of fantasy father-son bonding, Lucas tells Ray he has a "dream," a "secret," and whispers it in Ray's ear. This dream then becomes the focal point of the episode's second salvation narrative: if the attempt to save King and resurrect his dream *fails*, Ray at least gets to save Lucas's dream by fathering him. When Ray laments, "I didn't save King," Lucas pleads, "but you saved me, Ray. Thank you for saving *me*." In exchange, Lucas's dream of becoming a surgeon saves Ray: transported back to the present, Ray awakes to find the adult Lucas—identified by the distinguishing birthmark—performing the experimental treatment that the old Memphis doctor has informed Ray will save his life for free.

The substitution of one dream—King's—for the other—Ray's—participates in what Wahneema Lubiano has referred to as a conservative family values discourse in black popular culture. Black family values discourse, for Lubiano, is nothing more than the "aesthetics of state repression dressed up in blackface, in slogans of black responsibility, in increased attention to black self-help . . . in the valorization of black male self-reassertion predicated on the silencing of women . . . of anyone who falls outside of the parameters of the black nationalist 'family.'"[51] When Adelaide returns from the bank having successfully used Ray's legal advice to save the house, she tells Ray and Lucas, "Now I'm about to walk through my front door and into my kitchen, and I'm about to cook y'all the best meal y'all ever had!" when only moments earlier, when Ray meddles in the affairs of the household, she tells him, "I have a mind to put you out right now." Ray wins Adelaide's affection by saving her house in both the literal and figurative senses: from foreclosure and from single-mother pathology.

The family salvation narrative of "Memphis" captures the conservative motives that civil rights memory often serves. Romano and Raiford write about the "divergent and often contradictory ways" that civil rights memorializations often work: "President George W. Bush appealed to King's spirit on the 2004 King holiday to sell his 'compassionate conservatism' agenda, while former President Bill Clinton spoke of the movement as an 'American crossroads' at the 2004 Democratic National Convention in his effort to build support for Democratic presidential candidate John Kerry."[52] In a similar spectacle that same year, an estimated twenty-five thousand people participated in a march called "Reigniting the Legacy," a procession from Atlanta's Martin Luther King Jr. Center for Nonviolent Social Change to the city's Turner Field. The December 2004 march was staged in support of a federal constitutional amendment banning same-sex marriage. The march, led by Bishop Eddie Long, the pastor of New Birth Missionary Baptist Church, a megachurch outside of Atlanta, and Bernice King, the youngest daughter of Martin Luther King Jr. and an elder in the church, illustrated how postmortem charisma can be used to police African American sexuality, to align black religious groups with the "family" or "moral values" agenda of the Right, and to keep ideas of manhood tied to a model of religious and political leadership that relies on unyielding categories of sexuality and gender.

King's role as charismatic exemplar was at the center of the "Reigniting the Legacy" march's claim to social authority. The use of the King Memorial as the starting place, at which the leader lit a torch from the memorial's eternal flame, the circulation of King's rhetoric in quotes included in publicity and speeches, and the location of the march in King's childhood home, Atlanta's Sweet Auburn neighborhood, all exemplified the organizers' deliberate alignment with the cultural memory of King.

The march's goal was reportedly to "get back into the conversation of the nation," to introduce black Christians as vocal participants in the national discourse on marriage and sexuality. Framed, ironically enough, as a coming-out story, march participants appeared in news photographs wearing shirts that read "Stop the Silence," and the event was touted in one news story as an opportunity to speak in "one voice," to articulate "a unified vision of righteousness and justice."[53] Less than one month after voters in eleven U.S. states, including Georgia, approved of state constitutional bans on same-sex marriage, and in a state that had passed a Defense of Marriage Act nine years prior, the march's leader, ostensibly alarmed by the *suppression* of antihomosexual sentiment, told a reporter, "This is our coming out day. We are here to stay and will be heard."[54] Bypassing a counterdemonstration of fifty gay rights activists, the march proceeded from the King Center to Turner Field, where a recorded speech by Bishop Long played over the loudspeakers to greet the marchers entering the stadium. In her introduction of Long, Bernice King said, "I believe this day will go down in the history books as the greatest showing of Christ and his kingdom in this century," and she designated Long "the prophet appointed by God to speak the mind, heart, and gospel of God."[55]

The "Reigniting the Legacy" march made use of at least four powerful symbols in its production of the charismatic scenario.[56] First, the site of departure, King's burial site, indexed a primal source of mourning for African American leadership. The march was, indeed, a tomb-raiding mission that dug up the remains of King's authority for its own use, hence Rudolph Byrd and Nathan McCall's assessment that the "strange and misguided" march, a "hate crusade," ignored King's dream.[57] The fact that the march was a raising of the dead dressed up as a ritual of mourning was shored up by the all-black attire of the majority of the marchers.

Second, Bishop Long's physical presence typified how political authority is tied to the male body. The domain of charismatic authority, particularly in the civil rights tradition, is most often a masculinist sphere of influence—Steve Estes suggests as much when he argues that the masculinist rhetoric of political speakers "rallies supporters by urging them to be manly or to support traditional ideas of manhood."[58] In this instance, charismatic performance—the acting out of a privileged connection to the divine—plays out as a bourgeois, heteronormative family romance: Bernice King gestures to Long as her deceased father's substitute and successor, and in the drama, Bishop Long plays father not only to her but to all. As much as it was purported to "reignite" the legacy of civil rights, the march represented an Oedipal performance that required those involved to slay King's dream of egalitarian social life so that Bishop Long could be inaugurated as a new king for the race. The public family drama fortified the march's homophobic appeal to the union between one man and one woman as the prime marker of "righteousness" and "justice."

Finally, both the torch and the march forward, like the tomb and the bishop's physical positioning, functioned symbolically to attach charismatic leadership to a rigid, masculinist, heterosexist conception of black Christian identity. The torch is a common emblem of enlightenment and tradition that signifies the transferability of power: the Olympic torch, for example, is carried along from one location to the next to signify the passing on of unquestioned eternal values. In this scene, King's power is kept alive eternally in the memorial flame, and Long accesses it to possess King's authority. Further, the historical function of the march for blacks in America, Eddie S. Glaude has suggested, is to perform or "to continuously retell the story of bondage, the march toward liberation, and the discipline necessary to remain free."[59] The torch confers the power to free *and* to discipline, to liberate *and* to police the criteria for living freedom out.

The recuperation of the black family through the recovery of the black male head of household in the "Reigniting the Legacy" march and in the "Memphis" episode dramatizes what Hortense Spillers classically critiqued in "Mama's Baby, Papa's Maybe: An American Grammar Book": the Moynihanian myth of the pathological black matriarch.[60] The restoration of the father figure to his rightful place in the home in post–civil rights black culture plays out in a more fatalistic way in a film like 2005's *Hustle & Flow*, in which a Memphis pimp laments the absence of his father who, once "standing for right," has now disappeared.[61] In the latter, the patriarchal romance is written in the language of film noir, in which the desolation of the post–civil rights Southern urban landscape generates a malaise that persists despite the protagonist's successful attempt to become a rapper and his insistence that "everybody gotta have a dream." All three texts—"Memphis," the march, and *Hustle & Flow*—dramatize a kind of political "fatherlack," the anxiety of "Papa's maybe" projected onto postpolitical fantasy, a rejection of political activism in favor of conservative, individualist rhetorics of family values and career "dreams."

When Lucas begs Ray to remain in 1968, telling him, "You're supposed to be here with us. I know it," Ray tells him, "Don't forget what I told you, OK?

You fight for what you want! Don't forget that." "Don't forget" is a refrain that will be repeated throughout the episode, as Lucas later reminds Ray not to forget to fight from his heart. This symbolic father-son exchange of *unfor-getting* the new dream—the rehabilitated family and the upward mobility it enables—makes the matter of King's undeath itself a flight of fancy; the ghost of King returns to the sealed crypt, and the two men go about uplifting the race through a kind of masculinist self-assertion that straddles the time gap.

The ghosts of the past in contemporary culture, Huyssen writes, reveal "an attempt by ever more fragmented subjects to live with the fragments, even to forge shifting and unfixed identities out of such fragments, rather than chasing some elusive unity or totality."[62] I would argue, however, that the "Memphis" episode of *The Twilight Zone* forecloses the radical possibility of resurrection in favor of the more conservative move toward historical erasure and patriarchal romance. The loss or killing of historicity—the final laying to rest of Dr. King—so exorcises that past that, to return to Reed, "only a reified present seems to organize life," and the past very well functions as a "Mardi-Gras image" that is resurrected only to be thrown away. The ultimate marvels promised by twilight, in that case, have yet to be seen.

# NOTES

This chapter contains material first published in Erica R. Edwards, "'Welcome Back to the Living': Twilight Memories of Martin Luther King Jr. in Contemporary American Television," *South Atlantic Quarterly* 112, no. 2 (2013): 241–260. Copyright 2013, Duke University Press. All rights reserved. Republished by permission of the copyright holder, Duke University Press. www.dukeupress.edu.

1. Charles Taylor, *A Secular Age* (Cambridge, Mass.: Belknap Press of Harvard University Press, 2007), 3.
2. Saba Mahmood, "Secularism, Hermeneutics, and Empire: The Politics of Islamic Reformation," *Public Culture* 18, no. 2 (2006): 323–47.
3. Christopher Reed, *All the World Is Here! The Black Presence at White City* (Bloomington: Indiana University Press, 2000), 107.
4. Erica R. Edwards, *Charisma and the Fictions of Black Leadership* (Minneapolis: University of Minnesota Press, 2012).
5. See Vincent W. Lloyd, introduction to this volume.
6. "Vanessa's Bad Grade," dir. Jay Sandrich, NBC (1986). On the place of the King holiday and the "I Have a Dream" speech in American public memory, see Edward P. Morgan, "The Good, the Bad, and the Forgotten: Media Culture and Public Memory of the Civil

Rights Movement" in *The Civil Rights Movement in American Memory*, ed. Renee Christine Romano and Leigh Raiford (Athens: University of Georgia Press, 2006).

7. Cosby lamented "people getting shot in the back of the head over a piece of pound cake" as he spoke of the black struggle at the NAACP Legal Defense Fund's commemoration of the fiftieth anniversary of *Brown v. Board of Education*. Felicia R. Lee, "Cosby Defends His Remarks About Poor Blacks' Values," *New York Times* (May 22, 2004).

8. Avery Gordon, *Ghostly Matters: Haunting and the Sociological Imagination* (Minneapolis: University of Minnesota Press, 1997), 51. For Gordon, "haunting describes how that which appears to be not there is often a seething presence . . . often meddling with taken-for-granted realities" (8).

9. Todd Boyd, *The New H.N.I.C. (Head Niggas in Charge): The Death of Civil Rights and the Reign of Hip Hop* (New York: New York University Press, 2002), xix.

10. Houston A. Baker, "Generational Shifts and the Recent Criticism of Afro-American Literature," in *African American Literary Theory*, ed. Winston Napier (New York: New York University Press, 2000), 179.

11. Mark Anthony Neal, *Soul Babies: Black Popular Culture and the Post-Soul Aesthetic* (New York: Routledge, 2002), 3.

12. Ibid.

13. Jameson considers the present's nostalgic relationship to the past, referring to what Reed calls a loss of historicity as the "waning of affect," "a new kind of flatness or depthlessness, a new kind of superficiality in the most literal sense." Frederic Jameson, *Postmodernism, or, The Cultural Logic of Late Capitalism* (Durham, N.C.: Duke University Press, 1994), 9. See also Frederic Jameson, "Postmodernism and Consumer Society," in *The Anti-Aesthetic: Essays on Postmodern Culture*, ed. Hal Foster (Seattle: Bay, 1983), 111–125; Frederic Jameson, "Periodizing the '60s," in *The Sixties Without Apology*, ed. Sohnya Sayres et al. (Minneapolis: University of Minnesota Press, 1984), 178–209.

14. Neal, *Soul Babies*, 17.

15. Andreas Huyssen, *Twilight Memories: Marking Time in a Culture of Amnesia* (New York: Routledge, 1995), 8.

16. Ibid., 9.

17. Ibid., 3.

18. Max Weber, *Economy and Society: An Outline of Interpretive Sociology*, ed. Guenther Roth and Claus Wittich, trans. Ephraim Fischoff et al., 3 vols. (New York: Bedminster, 1968), 1:3.

19. Leo Lowenthal and Norbert Guterman, "Self-Portrait of the Fascist Agitator," in *Studies in Leadership: Leadership and Democratic Action*, ed. Alvin Ward Gouldner (New York: Harper, 1950), 99.

20. Ibid.

21. Clayborne Carson, "Martin Luther King Jr.: Charismatic Leadership in a Mass Struggle," *Journal of American History* 74, no. 2 (1987): 448.

22. Baker is careful to distinguish between "nostalgia"—a kind of homesickness or "purposive construction of a past filled with golden virtues, golden men and sterling events"—and "critical memory" ("the very faculty of revolution") in his discussion of King, but he is satis-

fied to leave King at the center of the civil rights imaginary, elevating King as "the King of the Black Public Sphere." Houston A. Baker Jr., "Critical Memory and the Black Public Sphere," in *The Black Public Sphere*, ed. The Black Public Sphere Collective (Chicago: University of Chicago Press, 1995), 13.

23. Ann Ruth Willner, *The Spellbinders: Charismatic Political Leadership* (New Haven, Conn.: Yale University Press, 1984), 199.

24. Ibid., 201.

25. Payne's argument that journalists covering the Civil Rights Movement preferred to represent the movement as a spectacle of singular, national leadership rather than to chronicle the unglamorous work of grassroots political organizing in part explains why the work of female activists like Ella Baker, who critiqued elite male leaders, has gone unrecognized in the public narrative of the movement. Charles Payne, *I've Got the Light of Freedom: The Organizing Tradition and the Mississippi Freedom Struggle* (Berkeley: University of California Press, 1995).

26. Other critics have discussed the way that the film *Barbershop* (2002; dir. Tim Story) ignited a debate about the civil rights legacy when one of the film's characters asserted that "Rosa Parks didn't do nothin' but sit her black ass down" and that "Martin Luther King was a ho." In pointing to the ways that contemporary black popular culture literally defac(at)es the civil rights legacy, I would also point to the skit on *Chappelle's Show* (2005; season 2) in which a character desegregates a whites-only bathroom, becoming "the first black person to take a shit on a white toilet" in 1954. These texts' scatological humor, I would argue, emphasizes the ordinary embodiedness of charisma's sacred heroes and attempts to deconstruct charisma as the otherworldly "gift of grace." See also Leigh Raiford and Renee C. Romano, "Introduction: The Struggle Over Memory," in *The Civil Rights Movement in American Memory*, ed. Renee C. Romano and Leigh Raiford (Athens: University of Georgia Press, 2006), xi–xx.

27. Alderman shows that more than seven hundred U.S. cities boast streets with King's name. Derek H. Alderman, "Street Names as Memorial Arenas: The Reputational Politics of Commemorating Martin Luther King Jr. in a Georgia County," in *The Civil Rights Movement in American Memory*, ed. Renee C. Romano and Leigh Raiford (Athens: University of Georgia Press, 2006), 67–95.

28. Cedric Robinson deconstructs the "metaphysics of leadership," pointing out that it is the cultural assumption of leadership as natural that authorizes what often amounts to a hierarchy that thwarts the West's most earnest attempts at democratic governance. Cedric J. Robinson, *The Terms of Order: Political Science and the Myth of Leadership* (Albany, N.Y.: SUNY Press, 1980), 50.

29. Susan Strange, *Casino Capitalism* (Oxford: Blackwell, 1986).

30. Eugene J. Johnson and Robert Douglass Russell, *Memphis, an Architectural Guide* (Knoxville: University of Tennessee Press, 1990), 5.

31. Ibid., 7.

32. Ibid., 136.

33. Huyssen, *Twilight Memories*, 15.

34. Alderman, "Street Names as Memorial Arenas," 74.

35. Raiford and Romano, "Introduction," xii.

36. Thomas Kane, "Mourning the Promised Land: Martin Luther King Jr.'s Automortography and the National Civil Rights Museum," *American Literature* 76, no. 3 (2004): 568.

37. Ibid.

38. Marc Scott Zicree, *The Twilight Zone Companion*, 2nd ed. (Los Angeles: Silman-James, 1992), 3.

39. Sasha Torres, *Black, White, and in Color: Television and Black Civil Rights* (Princeton, N.J.: Princeton University Press, 2003).

40. M. Keith Booker, *Strange TV: Innovative Television Series from* The Twilight Zone *to* The X-Files (Westport, Conn.: Greenwood, 2002), 49–50.

41. Ibid., 51.

42. Ibid., 54.

43. Kane, "Mourning the Promised Land," 557.

44. Booker, *Strange TV*, 49–50.

45. Boyd, *The New H.N.I.C.*

46. Torres, *Black, White, and in Color.*

47. Alice Rayner, *Ghosts: Death's Double and the Phenomena of Theatre* (Minneapolis: University of Minnesota Press, 2006), 168.

48. Ibid.

49. Ibid., 169.

50. Kane, "Mourning the Promised Land," 568.

51. Wahneema Lubiano, "Black Nationalism and Black Common Sense: Policing Ourselves and Others," in *The House That Race Built: Original Essays by Toni Morrison, Angela Y. Davis, Cornel West, and Others on Black Americans and Politics in America Today*, ed. Wahneema Lubiano (New York: Vintage, 1998), 251.

52. Raiford and Romano, "Introduction," xiii.

53. Charles Odum, "Thousands Participate in Atlanta Unity March," Associated Press (December 11, 2004).

54. Ibid.

55. Ibid.

56. I'm drawing here on Diana Taylor's notion of the scenario as "a paradigmatic setup that relies on supposedly live participants, structured around a schematic plot, with an intended (though adaptable) end." Diana Taylor, *The Archive and the Repertoire: Performing Cultural Memory in the Americas* (Durham, N.C.: Duke University Press, 2003), 26. To theorize the scenario is to bring narrative analysis and performance analysis together: "The scenario includes features well theorized in literary analysis, such as narrative and plot, but demands that we also pay attention to the milieux and corporeal behaviors such as gestures, attitudes, and tones not reducible to language. Simultaneously setup and action, scenarios frame and activate social dramas" (ibid.). The scenario differs from the text in critical ways: it is ephemeral rather than enduring, and the repertoire that houses it hosts a set of performances rather than a concrete narrative. Building on Taylor's theorization of embodied

practice, I am drawing our attention to the African American charismatic scenario as a specific repository for widely held beliefs about authority and identity.

57. Rudolph P. Byrd and Nathan McCall, "The Other Opinion: New Birth Missionary Baptist March: King's Vision Ignored in Hate Crusade," *Atlanta Journal-Constitution* (December 9, 2004).

58. Steve Estes, *I Am a Man! Race, Manhood, and the Civil Rights Movement* (Chapel Hill: University of North Carolina Press, 2005), 12.

59. Eddie S. Glaude, *Exodus! Religion, Race, and Nation in Early Nineteenth-Century Black America* (Chicago: University of Chicago Press, 2000), 9.

60. Spillers argues with regard to the myth of black matriarchy that originates in American slavery, "When we speak of the enslaved person, we perceive that the dominant culture . . . assigns a matriarchist value where it does not belong; actually misnames the power of the female regarding the enslaved community. Such naming is false because the female could not, in fact, claim her child, and false, once again, because 'motherhood' is not perceived in the prevailing social climate as the legitimate procedure of cultural inheritance." Hortense J. Spillers, "Mama's Baby, Papa's Maybe: An American Grammar Book," *Diacritics* 17, no. 2 (1987): 80.

61. *Hustle & Flow*'s protagonist, a Memphis pimp named DJay, pens a song lamenting the decline of insurgent black politics in Memphis and blaming his father's disappearance for his entrance into the underworld of trafficking women: "When I was young, I witnessed my dad standin' for right / Black pride in him, even though he [was] passin' for white / Took years from my life, now I'm missin' the man / Moms on some other shit and now I'm missin' the plan / And so I'm . . . stuck in this fuck-the-world mode, / All the lessons to a young teen baby was cold / Then my pimpin'-ass Uncle put me up on the game / It really ain't no love, it's 'bout this paper, man."

62. Huyssen, *Twilight Memories*, 28.

# 5

## OVERLOOKING RACE AND SECULARISM IN MUSLIM PHILADELPHIA

Joel Blecher and Joshua Dubler

Have you considered what noble lineage is?
*The best of you in lineage is the best of you in manners.*
—A SAYING ATTRIBUTED TO THE PROPHET MUHAMMAD
CIRCULATING ON GERMANTOWN AVENUE, NORTH PHILADELPHIA

### THE PROPHET'S TOOTHBRUSH IS ON GERMANTOWN AVENUE

TRUE TO the Arabic sense of the word, *jum'a*, on the 4900 block of Germantown Avenue, is a day of assembly. Early Friday afternoon, after prayers have finished, the streets clog with people. All but a few are black. The men sport beards, some hennaed red, and they don white *thawbs* for prayer that overhang the high-water pants that leave their ankles bare on ordinary weekdays too. From their own separate entrance at the adjoining storefront, women, the majority draped head to toe in black fabric, mix in with the men and spill up to, around, and through a jagged commercial row. The vendors' wares have been displayed on tables, or have been laid out on blankets on the sidewalk, or remain boxed in the trunks of the cars that brought them. Items for sale include home-baked entrées and desserts indigenous alternatively to the Middle East or the American South, books and CDs, scented oils, and boxes of individually wrapped *siwak*—the bristled branch of an arak tree, the implement with which the Prophet Muhammad is said to have cleaned his teeth.

Though but a small piece of a materially rich cultural universe, the Prophet's toothbrush nonetheless makes for an apt introduction to contemporary Philadelphia Salafism. Imported from South Asia or the Arabian Peninsula, sometimes by way of Brooklyn, the *siwak* is embedded in a field of textually regulated norms. As a commodity, the *siwak* is a shibboleth. Its social function is as a partially concealed marker of a subculture styled in protest yet laden with universalistic aspirations. But to its practitioners, this sociological function is largely beside the point. Ask a man in front of the Germantown mosque about the *siwak*, and he will likely take one from his pocket, describe its proper use, and reference one or two traditions (*hadith*s) attributed to the Prophet Muhammad through which this use is recommended. In this case, as in every case, cues are said to be taken from the example of the *salaf*— the Prophet, his companions, and pious followers from the first three generations of Islamic history. Contemporary Philadelphia Salafis draw on and project upon these pious exemplars to manufacture an idealized code for daily life whose rigidity and concern with purity rarely flag. For these people, the straight path is as wide as a tightrope and flanked on each side by hellfire. Nothing in one's daily practice is extraneous to this code. If not to the existential degree of the rules dictating prayer, alms, and pilgrimage, how one brushes one's teeth or cares for his cuticles are matters no less subject to prophetic example.[1] And so, a short walk up the Germantown mosque's creaky stairs discloses a seminar table in a windowless library, where, in his spare time, a Yemeni-trained American prison chaplain devotes three two-hour sessions of his larger course on Islamic law to explaining the *hadith*s that govern the *siwak*'s proper use.[2] These sessions are only for men, but via simulcast, through the shared eastern wall, women may listen in.

Attention is not a zero-sum game. But if the intense concern paid by Salafis in Philadelphia to proper Islamic dental care illustrates a preoccupation with bodily and creedal purity, it also hints at the sorts of things to which this community, at least in its public discourse, turns a blind eye. Broadly conceived, what Philadelphia's Salafis do not talk about is race or politics. Considering the prominence historically of race and social-justice discourses within African American Islam, this would seem surprising, and indeed it is. That this community explicitly denounces those Muslims that do engage race and politics is even more surprising. How this curious configuration of religion and race came about and how it might be read are the questions with which our contribution to this volume will grapple.

On the one hand, the Salafis' overlooking of race and politics is a reflection of our secular moment, as Vincent Lloyd defines it in the introduction to this volume. While Martin Luther King Jr. and Malcolm X brought discourses of race and religion to public rallies, lecture halls, and living-room televisions across the country, contemporary Salafism in Philadelphia, by contrast, embraces a politics of quietism, discouraging any race-based mobilization and any explicit confrontation with or action against the state. By failing to name and directly oppose the secular and racial status quo and by condemning those Muslim movements that explicitly do this critical work, the Salafis have come to accommodate themselves snugly to a secular regime that regulates—and relegates—race and religion to the discursive margins.

On the other hand, Salafism's ascendency in Philadelphia may be attributed, at least in part, to how it presents its practitioners with a radical alternative lifestyle that pays no heed to the existing racial and secular order. Contrary to the standard liberal formulae for containing religion in the public sphere, Salafi creed neither protects any private personal space in which the individual is freed from the obligations of the Qur'an and the Prophet's example (*sunna*), nor would it concede any facets of public life upon which the *sunna*'s prescriptions are silent. By this reading, Salafism's silence about certain aspects of secular discourse is actually a willful silencing. In its silent repudiation, it offers a righteous and sacred rejection of its predecessors in the faith who fought religiously against racial and economic injustice but who, in the Salafis' account, failed to extricate themselves from a fundamentally secular framework that doomed them from the start.

From the Salafi perspective, then, religiously infused political movements that purport to reject the status quo are, in fact, inextricably bound to the secular statist order. These movements, the critique runs, are polluted by secular idols, ideas, and ideologies—like nationalism—that ignore and suppress God's commands. By this view, figures like Malcolm X—not to mention Martin Luther King Jr.—belong squarely to the secular apparatus, in so far as they willfully allow their religious commitments to intermingle with and, often, to be eclipsed by their secular drive for racial solidarity, economic uplift, and other false gods.

This rejectionist attitude is rife with historical irony and unintended consequences, but taken on its own terms, the Philadelphian Salafi mode of overlooking the politics of race poses an apt and abiding provocation. By exploring the contested and intersecting local, national, and transnational histories of contemporary Philadelphia Salafism, this case study has as much to teach us about our own normative racialized and religious assumptions about black politics as it does about race and secularism in Muslim America.

## SALAFISM IN AMERICA: A CONTESTED HISTORY

Secular scholars have been slow to document the emergence of Salafism in America.[3] Of late, however, in blogs, YouTube videos, and conferences, American Salafis have themselves begun to recount their history. In these oral and written narratives, heated disputes arise at certain historiographical flashpoints, one of which being how the community ought to be portrayed in relation to the politics of race. A recent debate between Umar Lee and Dawud Adib is particularly illustrative. Along with other members of the black vanguard, Adib, a former imam of the Germantown *masjid*, embraced Salafism in East Orange, New Jersey, in the 1980s. Lee, a white convert to Islam from St. Louis, joined the movement in the 1990s, and he became a high-profile Salafi dissident in 2007 when he posted in ten installments on his Wordpress blog, "The Rise and Fall of the Salafi Movement."[4]

To date, Lee's "Rise and Fall" is the closest thing we have to a historical description of what we might call "black Salafism" in America. In tone, Lee's textured and detailed account is much closer to lament than to polemic. The story is a familiar one. It is that of an idealist once activated but of late grown weary, a story of fervor fanned and snuffed out. Lee's history begins in the early 1990s during the Malcolm X revival that accompanied the release of Spike Lee's biopic. The film sparked a resurgent interest in Islam and the dissemination of the Salafi "call," or *da'wa*, by way of networks not dissimilar to the punk underground of the same historical moment. It was this movement, one nurtured by bootlegged tapes, surfed couches, and shoe-strung conferences, that called Umar Lee to Islam. Lee responded emphatically. These were halcyon days of zeal and idealist dreams of social justice. "The environment often was hypnotic," Lee remembered. "We believed with our very beings that this was going to be the answer to the world's problems."[5]

Not all of it was that heady. At the material surface of this righteous zeal, Salafism simultaneously became a visible force in the marketplace of black urban style. In Philadelphia especially, Salafi norms of speech, dress, and worship spread throughout the African American Muslim community. Even non-Muslims started growing beards in the Salafi style, what to this day is called the "Philly beard."[6] "It was," as Lee somewhat neutrally observed, "the latest trend."[7]

The 1990s saw the Salafi movement's rise, but for Lee, the new millennium brought about its fall. Some of this decline, Lee readily conceded, can be fairly attributed to the panic and persecutions of the post-9/11 period, but ideological infighting and schismatic acrimony were, for Lee, the greater culprits. Need one be loyal to the Saudi throne? Was one sufficiently connected to the proper religious authorities, the *'ulama'* of the Arabian Peninsula? Were one's practices free of innovation, *bid'a*? Depending on the answers to these questions, groups of Salafis were fractured, and dissidents were shunned. For those like Lee who had come to take—or, in retrospect, mistake—the world of the religious enclave for the world as such, the effects of this dissolution were devastating:

> Brothers like me made their full time jobs "being Muslim." We would just find an odd job here or there to support ourselves and our families and return to our Salafi world. Many others dedicated their time in trying to "go study" with no thought of what we were going to do when we got older. We had no idea that the world—the real world—was continuing to move on without us.[8]

Not all were so disillusioned. To some ears in the Salafi community, Lee's implicitly secular and materialist hierarchy between the "Salafi world" and "the real world" struck a dissonant chord. In 2011, at a conference that took place on the other side of the Ben Franklin Bridge in Cherry Hill, New Jersey, Dawud Adib delivered a two-part lecture entitled "The History of the Salafi Da'wah in America." As an explicit rejoinder to Umar Lee's "Rise and

Fall," Adib's address was very different in style and content. Adib was polemical, denunciatory, and rambling, and he dismissed any notion that the Salafi world was a world apart. He maligned Lee's ideals of secular engagement and social betterment and argued instead for an orientation of pious steadfastness.

Adib's address began ad hominem. That Adib believed Lee was a "*shaytan*" and a "criminal" was not atypical when considering the heated atmosphere of these exchanges. More provocative, however, was Adib's accusation that Lee was a "fed"— that is, on the government's payroll.[9] Given Lee's erudition and detailed knowledge of events for which Lee was not actually present, he must be, Adib conjectured, a federal informant and perhaps even an agent provocateur.[10] This accusation indicates both the culture of fear and suspicion in which Salafi discourses operate and the degree to which accusations of collaborating with the state can serve as a powerful cudgel in diminishing one's credibility. It also suggests that Adib may have been exploiting his audience's sense that there was some ideological overlap, however subtle, between Lee's goals and those of the state.

Philadelphia Salafism's delicate balance between quietism and protest was also evident in Adib's history's pronounced, and even advertised, lacunae. As Adib declaimed at the outset: "When we talk about *tarikh*—history—we have to have accuracy," and with the passage of time, such accuracy becomes difficult to obtain.[11] What historical claims Adib did make he substantiated with what little documentary evidence he could find: a newsletter from the 1980s, a list of contacts from the 1990s. Such characteristically Salafi textual scrupulousness aside, however, there were tactical reasons for these narrative gaps: he was "advised not to mention" certain persons and names. Advised by whom, and for what reason? Adib did not say.[12]

Were Adib to play by the same narrative rules as Lee—secular rules, we should note, for which Paul and Augustine forged the prototype—Adib might have begun his history of Salafism in America with autobiography. This would have entailed describing his own youthful encounter with black nationalist Islam, an era that Umar Lee could access only secondhand by way of Alex Haley and Spike Lee. Adib, after all, who was born in the 1950s, was a member of the Nation of Islam, and upon Elijah Muhammad's death in 1975, he followed Muhammad's son Wallace into Sunni Islam.[13] But Adib sidestepped this obvious narrative arc. Understandably, only fragmentary glimpses of Adib's own reckoning with the legacy of the Nation of Islam poked through. What for many black Muslims of his generation was *the* watershed event was for Adib, in retrospect, not half as transformative as they thought it was. As he and some of his brothers and sisters came to realize in the decades since the 1975 conversion to Sunnism, Wallace Muhammad's Islam "was as bad, and maybe even worse than what his father was teaching, and Allah knows best."[14] Proudly evincing the sort of divisive absolutism that Umar Lee decried, Adib was unequivocal: "You only have two things—*sunna* and *bid'a*"—the righteous path and blasphemous innovations. For Adib, there was only correct and incorrect, no in-between. Those who follow an alternative methodology or *manhaj*, whether it be that of Wallace Muhammad, the Muslim Brotherhood, or the Tablighis, were not, for Adib, true Muslims. What mattered, for Adib, then, were not the facts of history but the moral and ethical lessons contained therein. And these lessons were not to be found in the historical experiences of a man or his community. Like everything else in the present day, they were prefigured by—and to be found in—the prophetic *hadith*.

Rather than to the history advertised in his title, then, Adib dedicated much of the first hour of his oratory to the recitation and catechistic repetition of a supplicatory prayer contained in a well-known *hadith*. For the history of the Salafi *da'wa*, the lesser, recent history of Salafism in America is somewhat beside the point. The history that matters is that of the *salaf*, and it is their language that addresses the sources of his audience's being, their ethical obligations, and the divergent futures that unfold before them. First in Arabic, then in English, Adib recited a *hadith*: "*Ya muqallib al-qulub, thabbit qalbi 'ala dinik.* Oh, Controller of the hearts, make my heart firm on your religion."[15] For Adib, that religion was fixed in the seventh century. That Umar Lee had smuggled in a secularist, sociological framework—that he had termed Salafism a "movement"—was, for Adib, a key tell that Lee was "off the *manhaj*," the idealized methodology based on the model of Muhammad and the first three generations of Muslims. Salafism could not "decline," on this view, because it is an enduring path to proper conduct and beliefs, not a political group or a sociological trend. In characteristic Salafi fashion, Adib teased mighty stakes from this fine-grained terminological distinction. "Only Allah knows what will happen to us in the future. Sala*fiyya* [as a methodology] is safe, but no one knows what will happen to the Sala*fis*." Should their hearts weaken, they too might drift away. And so, again and again, the men present and the women listening in were repeatedly called upon to chant the declaration of their steadfastness: "*Ya muqallib al-qulub, thabbit qalbi 'ala dinik.*"

## SALAFISM COMES TO AMERICA: TOWARD A CRITICAL HISTORY

Philadelphia's Salafi callers occupy the intersection of two distinct historical arcs. The first arc, already alluded to, is the tradition of African American Islam. As conventionally reconstructed, black Islam came with the African slaves, died with their descendants, and was resurrected in the twentieth century by the religious leaders and rank and file in the Moorish Science Temple and the Nation of Islam. The heyday of the Nation, when Malcolm X might credibly speak for American Muslims, was ironically enabled by a racist immigration law that barred from naturalization peoples from Muslim-majority lands.[16] With the passage of the Immigration and Nationality Act of 1965 and the influx of Muslims from South Asia and the Middle East, African American Muslims were simultaneously educated about the broader Islamic tradition and marginalized from it. Driven by this dialectical pressure, the mass embrace of Sunni Islam following Elijah Muhammad's death—what Wallace called "the second resurrection"—played the role of synthesis.[17]

The second arc picks up where the first leaves off chronologically, but spatially it jumps the ocean. This arc pertains to the late twentieth-century transformation of the Salafi *'ulama'* in the Arabian Peninsula. These very *'ulama'* appear, albeit obliquely, in Umar Lee's description of American Salafism's first stirrings in the late 1980s. Certain "individuals," Lee wrote, "really took 'the dawah' to the converts where it was originally mostly a Gulf Arab thing."[18] Here, Lee explicitly namechecked Dawud Adib alongside other prominent African American Salafi callers. Although Adib would later balk at Lee's characterization of Salafism as "a Gulf Arab thing," Lee had hit upon a crucial connection.

Charted genealogically, Philadelphia Salafism has deep roots in the Arabian peninsula. Although one could trace its origin to the militant puritanical movement founded by the eighteenth-century Arabian preacher Muhammad ibn 'Abd al-Wahhab, the quietist articulation of Salafism that would ultimately find a home in Philadelphia arose in the Saudi Kingdom in the aftermath of the 1979 occupation of the Grand Mosque in Mecca. This quietist Salafism was first propagated in Yemen, other centers of Islamic learning in the Middle East, and then Southeast Asia, Europe, and North America. In fact, a particular network of Saudi and Yemeni shaykhs have, over the last generation, exerted a direct influence in Philadelphia. One place where this legacy is visible is in Philadelphia Salafis' interest in authenticated *hadith*s on issues evocative of bodies, politics, and race.

The practice of Muslim scholars scrutinizing the authenticity of the transmitters contained in a *hadith*'s chain of transmission ( *jarh wa-ta'dil*) stretches back to the classical period of Islamic history. After a period of relative decline among the Ottomans, however, the tradition was revived by a number of key figures in the eighteenth, nineteenth, and twentieth centuries. Most notable for our purposes was the iconoclastic scholar Nasir al-Din al-Albani, who rose to prominence and notoriety in the 1960s and died in 1999.[19] Responding both to internal and external charges concerning the authenticity of the *hadith* corpus, al-Albani reopened scrutiny over the authenticity of *hadith*s long thought settled. Inevitably, controversies arose as al-Albani and his colleagues deauthenticated certain *hadith*s upon which contemporary practices and beliefs relied and authenticated other *hadith*s that contemporary discourses had previously ignored. Many of these controversies circled around matters of personal and group comportment: attire, music, purity, and worship practices.

As a general rule, al-Albani and the larger movement he inaugurated endeavored to remove piety from the corrupting aims of modern political theories. He issued withering criticism, for example, of the Islamist political activism of Sayyid Qutb and the Muslim Brotherhood. One potentially subversive exception to this rule stood out. On the basis of his methodology in authenticating *hadith*s, al-Albani asserted that a Muslim ruler must hail from the Prophet's own tribe, the Quraysh.[20] Armed with this opinion and its correlative prooftexts, al-Albani and his students came into conflict with the authority of the Saudi royal family, which could claim no such tribal lineage.

Not by accident did the Salafis stir up this hornet's nest. Rather, the subversive potential of al-Albani's new approach to *hadith* dovetailed with a widespread perception among Salafis and others that the Saudi royal family had been co-opted and corrupted by the secular West. This Salafi rejectionism reached an extreme in 1979 with the militant seizure of the Grand Mosque in Mecca.[21] In a matter of weeks, this blunt challenge to Saudi rule was put down, and in the aftermath, al-Albani and his Salafi intellectual allies were driven underground or into exile.[22] A number of Salafi *ulama'*, however, forged an intellectual compromise that allowed them to remain in the Saudi Kingdom. They stood by al-Albani's insights on everyday matters of piety, attire, purity, worship, and manners, but they explicitly disavowed the Salafi challenge to the House of Saud. Sidestepping the question of a ruler's pedigree, they reasserted the longstanding Sunni tradition that as a citizen, a Muslim owed his or her obedience to those in authority.[23]

Among the Salafi scholars who charted this strategic course was Muqbil ibn al-Wadi'i, who died in 2001.[24] Earlier in his career, al-Wadi'i had taken a number of provocative positions that had driven him into exile even before the Grand Mosque standoff. In Yemen, al-Wadi'i cultivated an accommodationist attitude toward both the Saudi royal family and the Yemeni state. In theory, the position was essentially a quietist one. For al-Wadi'i, quite simply, a Muslim's obligation is to practice the *sunna*, and the politics of the secular world are not his or her concern. To al-Wadi'i's right, a Saudi shaykh named Rabi' al-Madkhali went even further by demonstrating fervent loyalty toward the Saudi throne.[25]

In the 1980s, a vanguard of African Americans, Egyptians, and Sudanese luminaries journeyed east to Mecca and Medina to deepen their knowledge of Islam. After cultivating a Salafi practice at institutions like the Islamic University in Medina and the Umm al-Qura University in Mecca, these scholars brought the *da'wa* to New York and the mid-Atlantic states through publications, magazines and conferences.[26] By the 1990s, al-Albani had become viewed as one of the group's most eminent authorities, and a cadre of shaykhs including al-Wadi'i and al-Madkhali had been taken up as gatekeepers.[27]

In Philadelphia, traces of this influence abound. A mosque named for al-Wadi'i, which is located on the 2700 block of Allegheny Avenue in North Philadelphia, was recently the site for a conference in which Rabi' al-Madkhali and his colleagues delivered a telelinked lecture.[28] The International Islamic Information Network (IIIN), a nonprofit "Authentic Islamic Audio

Warehouse" that sells predominantly English recordings of lessons delivered by speakers at the Germantown mosque and whose proceeds go directly to support the Germantown mosque, directs its web traffic to six Arabic-language websites, one belonging to Muqbil ibn Hadi al-Wadi'i, one to Rabi' al-Madkhali, and one to Rabi''s brother, Zayd.[29] To this day, African American Muslims continue to go to Medina for study, and an increasing number of prominent Salafi callers have received their training in al-Wadi'i's Dar al-Hadith in Dammaj, Yemen.

It would be a mistake to read reductively the Philadelphia presence of al-Madkhali's and al-Wadi'i's articulation of Salafism as being a Saudi or Yemeni export. Though initially cultivated in the Arabian Peninsula, Salafism's worldwide dispersal from Indonesia to the United States is a reflection of its catholic elasticity and its ability to resonate across a range of cultural divides. Enabled by a secular-age consumer culture in which individuals are adept at navigating an unprecedented mélange of traditions, its emphasis on austerity, bodily purity, dress, and creed has proven to have widespread appeal for a variety of divergently placed Muslims, who, around the globe, have taken up the Salafi method and made it their own.

But Salafism's positive appeal has been only part of its success. In Philadelphia and elsewhere, Salafism has thrived both for what it speaks to and for what it chooses to remain silent. In the American context, its principal lacunae are politics and race. That is to say that the Salafism of al-Madkhali and al-Wadi'i offers not only an approach to a body of authenticated texts and the correlative pietistic practices. Also, as informed by its formative experience of political overreach, this strand of Salafism offers a conception of Islam in which personal piety is best practiced when it is insulated from the macropolitical order.

Some Salafis who claim al-Madkhali as an influence have gone even further by explicitly condemning, as al-Albani did, those Muslims who seek involvement in the national politics of several Middle Eastern states, such as the Muslim Brotherhood. Since 2009, some English-speaking supporters of al-Madkhali have created, maintained, and updated a website polemicizing against those Islamist movements who do engage the secular political order. Singled out for special criticism is the Muslim Brotherhood, who, it is said, "come out in the name of refuting Secularism" but do so "through involvement in the current secular political apparatus" at the explicit expense of the Qur'an and the *sunna*.[30]

The Islamist Muslim Brotherhood, part of the secular political apparatus? Much as we saw in the dispute between Umar Lee and Dawud Adib, "secularism" in this case may simply be the discursive stuff of which ad hominem attacks are made. But this counterintuitive suggestion is worth entertaining. Is there a perspective from which the structures of secular power and the religiopolitical activists that prominently oppose it are mutually reinforcing? Has the entrenched antagonism of these oppositional forces left open a space at the margins for those who might seek radically to redescribe themselves wholly outside of secular discourses and practices? Is there a space for those who abstain from resisting secular authorities on the grounds that resisting is itself a kind of co-optation if not properly authorized by the Islamic foundational texts?

At the very least, this posture has done vital social work. In Philadelphia, this overlooking of politics and race has provided African American Salafis with a modicum of stability that could endure an American surveillance state that, beginning with the first World Trade Center attack in 1993 and intensifying exponentially since 9/11, has indiscriminately trained all of its powers of control on Muslim bodies prejudged as suspect. Needless to say, the swearing off of explicit and explicitly antagonistic political discourses has not ensured Germantown's black Muslims with "security" in any substantive way. For this, a host of structural changes would be necessary. But this abstention has significantly improved the chances that they would avoid the fate that following 9/11 befell the more bellicose Salafi preachers. For having preached Muslim politics to his community in northern Virginia, a politics in which jihad by the sword has its place, Ali al-Tamimi is currently serving life in a federal penitentiary.[31]

The value of the renunciation of politics for black Muslim survival in the post-9/11 era should not be underestimated. This, quite simply, may well be the difference between imprisonment and freedom, death and life. But there is also another value here, a soulful, psychic value. For Philadelphia's black urban poor men and women accustomed to malignant neglect and social control by the institutions of society and state, the good news that they them-selves are *not* responsible for fixing the broken systems that they are wholly disempowered to fix could only have come as a tremendous relief.

## PROPHETIC *HADITHS* IN CONDEMNATION OF RACISM?

The Salafi renunciation of politics also needs to be understood within a finer-grained and more intramural cultural context. In their self-fashioning as Muslim, both as individuals and as a collectivity, Philadelphia's black Salafis explicitly remove themselves from the "black Muslim" tradition that began with Noble Drew Ali, was refined and mainstreamed by Elijah Muhammad and Malcolm X, and which was preserved in a tempered form by Warith Deen (né Wallace) Muhammad. Nowhere is this sequestration clearer than in the Salafi redescription of the categories of "race" and "racism."

As is true of the black churches of their parents and grandparents, Phila-delphia's Salafism is a religious subculture at once richly oral but also steeped in the written word. These two tendencies are plainly on display on German-town Avenue following the conclusion of *jum'a*, where, on the vendors' tables, texts come in two varieties: CDs and paperbacks. Of the CDs, some are pro-fessionally produced and feature recitations of the Qur'an delivered by Saudi chanters. Other CDs have a more homemade look and feature recordings of local Salafi callers' Friday sermons and other public lessons. Judging from their titles, the CDs address a range of topics, some of them narrowly doctri-nal but many of them geared to instruct the listener on how to live his or her everyday life *Islamically* in an otherwise secular world: how to be a nurturing husband, a dutiful wife, a user of the new technologies. Among the printed works, some bear the imprint of Authentic Statements, a West Philadelphia publishing house, but many come from farther afield. The printed matter, in general, makes little attempt to address local racial and political issues and is more narrowly focused on issues of creed, *hadith*, and law. An exception that proves the rule is the sale and circulation of Sunnah Publishing's *Prophetic Ahadith in Condemnation of Racism*, initially published in 2012.

From its Grand Rapids, Michigan, home base, Sunnah Publishing has be-come a major contributor to the Philadelphia Salafi scene. Since 2010 it has sponsored biannual conferences in Philadelphia, and it translates and distributes works by many Saudi and Yemeni scholars in the networks mentioned above.[32] Some of Sunnah Publishing's translators are Philadelphia locals, such as Abul Hassan Malik, an imam from Camden, New Jersey, who claims a reading license (*ijaza*) that certifies he has studied under the Yemeni scholar al-Wadi'i.[33] The lion's share are produced by Maaz Qureshi, who, prior to founding Sunnah Publishing in 2004, was active in a Canadian Salafi association called "The Revival of Islamic Dawah" (TROID) and sold his print and audio media by way of a still vital online outlet called SalafiPublications.com. Qureshi has been a resident of Grand Rapids since 1997 and by day works as a data specialist for Pitney Bowes.[34] Like all translations, Qureshi's are not mere replications of the original. Rather, they are peppered through with novel aspects intended to make the translated work speak to the new context where it is received. As with *Prophetic Ahadith in Condemnation of Racism*, they often include translators' notes that explicitly address Western audiences and report al-Albani's grades on the *hadiths*' authenticity.

As is so often the case with books, there is reason to suspect that books on Germantown Avenue are sometimes bought more for their talismanic value than for actual engagement with the theological and legal claims contained between their covers. But in content, *Prophetic Ahadith in Condemnation of Racism* is both surprising and revealing. Against Philadelphia's urban backdrop, "racism" may bring to mind white flight, sprawling ghettos, school closures, and expansive prison projects and evoke flashpoints such as the firebombing of MOVE and the conviction of Mumia Abu-Jamal. The titular "racism" condemned by the Prophet in the Sunnah Publishing volume, however, is of a wholly different order. Authored by 'Abd al-Salam Ibn Burjis (d. 2004), a late Saudi national, the book not only ignores the African American intellectual tradition of W. E. B. Du Bois, James Baldwin, Martin Luther King Jr., Malcolm X, Angela Davis, Cornel West, and others, but it also speaks very little to the underlying concerns about injustice that animate these thinkers.[35] Indeed, if anything, by appealing to the familiar language of "racism," *Prophetic Ahadith in Condemnation of Racism* makes a strong play to erase that critical race discourse and to supplant it with another.

Almost immediately in *Prophetic Ahadith in Condemnation of Racism*, it becomes clear that the theme of the *hadiths* and their commentary is not *'unsuriyya*—the term in the title that Qureshi sensibly translated as "racism"—but, rather, *'asabiyya* and *nasab*—which Qureshi renders in turn as "tribalism/nationalism" and "lineage."[36] From the first eighteen *hadith*s out of twenty-two explored in the volume, the reader receives a heavy-handed presentation on Muhammad's musings on tribalism and lineage. At first, the message seems to be one of democratic universalism and divine meritocracy. As compared to the fear of God (*taqwa*) that one exhibits in his or her faith and works, markers of lineage are said to mean next to nothing. Indeed, the commentary explains, when accorded undue status at the expense of one's faith and works, a focus on tribe and line proves, in fact, harmful. Hence the translated *hadith*: "The noblest of you according to Allah is the one with the most *taqwa*. Have you considered what noble lineage is? The best of you in lineage is the best of you in manners."[37] Before God, it would seem, *taqwa* is the only measure of a person's value.

A second *hadith* hews closer to the "racism" suggested by Qureshi's title. Speaking directly to distinctions of race and ethnicity, the *hadith* reads: "Indeed, an Arab has no excellence over an Arab, nor does a white person have any excellence over a black one, nor does a black person have any excellence over a white one, except through *taqwa*."[38] Here, too, then, the message seems clear: earthly hierarchies and lineages hold no weight in the hereafter.

But in a seeming reversal, the collection's final two *hadith*s offer definitive proof of the very thing the volume is generally intent on dispelling. Apparently, in God's mind, a hierarchy among lineages *does* exist. To be sure, *taqwa* remains the principal measure by which Muslims are judged by God, but, as the *hadith* proclaims, a Muslim of nobler tribal lineage is divinely awarded twice the benefit of that given to a Muslim of lesser tribal lineage for the performance of the very same good deed.[39] This privilege cuts both ways. For his disobedience, a Muslim of nobler lineage is divinely punished at twice the rate as well. Analytically, however, the net result is the same: in the judgment of *taqwa*, God is not blind to lineage. Thanks to lineage, one's reward or punishment can be augmented or diminished.

The collection's final *hadith* grants a special designation to Arabs. More so than other peoples, according to the Messenger of God, Arabs, it is alleged, are naturally inclined toward goodness, are "more given to generosity, forbearance, courage and more given to fulfilling the trusts and other than that from [among the] praiseworthy manners."[40] With increasing precision, the *hadith* commentary continues with the further elevation of those descended from the Prophet's own tribe, the Quraysh, and further still of those who may be counted among the Prophet's actual family. As with the markers of material success for Weber's Calvinists, these genealogical designations are no guarantee of God's favorable judgment, but as external indicators, they tend to correlate positively.

In his commentary, Ibn Burjis rests conclusively on the following tension. On the one hand, "making tribes the epitome of excellence and aiding its individuals from them over another individual from them due to an action or a statement is far from the standards of the *shari'ah* of al-Islam."[41] What matters is not the doer but the deed. On the other hand, however, "it is obligatory to submit fully to Allah with regards to mentioning the virtues of the tribes which have been related in the *shari'ah*."[42] In other words, one is ultimately judged on one's *taqwa*—hence the pious predecessors' robust emphasis on creed and bodily purity—but at the end of the day, some lineages are, indeed, nobler than others, and pedigree plays a role in how God rewards and punishes Muslims in the end times, and it plays a role in how Muslims ought to govern themselves in the meantime.

When taken to its logical conclusion, this privileging of the Qurashi lineage, in fact, undermines the Saudi royal family's claims to legitimacy. But for a Salafi dissident like Umar Lee, the sort of plainly pro-Arabian bias that lies at the heart of *Prophetic Ahadith in Condemnation of Racism* would stand as further proof, as he put it in a video blog, that men like Dawud Adib are basically "Uncle Tom to the Saudi King." As Salafi Muslims, black people had simply moved "from the back of the bus to the back of the camel."[43]

Telling inferences about *'asabiyya* (tribalism) may also be derived from another source: a purported dialogue between the Saudi dissident al-Wadi'i and Abu Muslimah, a black Salafi caller who, as you may recall from Umar Lee's history, hailed from the same East Orange clique as Dawud Adib.[44] As it is reported in a 2003 post on an English-language discussion board in a Salafi corner of the Internet, Abu Muslimah went to Muqbil al-Wadi'i to help repair his reputation after al-Madkhali cursed and disparaged him for being a black nationalist. While this may sound harsh, Abu Muslimah's predicament was not an unusual one within his scholarly network. After all, al-Madkhali was well known for applying the procedures of *jarh wa-ta'dil* to evaluate the trustworthiness of living scholars, a controversial but not unprecedented practice. The resulting exchange between the African American caller and his Arab shaykh reveals a great deal about Salafi discourse: its style, its mechanisms of interpretive authority, and its embedded perceptions of nationality and race.

In the exchange, which likely occurred in Arabic, the Yemeni shaykh Muqbil al-Wadi'i probed at the root cause of al-Madkhali's grievance against Abu Muslimah. We will quote at length, and transcription, transliteration, and translation inconsistencies are reproduced *sic erat scriptum*:

SHEIKH MUQBIL: Some of the brothers say that you have (call to) nationalism?

ABU MUSLIMAH: And how is that?

SHEIKH MUQBIL: Meaning that you prefer the non-Arab over the Arab.

ABU MUSLIMAH: How do I prefer them? With my Dawah? My dawah is for my people.

SHEIKH MUQBIL: So this (nationalism) is not what you are on. I was sure that due to the many blessings and good that Allaah has bestowed (given) you, that there would be many envious people. People who would envy you because of that and if they found any of your shortcomings they would propagate it. And if they did not find any shortcomings, would create something just to divert the people from being around you.

ABU MUSLIMAH: My dawah is very clear, walhamdulillaah. I call to the book of Allaah and the Sunnah of his Prophet (saw) based on the understanding of the Salaf of this Ummah. I give daily classes in the masjid and all of my classes are recorded. So, if I am calling to any nationalism, then where is this call? The issue is that I am an American. I live among the American, I know their language, I know their culture and I am from them. So what is the sin that I committed teaching my people their religion?

SHEIKH MUQBIL: You are to be praised (commended) on that. We did not think you had any of this nationalism, as we were in Al-Madinah calling to Allaah and everyone around us was Saudi. And we used to tell them; if you have any racism we would not accompany you. The dawah of the

Messenger (saw) is for the white, the black, the Arab and the non-Arab, in any country without any differentiation.

**ABU MUSLIMAH:** Abdullah McCafee was one of my students and he is a white American.[45] Now he is one of your students. Also, the Sheikh (referring to Abu Hatim, one of Sheikh Muqbil's students who is attending this session) visited us in our masjid. If I claim that a black Muslim is better than the white one, what is my proof from the Book of Allaah?[46]

Whether a faithful transcript of an actual exchange or an apocryphal fancy, Abu Muslimah's defense of his *da'wa*'s colorblindness speaks volumes about how race discourse has been inflected for Salafi Muslims. We might expect race discourse here to serve its conventional function of making sense of and critiquing social injustice. From what we reflexively know about black people's historical status in America, it would be understandable if Abu Muslimah were uncomfortable with Salafism's tendency for privileging Arabs. In his exchange with al-Wadi'i, however, the roles one might have anticipated are reversed. That is to say, it is Abu Muslimah, the black caller, who is forced to defend himself from the charge that as a purported sectarian black nationalist he is prejudiced against Arabs. Abu Muslimah is portrayed as having repaired his reputation in the eyes of his Yemeni shaykh and having averred that he overlooks racial differences in accordance with the Qur'an.

At the conclusion to *Prophetic Ahadith in Condemnation of Racism* is appended a creedal statement from Muqbil al-Wadi'i. In language borrowed from al-Albani, al-Wadi'i offers a cultural diagnosis and a plea for Muslim unity: "We hold that this multiplicity of present-day parties is a reason for the division of the Muslims and their weakness. So therefore we set about 'freeing the minds from the fetters of blind-following and the darkness of sectarianism and party spirit.'"[47] While, in its original context, al-Wadi'i and al-Albani would have been referring to the party politics of the Muslim Brotherhood and other species of Islamism indigenous to the Middle East, the condemnation of race-based politics on Germantown Avenue is difficult to miss. And so, to a population predisposed to use the critical discourse of race and racism to make sense of their own material and social disadvantage and to argue publicly for remediation, the message of *Prophetic Ahadith in Condemnation of*

*Racism* is clear: racism is, indeed, something that black people must struggle to overcome *in themselves.*

## IS BLACK ISLAM SECULAR?

In *The Philadelphia Negro*, in a chapter entitled "The Present Condition of the Churches," W. E. B. Du Bois notes how among the members of Philadelphia's Negro churches he found a preoccupation with "social betterment":

> All movements for social betterment are apt to centre in the churches. Beneficial societies in endless number are formed here; secret societies keep in touch; co-operative and building associations have lately sprung up; the minister often acts as an employment agent; considerable charitable and relief work is done and special meetings held to aid special projects. *The race problem in all its phases is continually being discussed, and, indeed, from this forum many a youth goes forth inspired to work.*[48]

In the century to follow, perhaps nowhere in Philadelphia did the "race problem" inspire more original and vivacious religious "work" than among its black Muslims. By World War II, a University of Pennsylvania graduate student, Arthur Huff Fauset, was able to observe, among the urban cults catering to the glut of great migrants, the religious inventiveness of the red-fezzed Moslems in the Moorish Science Temple.[49] In 1954, a similar Islam would creep in further from the margin, when early adopters of Elijah Muhammad's Nation of Islam were corralled by a red-headed minister and installed in their officially sanctioned institutional home. Over the next generation, Philadelphia's Temple Twelve would become a Nation of Islam stronghold, ministered in turn by Malcolm X and Elijah Muhammad's son, Wallace. The temple grew to acquire half a dozen satellites. Businesses were launched, both above board and below, and eventually so too was a Clara Muhammad School.[50]

If contemporary Salafism in Philadelphia confounds one's expectations for what African American Islam ought to look like, that is because the above trajectory of what might ironically be referred to as the "more traditional" black Islam is far more consistent with the reigning paradigms for black religion in general. In this way, comparing Salafism in Philadelphia with its predecessors in Islam is instructive, although less for the purposes of provenance than for contrast. For as has been the standard account from Fauset's day to the present day, the movements behind the Moorish Science Temple and Nation of Islam are best construed in the same Du Boisian light in which they must have seen themselves: as religious collectives armed with a practical politics engineered for the economic and social betterment of black folks. To frame this religious ethos in materialist terms is not to deny these groups their religious ideas and concerns. To be sure, each sect was led by a charismatic figure who spoke earnestly of God, and the rank and file lived rigid ritual protocols and abided in prohibitions of diet and grooming.[51] But in the critical light shined by Philadelphia's Salafis, the Moorish Science Temple, the Nation of Islam, and Warith Deen Muhammad's American Society of Muslims appear to have been and to remain, at the end of the day, *secular religions.*

Indeed, arguably, never were these groups more secular in form than when they were being religious. Their metaphysics and eschatologies pointed not away from the modern world but back to it. As individuals and as collectives, members of the Moorish Science Temple and the Nation of Islam pursued involvement in public life with the utmost urgency, as if the political, economic, and social world was, for all intents and purposes, the only world there was. For these groups, the sacred lineages connecting them to their lost pasts—to Moab, Mecca, and Morocco for the Moors and to the Tribe of Shabazz for the Nation—were transparently deployed as counternarratives in service of a future, one apocalyptically imminent, in which the achievement of full emancipation and nationhood was soon at hand.[52]

For the Moors and the Nation, the modern state was both a precondition and a horizon. It was a precondition inasmuch as it set the stage historically for their disenfranchisement in the United States. It was a horizon inasmuch as a nation-state all of one's own appeared as the obvious solution to the precipitating problems. If, in the practical mean, members of the Moorish Science Temple and the Nation of Islam had played the game of American public life as every other ethnic group had learned to play it—by building their economic and political strength so as to engender for black people public power commensurate to their numbers—those at the doctrinal extreme would have still insisted on a state all their own. That is to say that even when they dreamt, brothers and sisters in the Moorish Science Temple and in the Nation of Islam dreamt in secular.

Unlike today's Islamists, then, who collapse politics into religion, Malcolm X, for one, projected a secular frame in which religion and politics were relegated to two separate spheres.[53] If and when priority was to be established, racial solidarity was to come first, and religious commitments were to follow after.[54] Or, better put, the differences inherent in the latter were to be subordinated to the project of the former. As Malcolm X told a crowd of "friends and enemies" in Cleveland, Ohio, in 1964:

> Although I'm still a Muslim, I'm not here tonight to discuss my religion. I'm not here to try and change your religion. I'm not here to argue or discuss anything that we differ about, because it's time for us to submerge our differences and realize that it is best for us to first see that we have the same problem, a common problem, a problem that will make you catch hell whether you're a Baptist, or a Methodist, or a Muslim, or a nationalist. . . . All of us have suffered here, in this country, political oppression at the hands of the white man, economic exploitation at the hands of the white man, and social degradation at the hands of the white man.[55]

Malcolm X was rallying his audience against a racial, political, economic, and cultural status quo entangled with the secular order, but he takes as self-evident and actively reaffirms the very crux of secularism: to stand in solidarity against social and economic oppression, matters of religious differences must be "submerged."

This same secular blood courses through the tradition of black Islam. At the heart of the black Muslims' Islam was a creative and critical vocabulary about race in America. It was by way of a brutal racist caste system that, as the Moors saw it, an august people had come falsely to conceive of itself as "Negro, Black, and Colored." It was in the eugenics burlesque about Yakub, the bigheaded mad scientist who invented white people, that the followers of Elijah Muhammad would manufacture a modern theodicy.[56] All at the same time, Elijah was the key for diagnosing social injustice, the marker for delimiting the boundaries of the collective, and the catalyst for mobilizing toward justice.

Blackness also inscribed an attitude of righteous refusal. As captured by its early chroniclers such as James Baldwin and C. Eric Lincoln and promoted by its own spokespeople including Malcolm X, black Muslims were heavily motivated by political concerns, even and especially during its heyday, when the movement swore off conventional modes of party politics. In prose and in person, the black Muslims were prophetically critical and combatively polemical. As a performative style, the black Muslim mode of being in public was to signal protest. In glossing this attitude, Sherman Jackson calls on Charles Long's category of "black religion."[57] Not the same thing as African American religion, "black religion" is characterized by a "lithic consciousness, a state of mind which in confronting a reality bent on domination invokes *a will to opposition*, a veritable cosmic 'No.'"[58] This Nietzschean refusal of the status quo's politics, society, and culture, a refusal at once reactive and affirmative, polemical and self-constitutive, is black religion's animating disposition. And from a secular standpoint, given the enduring history of black disenfranchisement in America, how could it be anything else?

## SAYING "NO!" TO BLACK RELIGION

In 1953, *Ebony* ran a multiarticle spread on Philadelphia's "Negro Moslems." One piece, entitled "Moslems Take Firm Stand Against Racism," detailed how a Philadelphia tenor saxophone player named Lynn Hope traveled widely through the South, from Atlanta to Birmingham, New Orleans to Nashville, Charleston, West Virginia, to Gadsden, Alabama. In Hope's telling, when he and his fellow jazzmen presented themselves as Muslims, "we are recognized as whites in the South and are not Jim Crowed."

> Hope and his men, wearing their turbans, enter a restaurant with superb aplomb, and are usually told very quickly, "We don't serve colored people here." Hope's answer is swift, calm and always the same: "We are not Negroes but members of the Moslem faith. Our customs are Eastern. We claim the nationality of our Arabic ancestors as well as their culture." Almost invariably, they receive courteous treatment.[59]

If Elijah Muhammad and Malcolm X hoped to bludgeon the forces of American racism into submission by painting Christian apocalypticism in the starkest black and white, these midcentury Philadelphia "Negro Moslems" tried their hand at something altogether different. They identified a loophole. Armed with turbans, swagger, and the conviction that their new identities were no mere surface performance, they managed to transcend blackness. The editors at *Ebony* called it "a firm stand," but, in fact, the stand was anything but firm. It was, rather, soft and pliable. As a mode of combating racism, it was jujutsu.

Times have changed. After 9/11, as a would-be social tactic for evading prejudice, being a Muslim for an African American has far more downside than up. But the disavowal of race that once served "Negro Moslems" down South remains for their direct Salafi descendants ready to hand. This is especially the case in the Salafi callers' interactions with the *'ulama'* in the Arabian Peninsula, for whom, as we have seen, the black nationalist legacy of African American Islam seemingly leaves an abiding taint. And they are not alone. Elijah Muhammad's *Message to the Blackman in America* offered a powerful counterhistory of race that galvanized many black folk and spoke effectively to others in the white cultural mainstream, but it came at the cost of legitimacy in the eyes of the Muslim immigrants, who, beginning with the passage of the 1965 immigration law, transformed American religious cityscapes. If, in the wake of this cultural sea change, brothers and sisters of the Nation of Islam were often surprised to hear their Islam dismissed as inauthentic, their African American Sunni counterparts were mortified to find themselves tarred with the same brush. Thus we find a residual resentment among the Salafi for the followers of Wallace Muhammad, a man whose vision of Islam was, according to Dawud Adib, "as bad, and maybe even worse than what his father was teaching."[60] For if the father was guilty of anathema of the most obvious sort—claiming that Fard Allah was God incarnate—the son's anathema was subtler and, therefore, more insidious. For even with his 1975 conversion to Sunni Islam, Wallace, according to the Salafis, never diverted from his father's religious orientation, an orientation according to which Islam is perpetually instrumentalized for sociological, political, and economic ends.

That Dawud Adib refused to put Salafi Islam to such instrumental ends is what troubles Umar Lee most of all. In Lee's words, Salafis ignore "political empowerment for African Americans," and they do no kind of "community organizing that will make the communities cleaner and safer here in America."[61] As Lee video blogged:

> Once the Salafi *da'wa* came into being, the concept of institution building totally left. No more institutions were to be built. The Muslims' time was to be dedicated to sitting around in classes, studying basic Islamic issues, declaring people deviants, seeing who is on and off the *manhaj*, but there would be no institutions established. And we can see in the long career of Dawud Adib, we can see that he has built absolutely nothing. He's been imam of storefront *masjid*s, hole-in-the-wall *masjid*s. He's built no schools. He's built no institutions of learning. He's built no clinics. He's built no economic foundation for the Muslim community. And the feds love this because he's been a corrosive force in the Muslim community, because he's built absolutely nothing.[62]

As was illustrated earlier by the exchange between Abu Muslimah and al-Wadi'i as well as by the circulation of the *Prophetic Ahadith in Condemnation of Racism*, Philadelphia's Salafi are flanked to their right by their Arab *'ulama'* who wonder aloud whether black callers have truly removed themselves from the politics of their race. Meanwhile, as evident in Umar Lee's complaint, Salafis are excoriated by some for their political and social disengagement from their local communities. In his polemic against Adib's inactivity on the material level, Lee channeled the Du Boisian expectation—one no doubt shared by many of our readers—that black religion is to be evaluated by its contributions to "social betterment." Part of this expectation holds that mosques and churches ought to be sites of political organization and that, to the extent that they are not struggling to improve the economic and social circumstances of their people, black religious leaders like Dawud Adib fail to perform their allotted role properly. Indeed, as Lee would have it, by refusing such momentous burdens, Adib effectively renders himself a de facto defender of the political, social, and economic order under which *his people* suffer.[63]

The Salafi beg to differ. What is the point of mobilizing for action if the correctness of that action has not been persuasively shown to be grounded in the Qur'an and the authenticated example of the Prophet? On this view,

Elijah and Wallace Muhammad, in their political self-assurance, offered a provocative counternarrative to Jim Crow America, but, in their secular acquiescence and theological ignorance, they led their followers into the most damnable sins: *shirk*, associating partners with God. Lifting people up is certainly a noble ambition, but without the proper *taqwa*, Salafis argue, any such effort can only go catastrophically awry. As one Salafi elder at Graterford Prison articulated his own quietism: "We need to get our own house in order, and become good Muslims before we can do anything else."[64]

Philadelphia Salafis' quietism is more than a failure of courage or a by-product of blind indoctrination. In the final analysis, Salafism in Philadelphia promises a radical alternative to the dynamics that have maintained the secularized and racialized political status quo for almost a century. This promise happens to overlap with the coerced accommodationism that the secular state and society demands, but it is not reducible to it. Through study, fashion, faith, and purity practices, Salafis overlook the cultural norms of the secular age. They reject social betterment for social betterment's sake, and they reject the pursuit of racial justice for racial justice's sake. If black religion's strength came in its willingness to say "No!" to American racism, Salafism's greatest power—and, for its critics, its greatest weakness—stems from its quietly emphatic insistence on negating this negation. With the Prophet's toothbrush in hand, Salafis call upon others to fear God and quietly look on.

## NOTES

1. To sample a number of such *hadith* on the *siwak* circulating in the Philadelphia scene and elsewhere, see Muhammad ibn al-Uthaymin, *Arousing the Intellects with the Explanation of 'Umdatul-Ahkaam: The Book of At-Tahaarah (The Ritual Purification)*, trans. Abdullaah MacPhee (Philadelphia: Authentic Statements, 2011), 53–61. For an overview of the history and social function of the *siwak* in classical and medieval Islamic culture, see Vardit Rispler-Chaim, "The *Siwāk*: A Medieval Islamic Contribution to Dental Care," *Journal of the Royal Asiatic Society* 2, no. 1 (1992): 13–20.

2. Field visit and interview with Anas Waters, Friday, February 22, 2012.

3. One important exception would be Sherman Jackson's *Islam and the Blackamerican: Looking Toward the Third Resurrection* (Oxford: Oxford University Press, 2005). See also Abdin Chande, "Islam in the African American Community: Negotiating Between Black Nationalism and Historical Islam," *Islamic Studies* 47, no. 2 (2008): 221–241; and Emily Goshey,

"Salafi Islam in Philadelphia" (BA honors thesis, University of Pennsylvania, 2012). It is telling that the most recent trade book on the subject is written by an FBI fellow: Chris Heffelfinger, *Radical Islam in America: Salafism's Journey from Arabia to the West* (Washington D.C.: Potomac, 2011).

4. See Umar Lee, "The Rise and Fall of the Salafi Movement," Wordpress, 2007, http://umarlee.wordpress.com/rise-and-fall-of-the-salafi-movement-complete/.

5. Ibid.

6. See Jenice Armstrong, "Philadelphia Locals Adopt Muslim-Inspired Menswear," Philly.com (August 23, 2011), http://articles.philly.com/2011-08-23/entertainment/29917726_1_beard-traditional-muslim-attire-mustache.

7. See Umar Lee, "The Rise and Fall of the Salafi Movement."

8. Ibid.

9. See Dawud Adib, "History of the Salafi Da'wah in America," YouTube (2011), http://www.YouTube.com/watch?v=tixXMlFkgms, http://www.YouTube.com/watch?v=n7mKE-7W6cw.

10. This is an accusation that Lee has vehemently denied. See Umar Lee, "Umar Lee Explains the Why and How of 'The Rise and Fall of the Salafi Movement,'" YouTube (July 4, 2011), http://www.YouTube.com/watch?v=ZC6H7pjUEJY.

11. Adib, "History of the Salafi Da'wah in America."

12. We speculate further on this question below, near the end of the third section.

13. See Edward E. Curtis IV, "Islamism and Its African American Muslim Critics: Black Muslims in the Era of the Arab Cold War," *American Quarterly* 59, no. 3 (2007): 703–704; and Clifton Marsh, *From Black Muslims to Muslims: The Transition from Separatism to Islam, 1930–1980* (Metuchen, N.J.: Scarecrow, 1984), 89–104.

14. See Adib, "History of the Salafi Da'wah in America."

15. Ibid.

16. See Ian Haney Lopez, *White by Law: The Legal Construction of Race* (New York: NYU Press, 1997).

17. For an overview, see Edward L. Curtis IV, *Islam in Black America* (Albany, N.Y.: SUNY Press, 2002); and Richard Brent Turner, *Islam in the African-American Experience* (Bloomington: Indiana University Press, 2003). On the ongoing black struggle to process this cultural assimilation, see Jackson, *Islam and the Blackamerican*.

18. See Lee, "The Rise and Fall of the Salafi Movement."

19. On al-Albani's contribution to the tradition of *hadith* criticism, see Jonathan A. C. Brown, *The Canonization of al-Bukhārī and Muslim* (Leiden: Brill, 2011), 301–334. On Salafism more broadly, see Roel Meijer, ed., *Global Salafism: Islam's New Religious Movement* (New York: Columbia University Press, 2009).

20. See Stéphane Lacroix, "Between Revolution and Apoliticism: Nasir al-Din al-Albani and His Impact on the Shaping of Contemporary Salafism," in *Global Salafism: Islam's New Religious Movement*, ed. Roel Meijer (New York: Columbia University Press, 2009), 72–73.

21. Ibid., 74–76.

22. Ibid.

23. Ibid.

24. For an overview of Muqbil ibn al-Wadiʻi, see Laurent Bonnefoy, *Salafism in Yemen: Transnationalism and Religious Identity* (Oxford: Oxford University Press, 2012), 54–78.

25. See Lacroix, "Between Revolution and Apoliticism," 76–77.

26. See Adib, "History of the Salafi Daʻwah in America." Among the scholars Adib names are Sharif ʻAbd al-Karim and Ibrahim ʻAbd al-ʻAziz, both African Americans from Brooklyn who studied at Umm al-Qura University in Mecca. Adib names, among other notable Egyptian and Sudanese scholars, Shaykh ʻAbd al-Rahman ʻAbd al-Khaliq, who was born in Egypt in 1939, educated at the Islamic University in Medina, and contributed to Islamic periodicals that were distributed in North America.

27. Adib claimed there was a nascent Salafi *daʻwa* in America since the 1950s, but the founding of Salafi institutions may be more usefully dated to 1982, which saw the establishment of the Islamic Center of East Orange and the convening of the first conference of the Qurʼan and Sunna Society in Landover, Maryland. See Adib, "The History of the Salafi Daʻwah in America."

28. See "Pre-Conference Schedule Philadelphia/New Jersey August 2012 CE," Sunnah Publishing (2012), http://sunnahpublishing.net/pre-conference-schedule-philadelphianew -jersey-august-2012-ce/. According to some online anecdotes, al-Wadiʻi apparently visited the United States during his lifetime. See Aboo Shaahir, "Naseeha to Abdul Munʼim: Fear Allaah and Stop Waging War Against the Salafees!," Salaftalk.net (September 27, 2002), http://www.salafitalk.net/st/viewmessages.cfm?Forum=6&Topic=213.

29. The other links are to the prominent Saudi state-appointed scholars Ibn ʻUthaymin and Bin Baz and to Sahab.net, a popular Salafi website. See "Catalog," IIN Bookstore, http://www.iiinbookstore.com/catalog/.

30. See "About the TheMadkhalis.com," TheMadkhalis.com, http://www.themadkhalis.com /md/about.cfm.

31. See Milton Viorst, "The Education of Ali Al-Timimi," *The Atlantic* (June 2006), http://www.theatlantic.com/magazine/archive/2006/06/the-education-of-ali-al-timimi/304884/.

32. For example, they published a number of works of al-Wadiʻi in translation, including a five-CD-set class on hadith that the shaykh authenticated and compiled. They also published a translation of a polemical treatise authorized by al-Madkhali. See "5 CD – Jaami'us-Saheeh of Shaykh Muqbil – Abul-Hasan Maalik," Sunnah Publishing, http://sunnahpublishing.net/products-page/hadeeth-cd/5-cd-jaamius-saheeh-of-shaykh -muqbil-abul-hasan-maalik/; and "A Clarification of the Errors and Bias Present in al-Nasīhah of Ibrāhīm al-Ruhaylī," Sunnah Publishing (June 29, 2013), http://sunnah publishing.net/a-clarification-of-the-errors-and-bias-present-in-al-nasihah-of-ibrahim -al-ruhayli-part-1-shaykh-rabi-ibn-hadi-al-madkhali/.

33. A brief biography is advertised by Abu Abdul Fattah Ali Mohamed, "Abul Hasan Malik al-Akhdar UK Dates and Venues for Lectures," Salafitalk.net (May 12, 2009), http://salafitalk.net/st/viewmessages.cfm?Forum=28&Topic=8670.

34. See Charles Honey, "Local Nonprofit Hopes to Educate Others About Muslim Faith," *Grand Rapids Press* (August 23, 2008), http://www.mlive.com/living/grand-rapids/index .ssf/2008/08/local_nonprofit_hopes_to_educa.html.

35. Ibn Burjis was a student of Ibn 'Uthaymin and Bin Baz and a prolific scholar and teacher in his own right. To access his official webpage, see "Website of the Shaykh 'Abd al-Salam Ibn Burjis," http://www.burjes.com/.

36. 'Abd al-Salam ibn Burjis Ibn Nasir al-Abd al-Karim, *Prophetic Ahadith in Condemnation of Racism* (Grand Rapids, Mich.: Sunnah, 2012), 8–15.

37. Ibid., 47.

38. Ibid., 28.

39. Ibid., 60–61.

40. Ibid., 70.

41. Ibid., 73.

42. Ibid., 74.

43. See Lee, "Umar Lee Explains the Why and How."

44. A brief professional biography of Abu Muslimah can be found at "Masjid Khalid Bin al-Walid," Khalidmosque.com, http://www.khalidmosque.com/english/index.php?option =com_content&view=article&id=101:speakers&catid=53&lang=en.

45. This reference is almost certainly to 'Abdullah MacPhee, who studied at al-Wadi'i's Dar al-Hadith in Dammaj for an extended period of time, perhaps ten years. Upon his return, MacPhee vied for but failed to attain the position of the imam of the Germantown Mosque. He remains an active translator for *Authentic Statements*, a Philadelphia-based Salafi press.

46. Posted by an author with the handle "Aboo Talhah" (January 28, 2003). Aboo Talhah claimed this was his translation of an audio recording but did not post the audio after another poster requested it. See Aboo Talhah, "A Meeting with Shaikh Muqbil ibn Haadi (rh) and Abu Muslimah," Siratemustaqeem.com (October 4, 2002), http://www .siratemustaqeem.com/phpBB/viewtopic.php?f=1&t=1203&hilit=abu+muslimah&start=0.

47. Ibn Burjis, *Prophetic Ahadith in Condemnation of Racism*, 85.

48. See W. E. B. Du Bois, *The Philadelphia Negro: A Social Study* (Philadelphia: University of Pennsylvania Press, 1996), 207. Emphasis added.

49. See Arthur Huff Fauset, *Black Gods of the Metropolis: Negro Religious Cults of the Urban North* (Philadelphia: University of Pennsylvania Press, 2002), 41–51.

50. On Temple Twelve, see Rubin Benson, ed., *Top of the Clock: Minister Jeremiah Shabazz, Exclusive Interview* (Philadelphia: First Impressions, 1997).

51. See Edward E. Curtis IV, *Religion in the Nation of Islam, 1960–1975* (Chapel Hill: University of North Carolina Press, 2006).

52. See Nathaniel Deutsch, "'The Asiatic Black Man': An African American Orientalism?" *Journal of Asian American Studies* 4, no. 3 (2001): 193–208; and Edward E. Curtis IV, "African-American Islamization Reconsidered: Black History Narratives and Muslim Identity," *Journal of the American Academy of Religion* 73, no. 3 (2005): 659–684.

53. See Curtis, "Islamism and Its African American Muslim Critics," 695.

54. Curtis writes that "his first duty in life was to work for the political liberation of all black persons around the globe." Ibid.

55. George Breitman, ed., *Malcolm X Speaks*, (New York: Grove, 1990), 24.

56. Nathaniel Deutsch, *Inventing America's "Worst" Family: Eugenics, Islam, and the Fall and Rise of the Tribe of Ishmael* (Berkeley: University of California Press, 2009), 140–154.

57. See Jackson, *Islam and the Blackamerican*, 32.

58. Ibid. Emphasis added.

59. "Moslems Take Firm Stand Against Racism," *Ebony* 8, no. 6 (April 1953): 107.

60. See Adib, "History of the Salafi Da'wah in America."

61. See Lee, "Umar Lee Explains the Why and How."

62. Ibid.

63. This is more or less Sherman Jackson's critique of Salafism and other modes of African American Islam that abandon the prophetic tradition of black religion. See Jackson, *Islam and the Blackamerican*, 70–73.

64. See Joshua Dubler, *Down in the Chapel* (New York: Farrar, Strauss and Giroux, 2013), 228.

# PART III
## INFLECTIONS

# 6

# TWO WAYS OF LOOKING AT AN INVISIBLE MAN

## RACE, THE SECULAR, AND RALPH ELLISON'S INVISIBLE THEOLOGY

M. Cooper Harriss

A **TESTIMONY** to the durability of Ralph Ellison's *Invisible Man* (1952) is the prominence that its titular metaphor of invisibility retains more than sixty years after the novel's publication. Indeed, "invisibility" now serves as political shorthand for marginality or liminality, an identity and agency overlooked or ignored by more canonical or "official" versions of humanity, spawning a significant trend in academic book titles.[1] It should come as no surprise that *Invisible Man* would find such a reading. The contemporary study of African American culture emerged, like Ellison's career, in the context of two intellectual turns during the second half of the twentieth century—one to the social sciences in the immediate postwar era, the other to cultural theory in the 1960s. Black studies institutionalized modes of protest and black power by framing their political urgency within the intellectual rhetorics and logics in circulation at the moment of their inception.[2] Both the intellectual currents of the 1960s and the institutionalization of black studies were closely tied to secularism. Therefore the legacy of "invisibility" remains largely secular, despite the term's obviously nonsecular connotations.

This essay emerges from a simple question about invisibility's interpretive legacy: What does Ellison's signal metaphor for racial identity derive from a not-so-secular concept like invisibility? Put differently, if the task of secular modernity is the disenchantment of the world, why invoke the supernatural? There is, in a manner of speaking, more to Ellisonian invisibility than meets the eye. Ellison's protagonist seems to anticipate such questions in the novel's prologue, assuring the reader that "I am not a spook like those who haunted Edgar Allan Poe; nor am I one of your Hollywood-movie ectoplasms. I am a man of substance, of flesh and bone, fiber and liquids—and I might even be said to possess a mind."[3] Yet this narrator, speaking from novel's end "in the beginning," is an ironist, a dissembler. He denies his supernatural qualities by punning on the racial epithet "spook," converging presumably oppositional properties of materiality and immateriality into a singular, cooperative, and secular reality.

Ellison puts a finer point on this postsecular reading in his introduction to the novel's thirtieth-anniversary edition. Invisibility, he writes, "seemed to tease me with allusions to that pseudoscientific sociological concept which held that most Afro-American difficulties sprang from our 'high visibility'; a phrase as double-dealing and insidious as its more recent oxymoronic cousins, 'benign neglect' and 'reverse discrimination.'" He continues: "Thus, despite the bland assertions of sociologists, 'high visibility' actually rendered one un-visible—whether at high noon in Macy's window or illuminated by flaming torches and flashbulbs while undergoing ritual sacrifice that was dedicated to the ideal of white supremacy."[4] Ellison not only points to invisibility's clear origins in direct response to the social-scientific turn well underway in intellectual circles at mid-century, but he also suggests an ironically critical disposition toward this turn's epistemological claims. His metaphor for racial identity stands in direct opposition to the more broadly empirical pretensions of high visibility. It also indicates a dual nature for invisibility—one material (suggested by the economic implications of Macy's) and one orienting the tangible lynching of the "highly visible" body toward ritual's metaphysical realm.

Significant work in secularism over the past decade hinges on the general assertion that "the secular" (in its various permutations) is not a-religious, as many have assumed, but in fact functions much as religion did in premodern contexts. Tracy Fessenden calls the secular an "unmarked [religious] category." Theodore Ziolkowski delineates it as a formal "surrogate" for religious faith that modernity has disenchanted. According to Charles Taylor, the secular represents an "immanent frame." John Lardas Modern points to environments of unconscious religious understanding that "become matters of common sense" in his study of the American nineteenth century.[5] This essay seeks in part to recover religious antecedents that contribute to a more capacious understanding of invisibility than the one we have inherited—religious dimensions that articulate an overlooked, or *invisible*, theology for which racial ideologies have served as secular surrogates.

While race, as a byproduct of modernity, remains secular, Ellison's metaphor of invisibility becomes a lens for observing the genuinely religious nature of such secularism. *Invisible Man*, then, becomes a secular novel that offers what I call an invisible theology of race. This is to say that while readers usually focus on the secular dimensions of invisibility (and so its theological dimensions have remained invisible), invisibility also bears a deeper, theological meaning as it conceptualizes race in Ellison's novel. Recovering this theological meaning of invisibility permits us to see how *Invisible Man* (whatever Ellison's specific allegiances and intentions) illuminates the theological significance of race, offering an alternative and more capacious conceptual framework than older secularisms have permitted.

This essay highlights the status of race as invisible theology by framing two representative ways of "looking" at invisibility and, accordingly, two ways of "looking" at *Invisible Man*. The first way considers biblical invisibility, emphasizing certain overtly religious antecedent conceptions of Ellison's now-secularized metaphor and illuminating fresh political and cultural implications for the new secularism to which Jonathon Kahn refers in the conclusion to this volume. The second way, which turns to the War on Terror and more specifically to drones, offers an example from the new secularity's present tense, gesturing toward future contexts of Ellison's reinscribed secular metaphor. These two ways are deliberately provocative. Through them I wish to spotlight the status of race as a secular surrogate that draws liberally upon religious and theological imaginations to address a formidable epistemological problem encountered by modernity: If "all men" are truly created equal, then what might account for their lack of equivalence in the most empirical of aspects? Ellison's invisible theology problematizes prominent racial orthodoxies grounded in social-scientific materialism and public discourse that he distrusted and that in many ways continue to inform racial politics and policies alike. Secularism, as Vincent Lloyd argues in this volume's introduction, manages what "counts" and does not "count" as appropriate forms of religion.

Race, correspondingly, manages *who* "counts" as human and who does not. Exclusion and marginalization, then, like religion, are not essential conditions but derive from and rely upon a variety of social and cultural factors. Highlighting invisibility's religious framework, implicit though it may be, does not simply offer new insights into Ellison's novel but also suggests that such historical relationships may speak to present and evolving domestic and global contexts involving race and secularism.

## FIRST WAY: BIBLICAL SOURCES

To speak of Ellison and the Bible may prompt for some readers certain associations that do not align with my goals here. Ellison's unfinished second novel, for instance, derived as it is from a black preacherly vernacular, offers a far richer resource for discerning biblical allusions and rhetoric at the heart of Ellison's African American vernacular—were it my goal to treat them in such a way.[6] In this section, however, I wish to explicate invisibility in Ellison's work against a biblical backdrop. I do not imagine that Ellison sought explicitly to mine the biblical examples that follow. Ellison's invisibility is not an essentially biblical concept. Yet biblical invisibility and its later interpretive debates do matter in terms of constructing a more expansive conception of Ellison's metaphor for racial identity. Ellison was biblically literate and counted the King James Bible as part of a cultural unconscious upon which his broader worldview was built. In one interview he pairs the King James Bible with "British literature"—especially "Shakespeare or the great poets"— and "Negro folklore" as formative influences.[7] Elsewhere he groups the Bible among "sources" including "the spirituals and the blues," literature, mythology, sermons, and the dozens.[8] In this way the work of excavation deals less with recovering and piecing together tiny potshards and more with unearthing and exploring the cultural and political infrastructure of Ellison's corpus and career.

A second reason that recourse to biblical invisibility matters is that Ellison in fact invokes a biblical category to characterize his effort to push beyond, or at least to mitigate in some way, the secular leftist politics in vogue during the 1930s and 1940s—formative years to his development as a critic and fiction writer. In "A Very Stern Discipline," an interview published in 1967, Ellison's interlocutors encourage him to revisit his own literary origins in Harlem of the 1930s and 1940s—"the *New Masses* experience," they call it, when Ellison was enlisted in the New York Writers Project, spending time with Richard Wright and the "League of American Writers crowd." Ellison notes that while he "wrote what might be called propaganda having to do with the Negro struggle," his fiction strove for different objectives. He continues:

> I never accepted the ideology which the *New Masses* attempted to impose on writers. They hated Dostoevsky, but I was studying Dostoevsky. They felt that Henry James was a decadent snob who had nothing to teach a writer from the lower classes, and I was studying James. I was also reading Marx, Gorki, Sholokhov, and Isaac Babel. I was reading everything, including the Bible.[9]

Ellison's inclusion of the Bible here among pointed, even archetypal, alternatives to the political reading he undertook offers an intriguing juxtaposition of religious and literary aspirations (achieved through the Bible and Dostoevsky, if not James). Beyond the secular left milieu Ellison wrote out of and has been subsequently read through, there remains another valence—one that has always interacted with the political realm but has, at the same time, been held in tension with it. Biblical invisibility recovers this alternative reading to the politically informed one that coheres more intuitively with a standard characterization of racial identity.

## NEW TESTAMENT

The English word "invisible" appears in the Geneva Bible and the King James Version (both of which offer English translations that date to sixteenth- and seventeenth-century Protestantism, respectively, and proved foundational to an American biblical imagination vital to Ellison's cultural lexicon) only in Pauline texts.[10] For this reason we begin with Christian New Testament sources before circling back to consider conceptual analogies in the Hebrew Bible. Romans 1:20 speaks of "invisible things of God," Colossians 1:15 and 1:16 mention "the image of the invisible God," 1 Timothy 1:17 also refers to an invisible God, and Hebrews 11:27 calls God "him which is invisible." Another implicit construction of invisibility, "not seen," yields a wider sample of passages, but, again, the Pauline texts shine: Hebrews 11:1: "Faith is the evidence of things hoped for, the evidence of things not seen"; 2 Corinthians 4:18: "We look not at the things which are seen, but at the things which are not seen: for the things that are seen *are* temporal; but the things that are not seen *are* eternal."[11] A clear line of demarcation distinguishes the invisible from its deficient analogue, the visible. The nature of invisibility occupied prominent theologians in the decades just prior to *Invisible Man*. A quick survey of readings by Karl Barth and Rudolph Bultmann—representatives of important Protestant factions in the years before *Invisible Man* who generally disagreed with each other—helps clarify the Ellisonian view.

The overall effect of the catalogue of usages cited above suggests that New Testament invisibility bespeaks a kind of theological authenticity that is characteristic of the Divine and therefore beyond ordinary human ken. In this way it bears a sense of religious privilege—an interpretation very much in circulation during Ellison's time. Writing on Romans 1:20, Barth invokes a platonic ideal as intrinsic to "the invisible things of God": "Behind the visible things there lies the invisible universe which is the Origin of all concrete things."[12] On this reading God is invisible because God (be it God's glory, nature, or reality) surpasses the limits of human perception, drawing on Job's whirlwind (which Barth mentions) and especially resonant of the Divine statement to Moses in Exodus 33:20: "Thou canst not see my face: for there shall no man see me, and live." In this way invisibility highlights an unbridgeable gulf between human (whose realm is the visible) and God (the realm of the invisible). This interpretation offers a primary theological resonance for the concept of invisibility, one that underscores the difference between Ellison's concept of race and the more standard, "secular" conception of race, distinguishing between the material (visible) and the immaterial (invisible). Already the religious legacy of invisibility stands at odds with the materialist conception that has characterized post–*Invisible Man* appeals to invisibility.

A more "secular" reading of the visible/human/material and invisible/supernatural/metaphysical divide may be found in Rudolph Bultmann's attempts to "demythologize" the New Testament according to scientific modernism. In his 1941 essay "Theology as Science," Bultmann characterizes the visible world as scientific in nature: objective, disinterested, observable. Theology, on the other hand, like the God it characterizes, presents a paradox because it tends toward the "otherworldly, invisible, incomprehensible, etc., the thought is expressed that God cannot be objectified."[13] This tension that Bultmann seeks to reconcile, or at least to problematize, mirrors the "secular" demarcation for social science that Ellison was beginning to challenge during this period.[14] Invisibility defies objectification, which itself represents a form of secularism, of the secular management of identity.

Consider Ellison's yokel who challenges the prize fighter in *Invisible Man*:

> Once I saw a prizefighter boxing a yokel. The fighter was swift and amazingly scientific. His body was one violent flow of rapid rhythmic action. He hit the yokel a hundred times while the yokel held up his arms in stunned surprise. But suddenly the yokel, rolling about in the gale of boxing gloves, struck one blow and knocked science, speed, and footwork as cold as a well digger's posterior. . . . The yokel had simply stepped inside of his opponent's sense of time.[15]

For all of science's epistemological merit, such materiality is not foolproof. What remains fascinating about Bultmann's demarcation (and Ellison's destabilization of its terms) is that, first, it establishes a connection with the social-scientific epistemology by which midcentury renovations of racial identity sought to distance African Americans from older, religious, "superstitious," immaterial religious models.[16] Second, it emphasizes the audacity of Ellison's decision to deploy invisibility as his governing metaphor for race as a secular property in a secular age. Barthean invisibility in a primary sense does not represent an authentic, Ellisonian invisible theology. The Ellisonian value of Barthean invisibility derives from its utility as a postmaterialist (or postsecular) rejoinder to Bultmann. Ellison's ideal, we might say, resembles the prize fighter in his *next* fight after losing to the yokel: certainly still reliant upon speed and scientific elegance yet also keenly aware of their limitations, of the fact that these advantages are not indomitable. To read it an iteration further: invisibility as Ellison's metaphor for race acknowledges a kind of extant, baseline materialism (recall Ellison's readings of Marx and Maxim Gorky and his association with *New Masses*) yet with the significant caveat (via Dostoevsky, James, Shakespeare, the Bible—and even the spirituals and the blues) that there is more in heaven and earth than can be dreamt of by the social-scientific imagination.

## HEBREW BIBLE

The Old Testament (as the Hebrew Bible is known in the Geneva and King James translations of the Christian Bible) contains no specific instances of the English word "invisible," though the "seen," "unseen," and "not seen" remain significant analogues. I would like to focus briefly here on just one example of *not seeing* in the Hebrew Bible—Moses's encounter with Yahweh in Exodus 33:20—as a trope that illuminates an "invisible theology" at play in the Hebrew Bible itself, the world that it depicts, and the process of creating religious coherence from a diversity of cultural and theological outlooks. Such a trope frames certain parallels between biblical attempts to deal with religious, cultural, and political diversities—representative tensions between one and many in the development of early Israelite religion and biblical theology— and Ellison's democratic concern with American pluribus and unum as a racial-political (and therefore *invisible*) theme in *Invisible Man*.

In Exodus 33:20 Yahweh tells Moses, who desires to see God's "glory" (33:18): "Thou canst not see my face: for there shall no man see me, and live." Details surrounding this exchange illuminate the point more fully. God offers a middle way between death and outright hiddenness: "Behold, *there is a* place by me, and thou shalt stand upon a rock: And it shall come to pass, while my glory passeth by, that I will put thee in a clift of the rock, and will cover thee with my hand while I pass by: And I will take away mine hand, and thou shalt see my back parts; but my face shall not be seen" (33:21b–23). We locate here, in one sense, an antecedent for the Pauline view that Barth rightly connects to a sense of Platonic essences.[17] On this reading Moses may not look on God's face because the glory is too magnificent for frail humanity. The distinction remains unbridgeable. Another line of interpretation suggests, however, that the invisibility of God in the Hebrew Bible, symbolized in this instance by Yahweh's compromise, renders human incapacity to "see" God's full glory as less a mortal failing than a pragmatic reality. It introduces political implications that proved important for the formation and survival of Israelite religion at a moment of radical rupture in the history of Israel. These political aspects, I suggest, are concordant with specific themes regarding American diversity in *Invisible Man*; in the process of exploring them I locate a deeper resonance of invisibility's biblical depictions and what we might recognize as a religious antecedent to Ellison's racial metaphor. I am less interested here in claiming a one-to-one correspondence between Ellison's work and ancient Israelite religion than I am in offering a glimpse at how the latter might stand as a religious antecedent to Ellison's invisibility and thereby establish it as an unmarked religious category.

As scholars have gained a clearer sense of the messy and fragmentary nature of our present access to the history of Israel, a greater sense of social, political, and theological diversity within this history has emerged. Such diversity produced the multivocality of the Hebrew text, which represents a composite of authors, gods, theologies, and social and historical contexts joined into a larger "book." The earliest, prehistoric religious orientations that would eventually contribute to the rise of Judaism were highly localized in nature, contributing to, if not a larger "polytheism" among these early groups, then certainly a plurality of local gods and practices for the preservation of a receding (if not forgotten) past.[18] Erhard S. Gerstenberger traces the evolution of these various "Old Testament theologies" according to a progressive set of sociological units: family, town, tribe, and kingdom, emphasizing that these categories do not necessarily point to a whiggish procession of more perfect theologies but do excavate the diversities inherent to early Israel—many of which remain evident, if fragmentary, in biblical texts.[19]

The extreme duress of the Babylonian exile, beginning in 587 BCE, transformed Israel's characteristic heterogeneity: "Within a community characterized by a considerable diversity, no group emerged from this period without experiencing considerable change, due in no small part to spiritual trauma that called into question some of the most fundamental principles of the Yahwistic faith."[20] Accordingly a new emphasis emerged, one focusing on "the common legacy shared by all these groups," offering a centripetal emphasis and fostering a stronger, more monotheistic character.[21] It was in this exilic period and particularly during the postexilic one to follow that the Hebrew Bible became recognizably "biblical," canonized. People who lived under oppression, and who sought to retain a sense of affirmation for the suffering they had endured, codified their history according to the theological orientations of the exile. Prophetic and particularly wisdom literature "enjoyed a heightened popularity" that synthesized extant traditions and practices.[22] Older diversities did not disappear but, as one commentator has put it, "biblical religion . . . insisted on comprehending the many aspects of God in a single image of divinity."[23] The God of this "emergent Judaism" (and particularly the textuality of this God) became singular yet variable, a universal entity containing diverse particular voices and visions of Divine characteristics and will.[24] Yahweh's face remains invisible, then, as a way of managing Israelite diversity within the identity of Israel's one true God.

Understanding the God of Exodus 33:20 (in Walter Brueggemann's words, "hidden—indirect and not visible") to negotiate singularity and plurality characterizes this God in terms of Ellisonian invisibility.[25] In the epilogue to *Invisible Man* Ellison reflects jokingly on whiteness as a cultural default setting (and in this way, itself, a form of invisibility): "Whence all this passion toward conformity anyway?—diversity is the word. Let man keep his many parts and you'll have no tyrant states. Why, if they follow this conformity business they'll end up forcing me, an invisible man, to become white, which is not a color but the lack of one. Must I strive toward colorlessness?"[26] Unconscious whiteness (which is a hallmark of whiteness as an object of contemporary academic study), like the invisibility of blackness that such whiteness imposes, obscures a larger tension in Ellison's ideal American identity: "Think of what the world would lose if [colorlessness] should happen. America is woven of many strands; I would recognize it and let it so remain. . . . Our fate is to become one, and yet many—This is not prophecy, but description."[27] Such a tension becomes a prominent theme of the novel: the one and the many, the pluribus and the unum, centripetal hegemony and centrifugal fragmentation.[28]

In this way invisible theology itself becomes a question of pluribus and unum: The God of Sinai, a God of covenant, demands coherence, submerging particular diversities for the sake of the larger theological picture. Moses, like any human, may only glimpse parts of a God who, in Walt Whitman's phrase, "contain[s] multitudes." The God of the Hebrew Bible contains the paradox of one and many: Yahweh is, at once, an unum significant of a common legacy shared by diverse factions of people (Gerstenberger's families, towns, tribes, etc.), unified by historical suffering, experience, and covenant that joins them to a larger common identity.[29] In this way it resists fragmentation. Such a multifaceted God may not be seen in full, however, only glimpsed in part, and so the imago encountered by particular factions corresponds to the specific identity that these representative factions, the pluribus, themselves bring to God. Other aspects remain hidden, "not-visible," unseen.

Still, they are present and must be accounted for. Accordingly, a certain theological reductionism—the draining of local "color" (to invoke Ellison's term) for the sake of empty conformity that characterizes whiteness—may be avoided. A major proposition of Ellison's concept of race insists upon co-operative antagonism among various racial groups for the ongoing formation and reformation of their respective identities. The protagonist's concluding observation in the same paragraph we have discussed at some length above asserts that "One of the greatest jokes in the world is the spectacle of the whites busy escaping blackness and becoming blacker every day, and the blacks striving toward whiteness, becoming quite dull and gray. None of us seems to know who he is or where he is going."[30] This sentiment echoes poignantly (and more hopefully) in the novel's closing line: "Who knows but that, on the lower frequencies, I speak for you."[31] This relationship resides at the heart of Ellison's invisible theology. Most harrowingly, its indeterminacy draws on a disciplinary gaze to enforce rigid, if artificial, boundaries among racial identities; at its best, however, we find a measure of symbiosis. This is Ellison's democratic risk. Consider, for instance, the common appeal of another biblical motif—the Exodus—to both English Puritans and enslaved New World Africans.[32] Particular differences should not be ignored, but the myth itself remains capacious enough to serve as an evocative singular touchstone that contains very different conceptions, experiences, and performances of "America."

By reflecting on a biblical "way" of looking on invisibility, this first section has introduced specifically religious antecedents for invisibility that, whatever Ellison's conscious appropriation of them may have been, nevertheless contribute ineluctably to the concept that he revises as he constructs his evocative and ironic metaphor for race. These biblical structures have inscribed Ellisonian invisibility and participate in the literary and cultural meaning that this secular novel generates toward understanding the conceptual, political, and secular exigencies of race as an invisible theology.

## SECOND WAY: DRONES AND THE WAR ON TERROR

We now turn from background concerns to selected manifestations of race's invisible theology in present-tense cultural and political realities that Ellison could not have foreseen.[33] How does invisibility's secularizing impulse operate in contexts of globalization and empire? Medievalist Valentin Groebner, writing of the September 11, 2001, attacks and their aftermath, offers a suitable point of embarkation:

> When the secretary of state of the most powerful country in the world painted a picture of the threat from invisible secret organizations whose members, running to the tens of thousands, are hiding everywhere—that is, are at once everywhere and nowhere—ready to do their worst, it may make sense to recall the historical circumstances of invisible enemies and faceless violence.[34]

In chiasmic rejoinder to Groebner—having attended to certain "historical circumstances"—we now look ahead. The second section of this essay, this other way of looking on invisibility, reflects on how the critical lens that Ellisonian invisibility offers proves useful for reading ongoing realities and emerging global contexts in the twenty-first century. Accordingly recast, Ellison's decades-old metaphor gains new currency for helping to conceive of the dark and obscure significance of the present U.S. War on Terror and its various domestic and international tributaries, an exaction of power that brings invisible theologies of the secular state to bear against religiously articulated terms of dispute, themselves political and economic motivations narrated in theological terms as a "clash of civilizations" between "secular" and "Muslim" worlds.[35] The present mode is one of hypervisibility, hypervigilance, which like the hypervisible signifier of phenotype—of racial *appearance*—designates one as socially and politically disembodied, consigned to global underground networks marked by the ambivalence of invisible terror.[36]

Terror's "invisibility" and these myriad permutations of sight and seeing offer two fascinating insights to terror and the "war" against it. First, invoking an Ellisonian dimension of invisibility spotlights the continuity of racial—particularly black—identity as Muslims, globally, find themselves managed and controlled by a newly articulated yet oddly familiar imperial gaze, a re-constituted Jim Crow. Second, as I shall address more fully in the conclusion but wish to denominate here, invisibility's ambivalent secularism as a racial metaphor offers an intriguing entrée for parsing the nature of a war on terror fought largely against racialized Muslim subjects by an ostensively postracial and secular state, many of whose own citizens claim, however, to bear some variety of "Judeo-Christian" identity.[37] What conflicts and contradictions do these layers of secularity obscure and render invisible?

Surveillance as a hegemonic exaction of power is not a new concept, of course, but its more recent and emerging implications both warrant renewed attention and benefit from the Ellisonian conceptions of invisibility (and visibility) highlighted above.[38] Revelations offered by Wikileaks and, more recently, Edward Snowden's exposure of NSA policies (among others) high-light two related and paradoxical realities: in service of the protection of cer-tain freedoms and in the name of "security," the lives of individual citizens in the United States and abroad have become increasingly visible even as the government that views them and the military operations performed in the name of their security have grown ever more invisible. In the attempt to thwart terrorist attacks on U.S. soil, security operations have gone global. Accordingly, the disciplinary gaze that, looking inward, has ironically helped cast African Americans and "others" as invisible in an Ellisonian sense now looks outward as well—and imperially so.[39] Operations tend to be covert and focused; "justice"—such as it may be—travels not through transparent chan-nels but, akin to the vigilante violence of another "Invisible Empire" from an earlier age, remains obscured, hidden, out of sight, de facto, under the radar, glimpsed only in shocking and ghostly fragments such as the haunting pho-tographs that emerged from Iraq's Abu Ghraib prison, published by the *New Yorker* in 2004.[40]

There is a protean quality both to the justifications for such invisibility in the War on Terror and the political, industrial, and military organizations that propagate it that calls forth Ellison's Rinehart character from *Invisible Man*, a figure for whom the protagonist is mistaken on a number of occasions, representing, as he does, various guises to different people ("could he be all of them: Rine the runner and Rine the gambler and Rine the briber and Rine the lover and Rinehart the Reverend? . . . What is real anyway?").[41] The neon sign for Rinehart's Holy Way Station claims: "HOLY WAY STATION / BEHOLD THE LIVING GOD."[42] A flier passed to the protagonist reads:

Behold the Invisible
Thy will be done O Lord!
I See all, Know all, Tell all, Cure all.
You shall see the unknown wonders.
—REV. B. P. RINEHART
*Spiritual Technologist*
The old is ever new
Way Stations in New Orleans, the home of mystery,
Birmingham, Chicago, Detroit, New York, and L. A.
No Problem too Hard for God.
Come to the Way Station
BEHOLD THE INVISIBLE!
Attend our services, prayer meetings Thrice weekly
Join us in the NEW REVELATION of the
OLD TIME RELIGION!
BEHOLD THE SEEN UNSEEN
BEHOLD THE INVISIBLE
YE WHO ARE WEARY COME HOME!
I DO WHAT YOU WANT DONE! DON'T WAIT![43]

Consider the varieties of invisibility that Ellison establishes through this characterization of Rinehart. First, we encounter an invisible theology: the reader finds repetition drawing "THE INVISIBLE" parallel to "THE LIVING GOD." Second, invisibility characterizes materially both what one knows but keeps hidden (the secret) and what one does not know (the unknown wonders). In this way Rinehart's promise (to see, know, tell, and cure "all"—a clause that nicely encapsulates the missions of the Department of Homeland Security, the National Security Agency, and U.S. foreign policy writ large) offers help yet also implies a certain encroachment of privacy, threatening exposure—and the veiled threat that attends such insight. Third, invisibility also refers to a metaphysical unknown: God's will, certain wonders, the stuff of Revelation (which suggests visions and apocalypse). Fourth, perhaps most significantly, Rinehart himself is invisible. This is true literally, of course, in that he never physically appears as himself in the novel—he is only referred to and instantiated secondhand through conversations, pieces of paper, recollections, and various characters' misperceptions of the protagonist (whose similarity to Rinehart the protagonist eventually wields to his own advantage). Within these vagaries resides a nexus of presence and absence, blindness and insight, appearance and reality, violence and protection—even the material and immaterial (note the juxtaposition inherent in Rinehart's title "*Spiritual Technologist*," uniting Bultmann's factions of myth and science).

Such indeterminacy also characterizes drones, the weapons associated with the War on Terror that, while not entirely "invisible" or "inaudible," do draw harrowingly on the terms of Ellison's metaphor.[44] Justification for the use of drones has relied in some measure on obfuscation. Much as Israelite theology, discussed above, focused by necessity on a more centripetal conception of God in the face of wide theological diversity, the name "al-Qaeda" has become "an ill-defined shorthand . . . to describe a shifting movement" of "nations," "Organizations," and "persons" authorized by Congress as targets of force, themselves sufficiently indeterminate to warrant new methods of warcraft.[45] In the wake of the marginal success (at best) of the ground wars in Iraq, Afghanistan, and elsewhere, coupled with the eroding will to endure U.S. casualties generated by such exercises, the new weapon of the War on Terror—particularly under the Obama administration—has become the drone.[46]

Alex Rivera describes the drone in evocative terms—especially for our present purposes—in an interview with *The New Inquiry*: "The drone is the most visceral and intense expression of the transnational / telepresent world we inhabit," marking "every facet" of contemporary life, occupying a "nonplace," a "transnational vortex" that is "ever present." Furthermore, "The military drone is a . . . disembodied destroyer of bodies," "the most beguiling expression of the transnational vortex."[47] It is "disembodied and disfigured in complex and fascinating ways."[48] It rains invisible death and renders its victims, if ever actually *seen*, remote pixels broadcast upon a screen from half the world away. "Warfare by remote control" has become a prominent metaphor in discussing drones.[49] In this way both appearance and reality have become *virtual* iterations. The language of drones also deals in invisibility. For instance, drones' primary benefit (according to both supporters and detractors among policy specialists) is their capacity to diminish "collateral damage": a euphemism that obscures the human reality of killing innocents, rendering their deaths invisible.[50]

Caroline Holmqvist, seeking to conceptualize drone warfare, speaks in terms that echo the central question of this essay: What does invisibility's metaphysical or theological nature have to do with materialist, secular critique? What is it about "terror" and declaring "war" on it that defies (or even augments) the scientific and material nature of warcraft and diplomacy? Holmqvist suggests that drones induce

> "embodied performances" by virtue of their "superhuman" qualities—the fact that hyper-vision provided by drone optics far extends human vision through an unblinking, "all-seeing stare." Accordingly, the distinction between tangible and intangible is obliterated: under conditions of omnipresent war, the boundaries between the corporeal and incorporeal become irreversibly blurred.[51]

We may recognize an impasse between the scientific, rational, material, and economic desire that characterizes U.S. policy and the metaphysical qualities of the response. Such aims are liberal (or at least couched in the language of liberalism), yet the realities these liberal aims generate acknowledge something more: In Ellisonian terms, the U.S. military and diplomatic complex represents the prize fighter, and "al-Qaeda," for all its amorphous sophistication, remains the yokel. The irony of the War on Terror, the punch(line) that may fell the prizefighter, is that the preservation of liberalism requires the suspension or even the annihilation of liberalism's core tenets. Such contradiction, of course, brings us back to the "high visibility" that, according to Ellison, renders African Americans invisible and suggests that the implications of twenty-first-century U.S. global policy reflect—nearly two-thirds of a century later—a uniquely Ellisonian irony (much like race's invisible theology) in the grander scheme.

## SECULARISM'S INVISIBLE THEOLOGY

By way of conclusion I would like to emphasize three related points concerning the religious dimensions of race as a secular concept in Ellison's work, the antecedents on which invisibility both explicitly and implicitly draws, and its wider implications for present and future critical occasions. First, despite its more recent materialist, secular co-optations, the long conceptual legacy of invisibility is shot through with religious and theological significance. Second, that invisibility, with its religious and theological valences, characterizes an indisputably "secular" writer and critic such as Ellison's conception of race. Third, as a consequence, this more expansive conception of race's secularity offers a significant, ironic critical apparatus for negotiating better the vagaries of present and future political issues even—or *especially*—at a time when the character of debates over race in many arenas continues to change. Questions of the "postracial" character of the twenty-first-century United States, while frequently misguided, ill-informed, or malignant in motivation, do point to a simple and apposite reality: The exigencies of race have changed dramatically over the past several decades, yet the conceptual, rhetorical, and political responses that remain in vogue derive largely from mid-twentieth-century notions of race and identity. Black/white paradigms, for instance, have given way to the "browning" of American identities thanks to the proliferation of immigrants from the Global South and the emergence of "biracial" possibilities.[52] Academic works such as Kenneth Warren's controversial *What Was African American Literature?*, Eddie Glaude's "The Black Church Is Dead," and the attendant controversies generated by these and related statements detect significant shifts in the way race is conceived of and practiced, if not understood or theorized.[53] As the second way of looking on invisibility discussed above reflects, what was once understood as an internal, domestic racial disciplinary gaze has also been cast outward, racializing Muslims through a diffuse global War on Terror. Problematizing the secularity of race broadens its conceptual spectrum and offers new critical lenses useful for framing these emerging contexts.

Likewise, despite (or perhaps because of) his canonical acceptance, wide appeal, and relative ubiquity in American letters since the publication of *Invisible Man* in 1952, Ralph Ellison has been dismissed by vocal factions as a sellout, an Uncle Tom, an anachronistic relic of a bygone age whose work does not harmonize with the political currents that gave rise to Black Studies in the 1960s and beyond. Recasting the secularism of Ellison's concept of race as neither the absence nor antithesis of religion but—conversely—an invisible theology augurs a far different narrative. Whatever Ellison's shortcomings, warranted or not according to the more narrow assumptions that have characterized the past half-century, such renovations of race and secularism mark Ellison's work and worldview as prescient and uniquely useful for challenges presented by changing racial contours in the present and future tenses.

I close with two points for moving forward, one geared toward domestic dynamics and the other toward the global scene. Thinking domestically: what does the status of race as invisibility—a metaphorical quality that encourages us to look beyond a secularized, visible, material notion of racial identity to discover obscure, hidden, even obfuscated antecedents derived from foundational theological principles—mean in light of stories emerging (even as I write) concerning the police killings of Michael Brown outside of St. Louis, Eric Garner in New York City, and Freddie Gray in Baltimore? The durability of oppressive racial animus highlighted by these and related incidents emphasize the embedded, programmatic nature of racial invisibility, illustrating the postracial fallacy. Consider the indelible split-screen image of a president who identifies as African American speaking of law and order, of the management of identity, and encouraging calm even as the other side of the screen shows protesters meeting militarized police in the Ferguson night. Obama's "high visibility" offers a tangible, material sign of racial "progress," of specific change since (for instance) the publication of *Invisible Man*. Nevertheless, the submerged realities and frustrations of race as an invisible political theology tell a different story. Outraged protesters see themselves in the dead men they memorialize, knowing that they remain invisible because (as Ellison's protagonist puts it)

> people refuse to see me. Like the bodiless heads you see sometimes in circus sideshows, it is as though I have been surrounded by mirrors of hard, distorting glass. When they approach me they see only my surroundings, themselves or figments of their imagination, [we might add Hulk Hogan in the case of Darren Wilson "seeing" Michael Brown,] indeed, everything and anything except me.[54]

Turning to global implications, secularism's invisible theology as traced through Ellison's work in particular offers an important rejoinder to presumptions by the United States to police regions populated by Muslims according to ostensibly secular principles. In the days that followed the attacks of September 11, 2001, President George W. Bush insisted that the nascent "War on Terror" should not and would not become a "War on Islam."[55] Bush's secularism sought to circumvent interpretations of violent retaliation in Afghanistan and regime change in Iraq as engagement in a holy war—an ambitious mission that was decidedly not accomplished. Whatever tangible, material objectives the United States proposed, longer Western colonial legacies consistently intervened. Whatever the intention may be, however objectively laudable, such secularized acts bear the indelible racial context of colonialism and its invisible theology rooted in, among other things, the legacies of the Crusades.[56] As mentioned above, the ghostlike visions that emerged from Abu Ghraib in 2004 offer visual support of the haunted, almost supernaturally inflected underside of secularism's invisible management.

These foregoing examples foreground the irony in Ellison's legacy and the quality through which his continued (and burgeoning) relevance abides: The old-fashioned novelist whose racial sensibility never quite fit the tenor of his age in fact offers a compelling model for understanding unique complexities of domestic and global implications for race and secularism in the twenty-first century. Invisibility, as his metaphor for racial identity, provides precisely the kind of capacious conceptual tool required for the vexing ambiguities of our present tense—even as it helps lend nuance and depth to the way we understand the past. Likewise it illustrates the abiding religious dimensions of the new secularism for a world that can never quite render itself fully secularized.

# NOTES

1. To deploy but one metric, a simple title search for the word "invisible" in my home institution's online catalogue yields more than 2,500 hits—a significant number of which (whether directly or not) allude to this received interpretation of *Invisible Man*—from James Pye's *Invisible Children: Who Are the Real Losers at School* (New York: Oxford University Press, 1988) to Armando José Prats's *Invisible Natives: Myth and Identity in the American Western* (Ithaca, N.Y.: Cornell University Press, 2002) or Donald Willett and Stephen Curley's edited volume *Invisible Texans: Women and Minorities in Texas History* (Boston: McGraw Hill, 2005).

2. Fabio Rojas, *From Black Power to Black Studies: How a Radical Social Movement Became an Academic Discipline* (Baltimore, Md.: Johns Hopkins University Press, 2010), 1. Rojas's first two chapters trace this process of institutionalization as a struggle between radicalization and accommodation, negotiating the need to remain on the vanguard with the broader aims of transforming important institutions such as universities and their models of education.

3. Ralph Ellison, *Invisible Man* (1952; New York: Vintage, 1995), 3.

4. Ralph Ellison, "Introduction to the Thirtieth Anniversary Edition of *Invisible Man*," in *The Collected Essays of Ralph Ellison*, ed. John F. Callahan (New York: Modern Classics, 1995), 478.

5. Tracy Fessenden, *Culture and Redemption: Religion, the Secular, and American Literature* (Princeton, N.J.: Princeton University Press, 2006), 6; Theodore Ziolkowski, *Modes of Faith: Secular Surrogates for Lost Religious Belief* (Chicago: University of Chicago Press, 2007); Charles Taylor, *A Secular Age* (Cambridge, Mass.: Belknap, 2007), see esp. chap. 15; and John Lardas Modern, *Secularism in Antebellum America* (Chicago: University of Chicago Press, 2011), 7.

6. Laura Saunders offers the best extant account of Ellison's religious background and use of biblical and liturgical resources throughout his work. Laura Saunders, "Ellison and the Black Church: The Gospel According to Ralph," in *The Cambridge Companion to Ralph Ellison*, ed. Ross Posnock (Cambridge: Cambridge University Press, 2005), 35–55, esp. 37–47.

7. Hollie I. West, "Ellison: Exploring the Life of a Not So Visible Man," in *Conversations with Ralph Ellison*, ed. Maryemma Graham and Amritjit Singh (Jackson: University Press of Mississippi, 1995), 245.

8. Ishmael Reed, Quincy Troupe, and Steve Cannon, "The Essential Ellison," in *Conversations with Ralph Ellison*, ed. Maryemma Graham and Amritjit Singh (Jackson: University Press of Mississippi, 1995), 373. For more on the foundational nature of biblical language, especially as it is modeled on the King James Version, see also James Alan McPherson's interview and overview from *The Atlantic* in *The Collected Essays of Ralph Ellison*, ed. John F. Callahan (New York: Modern Classics, 1995), 368–370.

9. Ellison, *Collected Essays*, 742. We should acknowledge that this represents a retrospective statement and, furthermore, that Ellison could be cagy about his past political identities. Still, he sets up a clear distinction between literary heroes (Dostoevsky and James) and the politically oriented writers he was supposed to have read. Interestingly, this is a similar tension pursued in *Invisible Man*, which offers a clear critique of political action and the New York left of the 1930s. Similarly, Ellison frequently discusses his aims for *Invisible Man* by citing Dostoevsky. See "The Art of Fiction," for instance, from the mid-1950s, in *Collected Essays*, 212.

10. "Invisible," spelled "inuisible" in the Geneva Bible, appears a total of five times (in precisely the same places) in both the Geneva (1587) and King James Version (KJV) (1611) English translations: Romans 1:20, Colossians 1:15 and 16, 1 Timothy 1:17, and Hebrews 11:27, all of which are discussed in some detail in this essay. Geneva was the primary English transla-

tion used by Protestants in colonial America through about 1640, at which point the KJV took over until the late nineteenth century, at least. See Paul Gutjahr, *An American Bible: A History of the Good Book in the United States, 1777–1880* (Palo Alto, Calif.: Stanford University Press, 1999), 92.

11. These and all biblical quotations cited in this essay come from the KJV.

12. Karl Barth, *The Epistle to the Romans*, trans. Edwyn C. Hoskyns (1933; New York: Oxford University Press, 1968), 46.

13. Rudolph Bultmann, *New Testament and Mythology*, trans. Schubert M. Ogden (Minneapolis, Minn.: Fortress, 1984), 49.

14. Ellison's most trenchant critique of social-scientific methods may be found in his review of Gunnar Myrdal's *An American Dilemma* (1944). Ellison takes especial issue with what one commentator calls "Myrdal's sterile 'scientific' approach as inadequate to capture the mercurial forces of myth and history that under-gird power and race in America." Note the disjuncture between clinical "sterility" and the resurrection of myth (also Bultmann's chosen term—"mercurial" itself is also a term derived from Roman myth) that marks Ellison's approach as distinct. See Richard Errol Purcell, *Race, Ralph Ellison, and American Cold War Intellectual Culture* (New York: Palgrave, 2013), 51. For Ellison's review of Myrdal, see *"An American Dilemma: A Review,"* in *Collected Essays*, 328–340.

15. Ellison, *Invisible Man*, 8.

16. We find evidence of this demythologizing impulse in Alain Locke's introduction to *The New Negro*, in which he depicts modern African American subjects who have moved away from the "myth" of the past, becoming in the process modern and increasingly secularized people with "idols of the tribe to smash." This new outlook is "scientific," not "sentimental." Alain Locke, ed., *The New Negro* (1925; New York: Touchstone, 1997), 4, 8.

17. W. Wesley Williams offers a helpful digest of various debates concerning God's (in)visibility in the Hebrew Bible over the past century. He suggests, citing the work of Christi Dianne Bamford and Benyamin Uffenheimer, that such a view actually imposes Greek and later anxieties about corporeality upon the Hebrew Bible text. In fact, the more salient question is not whether one *can* but, in fact, if one *may* see God. See W. Wesley Williams, *Tajallī wa Ru'ya: A Study of Anthropomorphic Theophany and Visio Dei in the Hebrew Bible, the Qur'ān and Early Sunnī Islam* (Ph.D. diss., University of Michigan, 2008), 21–25.

18. In addition to different names for God (Yahweh, Elohim, etc.), we see evidences in sources such as Job of a divine council (the *Bĕnê Elōhim*), offering not one god but a sense of plurality. See David Penchansky's *Twilight of the Gods: Polytheism in the Hebrew Bible* (Louisville, Ky.: Westminster John Knox, 2005), esp. chap. 3, *"Bĕnê Elōhim:* The Divine Council in the Hebrew Bible," for one take on this phenomenon (23–32). See also Mark S. Smith, *The Early History of God: Yahweh and the Other Deities in Ancient Israel* (Grand Rapids, Mich.: Eerdmans, 2002).

19. See Gerstenberger's essay "Conflicting Theologies in the Old Testament," *Horizons in Biblical Theology* 22, no. 2 (December 2000): 120–134. He expands upon these typologies in *Theologies in the Old Testament* (Minneapolis, Minn.: Fortress, 2002). On this point see esp. 19–24, though the entire volume discusses them in greater detail.

20. Paul D. Hanson, "Israelite Religion in the Early Postexilic Period," in *Ancient Israelite Religion: Essays in Honor of Frank Moore Cross*, ed. Patrick D. Miller Jr., Paul D. Hanson, and S. Dean McBride (Philadelphia: Fortress, 1987), 485.

21. John Day, *Yahweh and the Gods and Goddesses of Canaan* (Sheffield: Sheffield Academic Press, 2000), 233. See also David Noel Freedman's essay "'Who Is Like Thee Among the Gods?': The Religion of Early Israel," which traces the submergence of El into Yahweh, in *Ancient Israelite Religion: Essays in Honor of Frank Moore Cross*, ed. Patrick D. Miller Jr., Paul D. Hanson, and S. Dean McBride (Philadelphia: Fortress, 1987), 334.

22. John Bright, *A History of Israel*, 4th ed. (Louisville, Ky. Westminster John Knox, 2000), 438.

23. Stephen A. Geller, "The God of the Covenant," in *One God or Many? Concepts of Divinity in the Ancient World*, ed. Barbara Nevling Porter (Chebeque, Me.: Casco Assyriological Institute, 2000), 286.

24. "Emergent Judaism" is Bright's phrase (*A History of Israel*, 438). For the diversity/singularity of God, see Geller, "The God of the Covenant," 286.

25. Walter Brueggemann, *Theology of the Old Testament: Testimony, Dispute, Advocacy* (Minneapolis, Minn.: Fortress, 1997), 333.

26. Ellison, *Invisible Man*, 577.

27. Ibid.

28. Pluribus and unum also constitute a broader theme elsewhere in Ellison's criticism, particularly for the democratic function of the novel, bringing together particulars and universals. See especially Senator Sunraider's speech on the Senate floor in the second novel (*Three Days Before the Shooting . . .* [New York: Random House, 2010], 242) and the essays "Society, Morality, and the Novel" and "The Novel as a Function of American Democracy" in *Collected Essays*, 698–729, 759–769.

29. See, for instance, Daniel J. Elazar, *Covenant and Polity in Biblical Israel: Biblical Foundations and Jewish Expressions* (New Brunswick, N.J.: Transaction, 1995).

30. Ellison, *Invisible Man*, 577.

31. Ibid., 581.

32. It is also important to recognize in exilic experience (and the postexilic literature that tells its story) a model for the development of Afro-America. New World Africans would resonate with biblical legacies of captivity, enslavement, and exile that unite—meaningfully, if not completely—culturally and politically diverse people, beliefs, and customs, forging a new and unique sense of theological identity. Such biblical legacies and identities proved familiar, appealing, and useful in the formation of African American identity in the midst of enslavement and exile.

33. Kenneth W. Warren argues against this point in *So Black and Blue: Ralph Ellison and the Occasion of Criticism* (Chicago: University of Chicago Press, 2003). For Warren, readings of *Invisible Man* that "speak to and for the larger human condition" deflect attention from "the way that ascribed racial status reflects and is refracted through some of the central issues of particular historical moments" (3, 23).

34. Valentin Groebner, *Defaced: The Visual Culture of Violence in the Late Middle Ages*, trans. Pamela Selwyn (New York: Zone, 2004), 65. What I appreciate, especially, about Groeb-

ner's position is what it suggests about the approach that I advocate in this essay: There's something imperative in the history of race and its religious dimensions that represents a lacuna in various assumptions about the relationship between race and secularism. Without such recoveries, we shall remain at a disadvantage in comprehending these new valences and acting appropriately moving forward.

35. We find an interesting illustration here of the religious and theological antecedents of secularism by noting that many understand this clash to remain one between not secularism and Islam, or competing political ideologies, but uniquely and overtly as an impasse and war between Christianity and Islam. For many, and not solely for evangelical Christians, the clash between secular civilization and theocracy invokes an invisible Christianity.

36. In interesting ways one finds a long history of the racialization of Islamic and African American identities in the United States and, to an extent, in earlier colonial contexts. Groups like the Nation of Islam, for instance, assert that true black identity is Islamic as a critique of Christianity as the "white man's" oppressive religion.

37. For more on the "Judeo-Christian"—itself a secularizing impulse—see the special issue of *Relegere* ("Revisiting the 'Judeo-Christian' Tradition"), coedited by Benjamin E. Sax and Matthew Gabriele. Of particular interest is Brian M. Britt's "Secularism and the Question of the 'Judeo-Christian,'" *Relegere* 2, no. 2 (2012): 343–352.

38. The best (and best known) reading of surveillance in modernity is, of course, Michel Foucault's *Discipline and Punish: The Birth of the Prison*, trans. Alan Sheridan (New York: Vintage, 1995).

39. See, for instance, Andrew J. Bacevich's *American Empire: The Reality and Consequences of U.S. Diplomacy* (Cambridge, Mass.: Harvard University Press, 2004).

40. The long-standard account of the formation of the Ku Klux Klan during Reconstruction—Stanley Fitzgerald Horn's *Invisible Empire: The Story of the Ku Klux Klan* (Cambridge, Mass.: Riverside, 1939)—does not remain in favor today, yet the title is clearly significant for our purposes. I should note that I do not wish to invoke a one-to-one correspondence between U.S. military initiatives and the KKK, though levels of secrecy, adjudication outside of legally recognized and sanctioned courts, and certain tendencies toward racial profiling make the comparison more apt than it should be. On Abu Ghraib, see Seymour M. Hersh, "Torture at Abu Ghraib," *New Yorker* (May 10, 2004), http://www.newyorker.com/archive/2004/05/10/040510fa_fact. Susan Sontag's reading of the Abu Ghraib revelations argues that "the photographs are us" and therefore "representative of the fundamental corruptions" at the root of foreign occupation, even as they are usually hidden or invisible. See "Regarding the Torture of Others," *New York Times Magazine* (May 23, 2004).

41. Ellison, *Invisible Man*, 498.

42. Ibid., 495.

43. Ibid., 495–496.

44. Literature on drones and their broader implications grows daily. Future historians will do very well to trace the evolution of thinking about and attitudes toward drones in essays from the *New York Review of Books* and the *London Review of Books* since the middle of the 2000s' first decade. Other assessments that have proved useful in my own thinking include

Richard Whittle, *Predator: The Secret Origins of the Drone Revolution* (New York: Henry Holt, 2014); Medea Benjamin, *Drone Warfare: Killing by Remote Control* (New York: OR, 2012); and Michael J. Boyle, "The Costs and Consequences of Drone Warfare," *International Affairs* 89, no. 1 (2013): 1–29. For a good point-counterpoint exchange concerning the various efficacies and shortcomings of drones, see Daniel Bynum, "Why Drones Work: The Case for Washington's Weapon of Choice," *Foreign Affairs* 92, no. 4 (July/August 2013): 32–43; and Audrey Kurth Cronin, "Why Drones Fail: When Tactics Drive Strategy" in the same issue of *Foreign Affairs* (44–54).

45. Cronin, "Why Drones Fail," 48. Al-Qaeda inhabits its invisibility deliberately, relying on ignorance and ambivalence to generate indeterminacy. On September 12, 2001, President George W. Bush claimed: "The American people need to know that we're facing a different enemy than we have ever faced. This enemy hides in shadows, and has no regard for human life. This is an enemy who preys on innocent and unsuspecting people, then runs for cover. But it won't be able to run for cover forever. This is an enemy that tries to hide. But it won't be able to hide forever. This is an enemy that thinks its harbors are safe. But they won't be safe forever." http://www.pbs.org/newshour/updates/terrorism/july-dec01/bush _speech_9–12.html. The group known as the Islamic State (ISIS or ISIL, variably) has only recently emerged (and thus it is more difficult to speak of them authoritatively), yet they also deal in a kind of transnationalism whose invisibility to nationalistic colonial legacies has proved vexing and appears to have some measure of staying power. Also, while they offer visible evidence of heinous acts against human beings (beheadings) and humankind (the destruction of historical artifacts), the spectacles that they produce prove so grotesque as to challenge the very limits of visibility. Mr. Norton's shock at visiting the Golden Day or the nightmare visions of the Harlem riots at the end of *Invisible Man* offer interesting passages for thinking through certain Ellisonian implications of this new faction.

46. "During his first term, President Obama launched nearly six times as many drone strikes than President Bush did throughout his eight years in office." Boyle, "The Costs and Consequences of Drone Warfare," 2.

47. Malcolm Harris and Alex Rivera, "Border Control: An Interview," *New Inquiry* 6 (July 2012): 7.

48. Ibid., 9.

49. In addition to Benjamin's book, cited above, Cronin and others draw on this analogy.

50. See both Bynum, "Why Drones Work"; and Cronin, "Why Drones Fail." For more on collateral damage, see part 4 of Stephen Nathanson's *Terrorism and the Ethics of War* (Cambridge: Cambridge University Press, 2010), 247–287.

51. Caroline Holmqvist, "Undoing War: War Ontologies and the Materiality of Drone Warfare," *Millennium—Journal of International Studies* 41, no. 3 (2013): 545.

52. See Ronald R. Sundstrom, *The Browning of America and the Evasion of Social Justice* (Albany, N.Y.: SUNY Press, 2008).

53. Kenneth Warren, *What Was African American Literature?* (Cambridge, Mass.: Harvard University Press, 2011), argues that "African American literature" was "dismantled" amid the exigencies of *Brown v. Board:* "African American literature took shape in the context

of . . . racial subordination and exploitation represented by Jim Crow. Accordingly . . . with the demise of Jim Crow, the coherence of African American literature has been correspondingly . . . eroded as well." Intrinsic to Warren's thesis (which mirrors, in ways, Eddie Glaude's claim of the Black Church's demise) is a sense of unmooring from a system that, for all of the injustice it propagated, also held together out of necessity a relatively stable sense of African American identity. Resistance, endurance, and survival forged a complex and multivalent cosmos that, in the wake of *Brown*, fractured, leaving African Americans and the broader public grasping for new ways to order their social relationships and political organizations amid this crumbling cosmos, turning to broader questions of anthropology, citizenship, and civil religion.

54. Ellison, *Invisible Man*, 3.

55. Bush first used the phrase "War on Terror" in an address to Congress on September 20, 2001, in part to distinguish that while the United States would attack Islamic terrorists, the war itself did not intend to engage Islam. This sought to destabilize the Holy War narrative that many Islamic militants and U.S. Christian militants wished to promote. See http://www.washingtonpost.com/wp-srv/nation/specials/attacked/transcripts/bushaddress_092001.html.

56. Bush spoke of a U.S. "crusade" to avenge the September 11 attacks in a speech delivered on September 13, 2001, a term he quickly disavowed and apologized for using.

# 7

# SECULAR COLONIALITY

## THE AFTERLIFE OF RELIGIOUS AND RACIAL TROPES

William D. Hart

The Eurocentric version [of knowledge] is based on two principal founding myths: first, the idea of the History of human civilization as a trajectory that departed from a state of nature and culminated in Europe; second, a view of the differences between Europe and non-Europe as natural (racial) differences and not consequences of a history of power.

—ANIBAL QUIJANO

I conceptualize the coloniality of power as an entanglement of multiple and heterogeneous hierarchies ("heterarchies") of sexual, political, epistemic, economic, spiritual, linguistic, and racial forms of domination and exploitation where the racial/ethnic hierarchy of the European/non-European divide transversally reconfigures all other global power structures. What is new in the "coloniality of power" perspective is how the idea of race and racism becomes the organizing principle that structures all of the multiple hierarchies of the world-system.

—RAMÓN GROSFOGUEL

IN *THE RHETORIC OF EMPIRE*, David Spurr identifies twelve tropes of colonialism: surveillance, appropriation, aestheticization, classification, debasement, negation, affirmation, idealization, insubstantialization, naturalization, eroticization, and resistance.[1] Though these tropes often have a racializing dimension, there are tropes associated with imperial/colonial modernity that tie specifically to religious and secular constructions of blackness. In this chapter, I explore religious constructions of racial identity and the reproduction in secular discourse of colonial tropes that are common in both scholarly and popular accounts of religion. I call this secular reproduction the "afterlife" of colonial, religious, and racial tropes. This inquiry raises many questions, some that I can only pose for further consideration: Is race—like the closely related terms nation and ethnos—a religious discourse? Is the secular a colonial discourse? Assuming they are, what are the prospects of secularizing and decolonizing these discourses? Africana religion has been a prime object of religious and secular discourse. Africana religion is a cover term for African-derived religions and the distinctive religious practices of African-descended people. There are various tropes associated with Africana religion that accent the religious construction of race: race as blackness, black people as distinctively religious, black religion as especially primitive, a kind of "Pythian madness, a daemonic possession" as W. E. B. Du Bois writes in *The Souls of Black Folks.* I shall focus on three tropes: fetish, voodoo, and frenzy. They derive from three geopolitical contexts: Portuguese exploration, conquest, and slave trading on the western coast of Africa, French slave trading and colonization of the Haitian side of the island of Hispaniola, and accounts of the religious practices of African Americans both enslaved and free.

As with "religion, religions, and the religious," to use Jonathon Z. Smith's term, there are competing notions of secularization, secularism, and the secular. My comments are primarily about the adjective rather than the nouns. Without rejecting other notions, I regard the secular as an organic outgrowth of religious life. I do not see a radical break between those aspects of the culture that we call religious and those described as secular.[2] On the contrary, I regard the secular as the dialectical other of the religious, an internal other that over time differentiates and becomes external to its religious habitat. Secular culture (at least in the West) is religious culture sublated, that is, negated, preserved, and carried forward. Without denying that some people are genuinely indifferent to religion or live in ways that appear to be untouched by religion, the predominate modalities, I argue, are secularized experiences of religion and religious expression of the secular. I see the religious and the secular as conjoined twins. Secularism is not the opposite of religion; it is religion's internal other. So my approach rejects any stark religious-secular distinction.

## CIRCUMSCRIBING THE TOPIC

During the early period of imperial/colonial modernity, initiated by Western European voyages of exploration and conquest in the fifteenth century, the presence or absence of religion emerged as a differential marker of humanity. Europeans often remarked on the absence of religion among Africans and the native people of the New World.[3] By the time that Hegel wrote his lectures on the philosophy of religion in the late eighteenth and early nineteenth centuries, religion still marked this difference. Eventually religion became a universal category of European classification, with particular forms, such as "primitive religion," associated with racial others such as Africans.[4] Based on "ethnographic" data gathered from travelers and would-be anthropologists, early theorists of religion drew invidious distinctions between the rationality of Christianity and the irrationality of primitive religions. The Portuguese were among the earliest sources of this data. When they encountered Africans along the western coast in the fifteenth century, they were intrigued by cultural practices that they later described as fetishism.[5] This concept quickly became a mainstay in efforts to theorize African religions and all religions deemed primitive. Marx appropriated the concept of fetishism to criticize the relations between consumer and commodity in a capitalist economy. In effect, Marx claims that "civilized," European Christians in capitalist nations such as England and the United States behave like African fetish-worshipers when they mystify the nature of commodities by attributing human-like qualities to them.

Like his Portuguese predecessors, Marx presents an ill-informed account of African religions: African traditional religionists do not worship fetish objects any more than Christians worship the cross. But this misrepresentation is understandable given his limited knowledge of African cultural practices. Marx and his predecessors are wrong but not blameworthy. Epistemically, they did not have the information to know any better. Epistemic innocence notwithstanding, when Marx used the term "fetishism" to describe the mystifying powers of capital, he stereotyped an important trope of imperial/colonial modernity and its secular theories of religion. While Marx never refers explicitly to the racialized colonial subtext of this trope, it is clearly there, hidden in plain sight. Marx's appropriation of fetishism is an example of how colonial and racialized notions are carried over, unconsciously and uncritically, into secular discourse. Thus a trope within imperial/colonial theorizing of African religions becomes a racially coded secular term for mystification, ignorance of cause and effect, and irrational attributions of subjectivity to inanimate things.

Like Marx, all of us are seduced by such language even when we self-consciously oppose imperial/colonial relations and constructions.

*Item*: In his magisterial *The Problem of Slavery in Western Culture*, the progressive historian David Brion Davis casually refers to Africa as the Dark Continent. Without recognition, he repeats Henry Morton Stanley's (and Hegel's) racialized and imperial/colonial description of Africa as bereft of light, knowledge, and history.

*Item*: In an analysis that explicitly aimed at gender injustice, racism structured by white supremacy, and imperial practices of every kind, the black atheist feminist Sikivu Hutchinson uses the term fetishism without acknowledging its racializing origins in Portuguese explorations and colonization of Africa.

*Item*: During the high tide of imperial/colonial modernity, "exotic and primitive others" such as Sarah "Saartjie" Baartman, the so-called Venus Hottentot, and Ota Benga, the so-called Pygmy in the zoo, were displayed before Western audiences in cages, circuses, carnivals, zoos, and scientific societies. As contemporaries of Benga, Chang and Eng Bunker, conjoined twins of Siamese origin, were on display in P. T. Barnum's popular circus. The phenomena of conjoined twins became associated with these brothers, hence the term "Siamese twins." In 2003, I gave a presentation at Colgate University on colonial constructions of knowledge. The title was "Race, Religion, Nation." In describing some phenomenon I no longer recall, I used "Siamese twins" instead of the proper term "conjoined twins." One of the participants quickly pointed out the discrepancy between my anticolonial conceptual frame and my unselfconscious use of a colonial trope. I should note that my remark was not a Freudian slip. I meant to use the term and did not think about its connotations. So the listener, quite properly, called me out. Did the listener offer his remark in sympathy, out of concern for the consistency of my argument, or was he hostile? Whether the intervention was hostile or not, I pivoted quickly by acknowledging my own complicity, which I argued only underscored the power and scope of colonial and racist tropes even in the discourse of a critic.

During the 1980 presidential campaign, George H. W. Bush described Ronald Reagan's supply-side economic plan as "voodoo economics." The idea that reducing regulation and taxes would lead to greater revenue and productivity sounded like magic. What better description of such *mumbo jumbo* than voodoo economics? I should note parenthetically that mumbo jumbo is closely associated with voodoo. Both are derived from names of West African deities. As an English term, mumbo jumbo refers to gibberish and to superstitious (fetishizing) habits of mind associated with the racialized primitive other. Though these associations are old, the racialized and imperial/colonial subtext of Bush's comment went largely unremarked. Thirty years later, David Aronovitch published *Voodoo Histories: The Role of Conspiracy Theory in Shaping Modern History*. Aronovitch certainly knows that the "voodoo" in his title is an invidious adjective. Clearly he selects this adjective to cast conspiracy theory in a negative light. So normalized is this usage that Aronovitch seems oblivious to the religious, racial, and imperial/colonial subtext. The use of voodoo—an Anglicized version of Vodou, which is an Afro-Atlantic religion—has become an all-purpose trope for irrationality of any kind.

Voodoo has no descriptive much less an analytic presence in Aronovitch's text. Though George H. W. Bush used a colonial and racist trope, it had an analytical aim: to expose defects in Reaganomics that, presumably, mimic the magical thinking widely attributed to voodooists. In this regard, he gestures in the direction of Marx, my critique of whom is mitigated by his effort to turn a religious and racial stereotype of a subject people—so-called African fetishizers—against the subjugating power of capital and Christianity. In contrast, "voodoo" is not so much an empty signifier as a tropological black hole whose gravitational pull is so strong and, consequently, so full of meaning as to no longer require specification. Thus all Aronovitch has to say is "voodoo histories" for the reader to know more or less what he means. Though the term is merely a book title and page header, it channels hidden, submerged, and iceberg-like meanings. Invidious uses of voodoo by Bush and Aronovitch reveal a porous membrane between religious and secular discourses on race, especially when they depict the practices of African-descended people.

The use of voodoo as a trope for magic and superstition, for inferior, defective, and pseudo versions of religion emerged from the American marine-led occupation of Haiti from 1914 to 1934. The writings that emerged during this period "refined and disseminated a set of tropes about Haiti"—stereotypes of voodoo, especially the figure of the zombie—that still influences the popular imagination today. Thus zombies became a Hollywood staple. Given the Haitian peoples' history of enslavement, "zombie" had a culturally specific meaning for them. Zombies represented persons deprived of agency. We might even say that they are metaphors of Haitian slavery. But the conventions of Hollywood's gothic horror genre decontextualized and depoliticized the very idea.[6] I have argued that racialized tropes regarding religion pass over into secular discourse. In *Haiti: The Aftershocks of History*, Laurent Dubois underscores my claim about such fluidity when he remarks:

Indeed, it is the American zombie clichés that have functioned as a kind of intellectual sorcery. They took a religion developed in order to survive and resist slavery—one that had served as [a] central pillar in the counter-plantation system at the core of the Haitian struggle to secure autonomy and dignity—and transformed it into nothing more than a sign of barbarism, further proof that the country would never progress unless it was guided and controlled by foreign whites.[7]

To see how deeply colonial tropes penetrated accounts of religion even among the subjects of such descriptions, one need go no further than Du Bois and his classic American letter, *The Souls of Black Folk*. Consider this famous passage:

It was out in the country, far from home, far from my foster home, on a dark Sunday night. The road wandered from our rambling log-house up the stony bed of a creek, past wheat and corn, until we could hear dimly across the fields a rhythmic cadence of song,—soft, thrilling, powerful, that swelled and died sorrowfully in our ears. I was a country school-teacher then, fresh from the East, and had never seen a Southern Negro revival. To be sure, we in Berkshire were not perhaps as stiff and formal as they in Suffolk of olden time; yet we were very quiet and subdued, and I know not what would have happened those clear Sabbath mornings had some one punctuated the sermon with a wild scream, or interrupted the long prayer with a loud Amen! And so most striking to me, as I approached the village and the little plain church perched aloft, was the air of intense excitement that possessed that mass of black folk. A sort of suppressed terror hung in the air and seemed to seize us,—a pythian madness, a demoniac possession, that lent terrible reality to song and word. The black and massive form of the preacher swayed and quivered as the words crowded to his lips and flew at us in singular eloquence. The people moaned and fluttered, and then the gaunt-cheeked brown woman beside me suddenly leaped straight into the air and shrieked like a lost soul, while round about came wail and groan and outcry, and a scene of human passion such as I had never conceived before.[8]

Discounting the primitivism, this is a lovely account of a Southern black church. Du Bois has an eye for detail. His account is very descriptive and visual; it transports us to this historical stage, as if the scene was suddenly playing live before our eyes. The lyricism of the passage notwithstanding, Du Bois channels a culturally dominant idea that associated black people with irrational fervor and irrationality with "primitive religion." Following terror, Pythian madness, and demoniac possession, Du Bois refers to "the Frenzy" of black worship. We could regard these terms as merely a rhetorical flourish, as baroque, Victorian formulations. Or we could charge Du Bois with elitism.[9] While accurate as far as it goes, the elitism critique ignores the larger discursive context that positioned Du Bois as a writing subject. Earlier, I referred to progressive scholars and critics who unconsciously reproduced colonial and racist tropes. This same unconscious reproduction partly explains Du Bois's language. It was part of a broader discourse that he could not wholly evade. This is an explanation, not an apology. By way of comparison, one might juxtapose Du Bois's language with the discourse of the underclass and black urban nihilism. Some might suggest that the purveyors of this discourse exhibit the same defect as Du Bois's Victorian account; both Du Bois and his antiprimitivist critics are seduced by discourses that draw invidious distinctions between the black folk, whether rural or urban, and the black elite. But I digress.

Several years before Du Bois's foray into the discourse of black primitivism,[10] Edward Wilmot Blyden traded on the same primitivist idea in *Christianity, Islam, and the Negro Race*. Under the influence of colonial/imperial modernity, Blyden associates traditional African religions with fetishism and idolatry while Islam represents enlightenment.[11] In contrast to African fetishism, Islam stands shoulder to shoulder with its Abrahamic brethren, Judaism and Christianity, as vectors of cultural advancement. Several decades after the publication of *Souls*, Leopold Senghor, the leading proponent of Négritude, infamously remarked that "Emotion is Negro, reason is Greek." Thus he legitimized a trope that spanned colonial theories of religion and secular discourses on black identity. Though Blyden, Du Bois, and Senghor were pan-African freedom fighters, they were seduced by tropes of imperial/colonial modernity that transcend the religious/secular distinction.

Fetishism, voodoo, and frenzy are colonial, religious, and racial tropes that pass over and are reborn within secular discourse.

## DO COLONIAL TROPES HAVE A HALF-LIFE?

A commentator raised an interesting question. Do tropes such as fetishism, frenzy, and voodoo have a half-life? The question suggests that these tropes were or ought to have been radioactive. Though important, the question is premature. To quote Chou En-lai regarding the success of the French Revolution of 1789 or the French student protests of 1968, as the case may be, "It is too soon to say."[12] Paradoxically, it may be too soon and too late. I find little evidence that these terms have ever been radioactive. If these tropes have become radioactive, it has only been during the era of postcolonial critique. Insofar as there is any sense that these tropes are religiously and racially toxic, I find little critical commentary regarding frenzy[13] and voodoo. In contrast, fetishism has long been an important trope in progressive discourses influenced by Marxism and psychoanalysis. Fetishism has been baptized and haloed so to speak by the discursive creativity of Marx and Freud. Thus to consider rightly the half-life of this trope and the others, we must first acknowledge their radioactivity and grasp critically their place within the coloniality of power.

Here I follow Anibal Quijano as elaborated by Ramón Grosfoguel in the introductory epigraphs. On this view, "the coloniality of power" refers to a world system that emerged after the European "discovery" of the New World in the fifteenth century. Under the regime of imperial/colonial modernity, as artifacts of a then-emerging white supremacy, the ideology of race and the practice of racism became the structuring agent with respect to a broad range of pernicious hierarchies in politics and economics, gender and sexuality, knowledge and religion. The coloniality of power is the enabling condition for tropes such as fetishism, frenzy, and voodoo. The question of whether these tropes have or ought to have a radioactive half-life relates to the contemporary salience of the coloniality of power. Has the passage of time and an epistemic shift in anthropology[14] detoxified these tropes? Like the nonscientific expression "the sun rises in the east and sets in the west," are these tropes inoffensive if not innocent reminders and remainders of an obsolete worldview? Those who would deny the racialized expression of the phenomena that Quijano and Grosfoguel describe have a heavy burden. Virtually everywhere we look, a racialized division of labor, power, and prestige appears.

In this section, I take a second pass at fetishism, frenzy, and voodoo. In this iteration, I consider frenzy first because it is the most ambiguous and poses the most difficulty for my thesis that these tropes are racialized religious ideas that have passed over into secular discourse. Frenzy may be the least provocative of the three and certainly the least productive in terms of the discourse generated. This trope does not have the same genealogy in the practices of African-descended people that fetishism and voodoo have. Further, frenzy loses some of its distinctiveness when we consider closely related terms such as "ecstasy," Pentacostalism, and "enthusiasm," which was associated with post-Reformation Protestant sects. Frenzy was a religious trope before it became a racial trope under imperial/colonial modernity. Religiously dominant Europeans construed dissidents and minorities as emotionally unhinged and disposed to violence and perversion. Around the same time, Europeans began to encounter "anthropological others" whom they deemed barbarous, savage, and primitive. They construed such people, especially Africans and aboriginal Americans, as subjects of irrationality, affect, and emotion. Frenzy characterized their religious practices.

Since Du Bois has been the focus of my account of the frenzy trope, it is important that we distinguish between a subject-centered and a discursive critique. Insofar as we wish to make a normative judgment, the first approach fixes responsibility at the level of the individual subject. In contrast, the second approach targets the discursive context—linguistic, cultural, political, and material—that produces and positions a subject, such as Du Bois, and induces him to speak in a particular manner. Here Du Bois is a subject of and a node within the discourse and not its author. In short, this is not about Du Bois's intentions or a simpleminded attempt to blame or defend him. Rather, I attempt to understand how even critics, against their intentions, become puppets of a dominant discourse. In his magisterial biography of Du Bois, David Levering Lewis provides a detailed portrait of his Victorian formation and sensibilities.[15] While frenzy predates the Victorian age, it is certainly a word that fits nicely in such a time. Even as we accept Foucault's critique of the "repressive hypothesis,"[16] the Victorian age was concerned with various proprieties regarding emotional and bodily comportment that black ecstatic religiosity violated. Here Cornel West's remark about Du Bois's exoticizing anthropological gaze is apropos. In the same vein, Victor Wolfenstein likens Du Bois's account of the frenzy of black worship to the kind of exoticism "famously analyzed by Edward Said" in *Orientalism*.[17] I might annotate Wolfenstein's remark by saying that the discourse of primitivism is a better match for the point he wishes to make. Where the "exotic Oriental" is construed as decadent, the exoticism of Afro-descendants is labeled primitive.

As previously noted, Du Bois's use of frenzy has not generated much commentary pro or contra. Many commentators reference the phrase "the Preacher, the Music, the Frenzy," but few discern anything more than a bit of political incorrectness given contemporary sensibilities. This view is articulated well by the Reverend James Forbes:

> Some black people think that the worst thing Du Bois wrote in *Souls* was about the "frenzy of a Negro revival"—the dancing, the shouting, and the catching up into ecstasy. They think if white people or Europeans read that,

they would get the sense that we are victims of uncontrollable excess. I think that when I get touched by the spirit, my traditional rules and motor actions are transcended and a new freedom comes.[18]

In a way that Du Bois does not, Forbes acknowledges the discursive problem, that is, the white supremacist construction of black religious expressivity. In response, Forbes attempts to reorient our normative evaluations by reinterpreting standard Eurocentric interpretations of ecstatic bodily comportment. Given the ongoing construction of black people as irrational, where frenzied violence is the flipside of frenzied religious expression within a general economy of disordered passions, there is little reason to believe that the secular incarnation of this trope is less radioactive. I am not suggesting that reinterpretations such as Forbes's are meaningless. Rather, my point is that the dominant discourse canalizes the use and significance of the trope. Its dominant use still expresses a colonial disposition toward black people according to which black bodies signify chaos. With his account of the contemporary iconic status of African American worship, Geraldo Marti challenges my claim. Without skirting its roots in the essentialism of romantic racialism, Marti claims that an interracial consensus regarding the superior authenticity of black religious expression is now regnant.[19] This would suggest that not only has the radioactive half-life (negative constructions) of black worship ended but also that a complete normative inversion has occurred. That which was formerly degraded within the dominant discourse is now exalted. Of course, we should note that Marti refers, as far as I can tell, to perceptions within multiracial churches. It remains to be seen whether this perception is shared widely outside such churches. Further, he refers to attitudes toward music and not specifically to the ecstatic dancing and speech (shouting) that Du Bois calls frenzy. And of course there is the critical question that must be asked: Does this positive construction of black worship alter the underlying notion that black people are emotionally excessive, that is, irrational and dangerous?

I suggested at the outset that frenzy (a placeholder for several terms concerning emotional excess and irrationality) might pose greater difficulties for my thesis than voodoo and fetishism. Though I am still confident in the thesis, Forbes's testimony and Marti's analysis do pose challenges. Matters are clearer regarding voodoo. In her account of Haiti after the 2010 earthquake, the American journalist Amy Wilentz uses the British journalistic term "Fred Voodoo" to characterize ordinary Haitians. As she acknowledges, the term is pejorative. But she wants the reader to feel the full contempt with which international media and other opinion makers regard Haitians. As I read her, she realizes that the structuring power of discourse cannot simply be evaded by reference to the good intentions and transcending purity of an individual subject such as herself. She knows that the discourse implicates her against her will. She knows that a maligned religion, Vodun, through its English derivation, voodoo, operates as a metonym for a maligned people. If the colonial trope "frenzy" constructs Afro-descendants as emotionally unhinged and thus irrational, then "voodoo" casts them as zombies. On this view, Haitians have an unnatural relation to their emotions, history, and circumstances. They wait absurdly for white people to save them as if waiting for Godot. Whether her comment is ironic or not, it surprises Wilentz that people continue to construe Haitians, without reference to history or context, as "destitute, pathetic, uneducated, and probably irredeemable." These views recall the age-old attitude of France and the United States during the era of imperial/colonial modernity. These views compelled Frederick Douglass, America's first black envoy to Haiti, the first black republic, to conclude that the slave and colonial powers had not forgiven the island nation for being black.[20]

Discourse is not about the intentions of the individual subject; it's about the power to position, authorize, and signify regardless of the inner orientations of the individual. Clearly a person of good will who truly wants the best for Haiti as enlightened Haitians might conceive matters, Wilentz illustrates this point by transforming the zombie, a racialized religious figure within the colonial trope of voodoo, into a secular figure. "The zombie is something we all fear becoming, if we think about it. He is frightening in a primordial way, and in a modern way, too. He is dead but he's walking; he has to work even after death." As the living dead, the inanimate animated, this figure is both ancient and modern—"like the robot of industrial dystopias."[21] Wilentz adds:

> With perfect obedience and lack of any future, the zombie who cannot escape from servitude even in death, is the echt citizen in a dictatorship. He's great for fascism (one recent zombie movie was called *The Fourth Reich*). The

zombie is willing. He works for free. You feed him very little. He makes no demands. He's like Apple's Chinese factory workers; or like the refugees in Haiti's earthquake camps; or like guest workers in European countries; or like employees at call centers in India or the Philippines—except he is not desperate, he simply *is*; as such, he's devoid of hope and consciousness, and therefore unable to come up with a critique of the system he's trapped in, or a plan to rise up from his servitude.[22]

A minor figure in voodoo, the zombie has captured the Western imagination and become an all-purpose metaphor for the ultimate loss of agency, alienated consciousness, disordered emotions and affect, and political and economic subjugation. The logic of the zombie-as-voodoo trope operates as follows: first, observers from enslaving and colonizing nations, especially France and the United States, perceive the African-based religion of Haitians as negative and bizarre, that is, as *empirically other*;[23] second, they apply this trope to phenomena they regard as bizarre or suspect. Thus we have discursive figures such as voodoo economics, voodoo history, and Fred voodoo—the latter trope, again, establishing a metonymic association between voodoo as negative, bizarre, and zombie making and the comportment of the average Haitian.

## ELIZABETH MCALISTER ON THE "RACE AND RELIGION OF ZOMBIES"

In a fascinating account of the "tropics of zombie," Elizabeth McAlister traces the proliferation and the religious and racial transformations of this figure.[24] Zombies are now black and white, religious and secular, a philosophical conceit and a kind of blank. Zombie is the new Proteus, the god or "god-term"[25] of infinite transformation and signification. In contemporary Hollywood movies, the zombie has morphed from enslaved and colonized black worker into "hyperwhite" people cannibalizing everyone in sight. In turn, black males in movies such as the *Night of the Living Dead*, *Dawn*, and *Day* trilogy and *I Am Legend* have emerged as messianic zombie fighters. In many respects they conform to the romantic (allegedly positive) stereotype of the "super-duper magical Negro" saving civilization from the living death of an all-consuming whiteness.[26] Regarding these misappropriations of the zombie figure, especially as hyperwhite and secular, she points to the very different figure that appears in Haitian Vodun. Within "the colonial 'space of death'" and "'culture of death' of the plantation," the zombie presents as a politically ambiguous and ambivalence-inspiring figure of collusion and rebellion.[27] By making zombies, enslaving disembodied souls or soulless bodies, Haitians reproduce *and* seek to repair the trauma of slavery and colonialism.[28] According to McAlister:

> Zonbi-making is an example of a nonwestern form of thought that diagnoses, theorizes, and responds mimetically to the long history of violently consumptive and dehumanizing capitalism in the Americas from the colonial period until the present. Zonbi can be understood as a religious, philosophical, and artistic response to the cannibalistic dynamics within capitalism, and a harnessing of these principles through ritual.[29]

She adds:

> Zombie mythmaking began in Haitian colonialism as a complicated engagement with slavery and death-dealing capitalist formations. In white American books and films, zombie mythmaking became articulated through, and into, a sign for black barbarism, only to re-emerge recently as a cipher whose meaning has to do with the death-dealing qualities of whiteness itself. The zombie has been part-human, inhuman, slave, revolutionary, cannibal, monster, destroyer, and that which it is moral to destroy. Insofar as the zombie is a cipher, it can be cast to form any number of meaning-sets; it is always shifting signification and yet it can be said to hint at something of the original. After all, we all know what a zombie is.[30]

Does the general use of "voodoo," a historically specific term, as an adjective for all things bizarre render it inoffensive? Has the generality of the term drained its religious and racial specificity, disembedding it from a white supremacist economy of perception? Considering a history of pejorative constructions of voodoo—as the bizarre, zombie-infested religiosity of an Afro-descendant people—has the broad adjectival usage effectively produced the equivalent of radioactive decay in the religious and racial semiotics of the word, thus eliminating its toxic half-life? When we think voodoo in the first instance, is it the case that we no longer imagine and perceive black people negatively? These questions are apropos of all three tropes: frenzy, voodoo, and fetishism.

By way of comparison, consider another racialized religious trope, namely, "Jewing-down." Embedded in a history of Christian-inspired anti-Judaism, Jewishness, and anti-Semitism, this trope expresses the stereotypical notion that Jews are inordinately fond of money, will go to great lengths to acquire it, and part with it only grudgingly. It is hard to imagine under what scenario this trope might be regarded as having outlived its toxic effects. Critics might argue that the metaphor cluster of radioactivity, decay, and half-life do not apply to the concept. Despite its common use by older generations of Americans to describe "money-grubbing" people regardless of nationality, race, and ethnicity, it seems unlikely that many, upon reflection, would regard the term "Jewing-down" as inoffensive to Jews. Despite its general application, they would recognize the particularity of its signifying power as an anti-Semitic concept. The notion that the passage of time has, or ought to have, diminished the religious and racialized specificity of the trope would be vigorously contested. The fact that many Americans are inured to the "Washington Redskins" and the "Cleveland Indians" (as they once were to black "lawn jockeys" and the "little black sambos" that inhabited their curios) does not mean that they are not toxic locutions ensconced in a settler colonial way of life.[31] Other than the coloniality of power, the *colonial difference*, including the comparative social status of Jews and Haitians[32] within the international division of labor, power, and prestige, it is hard to see the logic underlying different perceptions regarding the use of "Jewing-down" and voodoo.[33]

Our exploration of the voodoo trope, with zombie as metonym, overlaps and interpenetrates the discourse of fetishism. Tropologically, fetishism operates like voodoo. Channeling the scholarly discourse regarding fetishism, Du Bois remarks: "The religion of Africa is the universal animism or fetishism of primitive peoples, rising to polytheism and approaching monotheism chiefly, but not wholly, as a result of Christian and Islamic missions. Of fetishism there is much misapprehension. It is not mere senseless degradation." On the contrary, fetishism is the life philosophy of primitive Negroes. He adds that primitive people do not divorce religion and practical life as civilized people commonly do. "Religion is life and fetish an expression of the practical recognition of dominant forces in which the Negro lives."[34] Fetishism is the most complicated of the tropes under consideration. We can hear Du Bois struggling with the concept in this passage. Marx revolutionized critical thinking with his notion of the fetishism of commodities. Alfred Binet and Freud revolutionized critical thinking a second time by applying the concept of fetishism to eroticized objects of desire. Popular understandings are almost exclusively of Freudian derivation. In the practice of "foot worship" (foot fetishism), we encounter an easily recognizable set piece in popular culture. It is a standard way of speaking about "deviant" forms of sexual desire. So when media outlets reported in late 2010 that Rex Ryan, the coach of the National Football League's New York Jets, and his wife engaged in foot-fetish eroticism, there was little need to explain to the reader what they meant.

The fetishizer is under the *spell* (Portuguese: *feitico*) of the foot—or any object that inspires desire, to which he attributes erotic powers. While the term can partially be traced to this Portuguese word, William Pietz argues that "fetishism" derives from a pidgin term, *Fetisso*, that emerged in the interspace created by the cross-cultural encounter between West Africans and Portuguese—that is, the term is not native to either culture.[35] Portuguese colonizers drew in part on invidious Arab representations of black Africa. They perceived African societies as burdened by a primitive, magical understanding of efficient causality, as chaotic, and as generally devoid of standard institutions of governance. Driven primarily by the desire for gold and commercial exchange, Europeans groped for a language that would allow them to make sense, as they saw it, of the African's disordered relation to materiality, spirituality, and economic value. To paraphrase Freud, where fetishism was, there European-style social institutions should have been. On this European view, rooted in Greek and Christian metaphysics of matter and spirit, the African sense of value was trifling. Africans valued the wrong things. They invested trivial material objects, "fetishes," with attributes they did not have—with social, economic, and spiritual value.[36] Under the medieval fourfold model of religion classification—Christianity, Judaism, Islam, and idolatry—African religions had long been relegated to the last category. Though obviously related, the practices called fetishism appeared to exceed the logic of this classification. Where Europeans construed an idol as "a freestanding statue representing a spiritual entity (a 'false god')," fetishes adorned the body, were regarded as embodying actual power, and through ritual practices were instrumental in achieving material ends.[37]

Seventeenth-century merchants wanted "a clean economic interaction"[38] with the Africans they encountered. Instead, they had to negotiate "social relations and quasi-religious ceremonies that should have been irrelevant to the conduct of trade."[39] On their view, perverse superstitions got in the way of a normal commercial relationship. Pietz claims that a "general theory of fetishism" emerged in the eighteenth century in response to this problematic and novel situation.[40] Within this theory, the "African fetish worshiper became the very image of the truth of 'unenlightenment,'"[41]—they personalize the impersonal, attributing sickness and death to supernatural malice; they spiritualize matter, attributing animate and anthropomorphic qualities to it; they confound religion and trade, where the former, "grounded in mercenary motives," is little more than the pursuit of the latter;[42] they eroticize social relations (is this the taproot of the nineteenth-century psychoanalytic appropriation of the concept?), injecting desire where it should not be, which explained African women's disposition to promiscuity.[43] On the view that Pietz derives from the writings of Bosman, "the religion of fetishes" undermines the spontaneity of natural market activities on which economic health and "a truly moral social order" depend.[44] In the absence of this market, priests of fetish religion exploited the superstitious masses. Though the priestly class operated from the same motives of rational self-interest that drove merchants, mercantilism was honest and moral by comparison.[45] Construed as superstitious and terror driven, the fetish-worshipping populace, standing metonymically for all Africans, embodies irrationality and absolute political abjection. The religion of fetishism undermines both autonomous subjectivity and the kind of politics suitable to a free people.[46] As Pietz remarks earlier in the essay, the slavishness attributed to the fetish worshiper, their infantile, unenlightened submission to heteronomous authority, dovetailed with the transatlantic enslavement of Africans.[47]

Marx appropriated this Enlightenment and post-Enlightenment usage. His "theory of commodity fetishism describes how objects appear to be autonomous and independent of the human subject."[48] Like agents with intentionality, commodities appear to have social relations. Thus, fetishism refers to the "social properties of material things."[49] Working within the constructivist tradition of Feuerbach, where God is alienated (externalized) human subjectivity, Marx discovers the same alienation in our perception of commodities: we misattribute our social relations as workers to the commodities we produce. Whether g/God[50] or commodities, there is a misattribution of human relations and powers to objects of human mental and physical labor. As Christopher Wise remarks: "A commodity fetish is often an object from which all evidence of human labor has been erased, which is why it is easy to mistakenly project autonomy upon it. In the end, however, the commodity is made by human beings and is hardly independent from those who made it."[51]

Can we save Marx and Marxism from complicity with the propagation of a colonial trope and a history of pejorative use? Perhaps we can. Under a construction that might save them, fetishizing is not some prelogical atavism. Rather, it is a necessary mode of human perception, the social psychology "of commodity production systems" that forces people to attribute inherent rather than relational properties to material things.[52] My desire to disassociate Marxism from the pejorative history of the trope arises from the fact that fetishism names something that needs to be named. The requirements of critical thinking demand that the phenomena that Marx names the "fetishism of commodities" be disclosed. So my critique of the fetishism trope should not be confused with the assertion that we ignore the phenomena it describes. Describing the phenomena is a critical necessity; using fetishism as descriptor is not. The argument against fetishism as descriptor should be juxtaposed to the claim that the phenomena described is "a necessary mode of human perception." This argument from psychological necessity is not the standard reading of the theory. Even if we assert that this reading should be the standard—that phenomena described as commodity fetishism should be understood as necessary in a commodity-producing system, that its association with pejorative perceptions of African people is contingent and not necessary—there is still the question of why Marx glommed onto this racialized religious trope in the first place. He had other tropological resources ready to hand. What did this trope enable him to do that Feuerbach's notions of alienation, externalization, and projection did not? However we answer this question, the Marxist tradition bears heavy responsibility for the dissemination of a colonial trope that constructs African-descended people as archetypical fetishizers. Marxist discourse reproduced this culturally dominant perception.

Marxist uses of the fetishism trope were soon joined and quickly superseded by psychological appropriations. Alfred Binet introduced the trope in 1887, and Freud's short essay of 1927 stereotyped usage. Under Freud's psychoanalytic interpretation, the fetish, prototypically, is a penis substitute.[53] The fetish protects the male subject from his fear of castration. Or, as subsequent psychoanalytic theories suggest, fetishism arises from, among other causes, early childhood anxiety triggered by separation from the mother, humiliation by parents, attachment to a transitional object, or feelings of sexual inadequacy.[54] As the displaced object of desire, sexual fetishism, prototypically, presents as foot worship. If African fetishizers mistakenly attributed spiritual significance to material objects and commodity fetishizers perceived economic objects as having social relations independent of human agency, then sexual fetishizers constructed feet, other discrete body parts, or inanimate entities of various kinds as sexual objects. In all three cases, fetishism is constructed as lack: deficient knowledge of natural causation, absence of critical insight, a misdirected form of sexual desire.

Thus far, I have argued that religious and racial uses of the fetishism trope rooted in the colonial encounter continue to signify in Marxist- and psychoanalytic-inflected discourses. Drawing on psychoanalytic uses of the trope, Nina Cornyetz explores the fetishizing of blackness in contemporary Japanese culture. She refers specifically to skin color, hair styles, and hip-hop modes of bodily comportment, the metonymic association of black males and the phallus, and the way these features continue to signify in post–World War II Okinawa. She remarks: "To possess the black phallus is to wield the weapon that threatens white masculinity; a black phallus affixed to the Japanese body would invert the "feminization" imposed by the occupation troops."[55] Fetishizing blackness is a way of recreating Japanese identity and reasserting masculine agency after military defeat and occupation by a white-identified United States. In appropriating blackness, the Japanese express an erotic desire for the black male body and its imagined capabilities *and* thereby reproduce a history of antiblack perception.[56] They rearticulate the old association of black people with primitive sensuality and sexuality. Along with the construction of African fetishism as primitive religion, the attribution of inordinate sexual desire and prowess constitutes the common ancestry of the psychoanalytic fetishism that Cornyetz describes and the commodity fetishism that Marx discerns in his critique of capitalist political economy. Through the appropriation of hip-hop culture as capitalist commodity and of blackness as a psychoanalytic object of erotic desire, the Japanese marry the dominant modes of fetishism discourse. In each case, fetishizing refers to an atavistic developmental mode of human perception associated, archetypically, in theories of religion, with people of African descent.

One critic suggests that "fetishism has itself become a fetish," a cultural objectification and representation that we no longer control and that conceals as much as it reveals.[57] This observation supports my claim that fetishism, like frenzy and voodoo, signifies in ways that conceal its colonial origins in the encounter with and subjugation of African people and that mystify the ongoing operations of the coloniality of power. As an example, I wish to consider briefly an essay that I admire: Jon Goss's "Once-Upon-a-Time in the Commodity World: An Unofficial to Guide to Mall of America." Regarding fetishism, Goss provides some useful distinctions: the anthropological sense of animating the object world, "the psychoanalytical sense of displacing and condensing repressed desire," and the Marxist sense where the commodity is "severed from its relations of production and distribution" and haloed with authenticity and innocence.[58] Though I share most of his intuitions and conclusions, I shall offer a negative observation regarding his use of fetishism. I hope readers do not interpret my comment as a "gotcha" remark. Though meaningful distinctions can be made between particular cases, we are all complicit in perpetuating the use of colonial tropes. This *discursive guilt*, so to speak, where we find ourselves having already spoken before understanding the conditions (positionality) of that speech, is the import of my earlier remark about my unthinking use of "Siamese twins." With this point in mind, I cannot resist remarking on the way that Goss's careful analysis of the many forms of fetishism in the Mall of America reproduces the very phenomena it describes. Goss describes the way that the mall expresses an imperial nostalgia and reduces colonialism to a fashion show through stores such as Banana Republic and Timbuktu Station. He notes that stores such as Pueblo Spirit, Rainforest, Congo Mogambo, and Rasta Pasta fetishize the past and the exotic.[59] Yet he does not remark on the fact that the analytic category of fetishism itself is a contaminated product of a colonial encounter. Goss conflates sexual fetishism and commodity fetishism and constructs both as simultaneously denying and affirming "the lack of the real" but does not remark upon that lack of the real that European observers *discovered* in the religious practices of African people.[60] If the Mall of America exhibits imperial nostalgia, then Goss's use of fetishism pulls a veil of imperial forgetfulness over its own conditions of emergence, over the colonial encounter between European Christian and traditional African religionist. Goss's forgetfulness regarding the coloniality of fetishism—its relation to the transatlantic subjugation of African people— parallels my thoughtless use of Siamese twins. It shows how deeply colonial tropes have insinuated themselves into everyday speech.

Like frenzy and voodoo, fetishism is subject to question. Does this trope have a radioactive half-life? Should it have a half-life? Has the widespread use of the term in Marxist and psychoanalytic discourses effectively severed the trope from the conditions of its historical emergence—colonialism, white supremacy, and the association of Africa, in modern theories of religion, with the most primitive (childlike, heteronomous, and prelogical) stage of human development? Does common usage detoxify the effects of these historical conditions and associations? Does fetishism function differently than Jewing down? Is there an innocent use of the trope? Or is the trope haunted by the afterlife of denigrating perceptions of African-descended people? As with frenzy and voodoo, these rhetorical questions signal my conclusions regarding fetishism.

## COLONIALITY AND THE RELIGIOUS-SECULAR CONTINUUM

In this chapter, I advanced a claim regarding the secular afterlife of three racialized religious tropes: frenzy, voodoo, and fetishism. Of the three, the evidence is weakest for frenzy. It is easiest to make the case regarding voodoo. Fetishism is the most complicated of the three owing to the specificity of its history as an object of Marxist and psychoanalytic discourses. Marxism and psychoanalysis *reoccupied* this colonial notion. Reoccupation is Hans Blumenberg's term for the discursive practice of resignifying culturally significant paradigms. For example, the modern notion of progress reoccupies the medieval Christian concept of "a providentially guided 'story of salvation.'"[61] The secular reoccupation of fetishism may very well have distanced the trope from its pejorative racial uses. To understand this possibility, consider the minstrel tradition, the most popular form of entertainment in the second half of the nineteenth century,[62] in which white performers in blackface lampooned the lives and manners of black people. Taking common stereotypes to the extreme, they depicted black people as foolish, lazy, happy, and harmless darkies who pine for the good ole days of plantation slavery. As depicted, black people had an inordinate love of fried chicken and watermelon and would resort to thievery to get them. The burnt cork they used to blacken their faces was designed to exaggerate the facial features of black people in the most cartoonish fashion. In the iconography of the time that corresponded to depictions on stage, black people had jet-black skin, humongous ruby-red lips, a wide toothy grin, and bulging eyes that appear ready to explode.[63] The white minstrel tradition flourished during a turbulent period that encompassed the last decades of slavery, the Civil War and Reconstruction, and the mass violence and terror against free black people—racial cleansing, white riots,[64] and lynching—that defined the Nadir (1880–1940). White minstrelsy was an exercise in nostalgia that construed the lives of black people as carefree and made it impossible to take their actual lives and interests seriously. In this construction of primitive freedom, there was a good time to be had, and that was the point.[65] Black minstrelsy is black people acting like white people acting like black people.[66] At its best, black minstrelsy signifies on white minstrelsy, cleverly and ironically undermining its worst excesses and creating a space of freedom.[67] If black minstrelsy reproduced and transcended the stereotypes of white minstrelsy, then twentieth- and twenty-first-century black comedic traditions reproduce and transcend black minstrelsy. However ambivalent the relationship, these traditions are rooted in black minstrelsy. Whether the subject is Lincoln Perry (Stepin Fetchit), Jimmy Walker (J. J. Evans Jr. a.k.a Kid Dy-No-Mite), William J. Drayton Jr. (Flavor Flav), or Tyler Perry (Madea), black audiences disagree bitterly about the manner in which black comedians represent the race. Their comedic genius produces a carefree space of creative freedom by transcending the worst stereotypes. But their minstrel-derived routines also undermine the dignity of black people by reproducing those stereotypes.

It may be the case that the secular reoccupation of colonial tropes works in an analogous manner, both reproducing and transcending imperial scorn. One thing is clear: secular discourse did not kill these tropes. It gave them a second life, an expanded and endlessly productive life. Rooted in a colonial relation, in Europeans' pejorative construction of African people and their religion, fetishism is so firmly ensconced in the discourse that it is hard to imagine things otherwise. I can hear people now, across the ideological spectrum, rejecting the implications of my critique. I am reminded of Daniel Snyder, the owner of the Washington Redskins, who vowed never to change the team's name. He dismissed any concern about redskins as a racist slur by citing the "great tradition and what it's all about and what it means."[68] We only know too well what he means. He doesn't mind the racist connotations, and Indians don't matter.[69] Snyder's comments tell us who does and does not count as a subject of honor and respect. This fact cannot be separated from the ongoing reality of the coloniality of power, the national and international division of labor, power, and prestige. With this claim in mind, I attempted to answer the question of how frenzy, voodoo, and fetishism signify now. In their secular incarnations, did they cease being racialized religious tropes? I conclude that they did not. Even though these tropes transcend their colonial constructions, they continue to signify on African-descended people in pejorative ways. In this regard, they are like black minstrelsy. Fetish, voodoo, frenzy, bulging eyes, watermelon rinds scooped clean, step and fetch that chicken, Jump Jim Crow, dance.

## CONCLUSION

Frenzy, fetish, and voodoo are racialized religious tropes associated with African-descended people. Historically, they derive from transatlantic slave trafficking and colonial encounters between black people and white people, respectively, in the United States, West Africa, and Haiti. These tropes construct black people as deficient (abnormal) with respect to the putative white norm of rationality, self-possession, and control. Black people prototypically are slaves to their passions, and this captivity expresses itself in ecstatic religious practices: emotionally unhinged (frenzied) bodily expressions, the inability to properly distinguish objects from agents (fetishism), and bizarre ideas (voodoo) about the living dead.[70] This religiously expressed deficiency in rationality and self-control flows naturally into all kinds of riotous behavior, especially criminality.

This analysis channels divergent streams that converge and pool around a singular logic: the logic of sublation, the German *Aufhebung*, where a set of racialized religious tropes is simultaneous negated, preserved, and elevated within secular coloniality. Rather than detoxifying the tropes of frenzy, fetish, and voodoo, secular coloniality has only generalized their poisonous effects. There is a willful amnesia regarding these tropes, much like "redskins," the historical reference of which, according to one source, is the red appearance of "the mutilated and bloody corpses" left behind by scalp-hunting Indian killers.[71] Redskin refers graphically to a genocidal practice: a redskin is a dead Indigenous American. A popular nineteenth-century aphorism captures this reality in a pithy formula: "the only good Indian is a dead Indian." Amnesia notwithstanding, redskins are an iconic sign of genocide. Thus the tropological careers of frenzy, fetish, and voodoo expose the defect of any claim that religion and secularity are radically distinct. The history of these tropes undermines the notion that the secular order represents a fundamental emancipation from the powers and practices of religious order, that a *cordon sanitaire*, a decontaminated zone, separates the two. Conversely, this analysis challenges forms of postsecularist thinking that attempt to relocate and quarantine colonialism and other disagreeable practices within secular spacetime. Where racial tropes are concerned, religious and secular practices are two sides of the same colonial reality.

## NOTES

1. David Spurr, *The Rhetoric of Empire: Colonial Discourse in Journalism, Travel Writing, and Imperial Administration* (Durham, N.C.: Duke University Press, 1994).
2. For a similar view, see Martin Marty, "Our Religious-Secular World," *Daedalus* 132, no. 3 (2003): 42–48.
3. See David Chidester, *Savage Systems: Colonialism and Comparative Religion in Southern Africa* (Charlottesville: University of Virginia Press, 1996).
4. Originally published in 1965, E. E. Evans-Pritchard, *Theories of Primitive Religion* (New York: Oxford University Press, 1968), is a classic example.

5. William Pietz, "The Problem of the Fetish, I," *RES: Anthropology and Aesthetics* 9 (1985): 5.

6. Laurent Dubois, *Haiti: The Aftershocks of History* (New York: Metropolitan, 2012), 296.

7. Ibid., 298.

8. W. E. B. Du Bois, *The Souls of Black Folk* (New York: Vintage, 1990), 137–138.

9. Cornel West, *The Cornel West Reader* (New York: Basic Civitas Books, 1999), 91.

10. Jonathon S. Kahn, *Divine Discontent: The Religious Imagination of W. E. B. Du Bois* (New York: Oxford University Press, 2009), 55–56.

11. Edward Wilmot Blyden, *Christianity, Islam, and the Negro Race* (Edinburgh: Edinburgh University Press, 1967), 6.

12. See Richard McGregor, "Zhou's Cryptic Caution Lost in Translation," *Financial Times* (June 10, 2011).

13. Donald H. Matthews, *Honoring the Ancestors: An African Cultural Interpretation of Black Religion and Literature* (New York: Oxford University Press, 1998). "For DuBois, these three features of the preacher, the music, and the frenzy constitute the major features of African American religion. All are descendants of African traditional religion. DuBois even goes so far as to relate the frenzy to the ancient oracular manifestations of Delphi and Endor. This placed frenzy—probably the most 'heathenish' feature of African American religion—on a par with classical religious expressions and gave an elegant status to a much-maligned feature of black religion" (55). "What Du Bois calls 'the Frenzy' refers to the call-and-response of the black service, the 'Shouting.' This might be a low murmur from somewhere in the pews or a scream, entail clapping or stomping, even a 'wild waving of arms.' Always ready to historicize, Du Bois notes that this behavior was nothing new, reaching as far back as Delphi or Endor." Jay Parini, "*The Souls of Black Folk*: A Book That Changed America," *Journal of Blacks in Higher Education* 62 (Winter 2008/2009): 72–80. Referring to the preaching style of a 1930s Chicago preacher he calls "Reverend F," which combined appeals to reason and emotion, Wallace Best remarks: "As a mixed-type sermon progressed, the minister moved from text to extemporaneous speaking, the volume of his voice rising steadily. Decorum would soon be cast aside as he worked himself, and at least a portion of the congregation, to an emotional frenzy." Wallace D. Best, *Passionately Human, No Less Divine: Religion and Culture in Black Chicago, 1915–1952* (Princeton, N.J.: Princeton University Press, 2005), 97. David Levering Lewis construes Du Bois and those for whom he spoke as follows: "Alienated as blacks often were by what seemed the desiccating conventions of whiteness but also by the irrational frenzy of black religion, Du Bois exhorted them, nevertheless, to cherish the ceremonializing of 'Birth, Death, Pain, Mating, Children, Age.' Ever and anon we must point to these truths," he insisted. David L. Lewis, *W. E. B. Du Bois: The Fight for Equality and the American Century, 1919–1963* (New York: Henry Holt and Company, 2000), 222. According to Jonathon Kahn, "The 'Frenzy' turns into a rendering of religion as the place where the community—black folk—conducts moral, aesthetic, and civic business." Jonathon Kahn, *Divine Discontent: The Religious Imagination of W. E. B. Du Bois* (New York: Oxford University Press, 2009), 59. By wedding frenzy to these activities Kahn effectively decontaminates the trope.

14. For an excellent survey of the topic, see Lee D. Baker, *From Savage to Negro: Anthropology and the Construction of Race, 1896–1954* (Berkeley: University of California Press, 1998).

15. David Levering Lewis, *W. E. B. Du Bois: Biography of a Race* (New York: Henry Holt, 1993).

16. See "Part Two: The Repressive Hypothesis," in Michel Foucault, *The History of Sexuality*, vol. 1: *An Introduction* (New York: Vintage, 1990).

17. Victor Wolfenstein, *The Gift of the Spirit: Reading* The Souls of Black Folk (Ithaca, N.Y.: Cornell University Press, 2007), 98.

18. Rebecca Carroll, *Saving the Race: Conversations About Du Bois from a Collective Memoir of Souls* (New York: Harlem Moon, 2004), 175.

19. Geraldo Marti, *Worship Across the Racial Divide: Religious Music and the Multiracial Congregation* (New York: Oxford University Press, 2012), 52–53, 58–60.

20. Amy Wilentz, *Farewell Fred Voodoo: A Letter from Haiti* (New York: Simon and Schuster, 2013), 91.

21. Ibid., 96.

22. Ibid., 96–97.

23. Charles H. Long, *Significations: Signs, Symbols, and Images in the Interpretation of Religion* (Philadelphia: Fortress, 1986), 90.

24. Elizabeth McAlister, "Slaves, Cannibals, and Infected Hyper-Whites: The Race and Religion of Zombies," *Anthropological Quarterly* 85, no. 2 (2012): 457–486.

25. Kenneth Burke, *The Rhetoric of Religion: Studies in Logology* (Berkeley: University of California Press, 1970), 25–26.

26. McAlister, "Slaves, Cannibals, and Infected Hyper-Whites," 477–480.

27. Ibid., 461. She cites Michael Taussig's influential essay "Culture of Terror—Space of Death: Roger Casement's Putumayo Report and the Explanation of Torture," *Comparative Studies in Society and History* 26, no. 3 (1984): 467–497.

28. McAlister, "Slaves, Cannibals, and Infected Hyper-Whites," 464–465.

29. Ibid., 468–469.

30. Ibid., 483.

31. By way of preemption, let me say that the utterance "political correctness" is the piggish squeal of the bigot held accountable for his bigotry. The bigot inverts the meaning of the occasion and presents himself as the victim of other people's resistance to the plain truth or construes them as lacking a sense of humor.

32. I recognize that Jews and Haitians are overlapping categories whose members interpenetrate.

33. To be clear, I am not referring to "voodoo" as the name of Haiti's African-based religion but to a construction of that religion and its adherents that transforms the word into a trope for anything that the (white) observer regards as bizarre.

34. W. E. B. Du Bois, *The Gift of Black Folk: The Negro in the Making of America* (New York: Oxford University Press, 2007), 119. Regarding the scholarly consensus, compare Du Bois's remarks to those of Joseph Thomson in 1887: "Fetishism is a tremendous power throughout Africa, and cannot be put down by ridicule or contempt. We look at their fetish charms

and wonder how people can be so foolish, but these are but outward signs of what is of immense significance to the unfortunate native." Joseph Thomson, "Note on the African Tribes of the British Empire," *Journal of the Anthropological Institute of Great Britain and Ireland* 16 (1887): 182.

35. Pietz, "The Problem of the Fetish, I," 5.
36. William Pietz, "The Problem of the Fetish, II: The Origin of the Fetish," *RES: Anthropology and Aesthetics* 13 (1987): 41–42.
37. Ibid., 36.
38. Ibid., 45.
39. Ibid.
40. Ibid.
41. William Pietz, "The Problem of the Fetish, IIIa: Bosman's Guinea and the Enlightenment Theory of Fetishism," *RES: Anthropology and Aesthetics* 16 (1988): 106.
42. Ibid., 117.
43. Ibid., 112.
44. Ibid., 121.
45. Ibid.
46. Ibid., 119.
47. Ibid., 112.
48. Christopher Wise, "Saying 'Yes' to Africa: Jacques Derrida's *Specters of Marx*," *Research in African Literatures* 33, no. 4 (2002): 130.
49. Haskell Lewin and Jacob Morris "Marx's Concept of Fetishism," *Science & Society* 41, no. 2 (1977): 188.
50. This neologism refers to "gods and God."
51. Wise, "Saying 'Yes' to Africa," 130.
52. Lewin and Morris, "Marx's Concept of Fetishism," 173.
53. Sigmund Freud, "Fetishism," in *Miscellaneous Papers, 1888–1938*, vol. 5 of *Collected Papers* (London: Hogarth Press and Institute of Psycho-Analysis, 1924–1950), 198–204. Regarding the politics of fetishism and debates concerning dildo use among lesbians, an observer remarks that "Critics of the dildo claim that it is a penis replacement, and its proponents claim that it is not." See Heather Findlay, "Freud's 'Fetishism' and the Lesbian Dildo Debates," *Feminist Studies* 18, no. 3, "The Lesbian Issue" (1992): 563–579.
54. D. Richard Laws and William T. O'Donohue, *Sexual Deviance: Theory, Assessment, and Treatment* (New York: Guilford, 2008), 115.
55. Nina Cornyetz, "Fetishized Blackness: Hip Hop and Racial Desire in Contemporary Japan," *Social Text*, no. 41 (1994): 124.
56. Cornyetz, "Fetishized Blackness," 126–127.
57. Robert Pool, "Fetishism Deconstructed," *Etnofoor* 3, no. 1, "Fetishism" (1990): 125.
58. Jon Goss, "Once-Upon-a-Time in the Commodity World: An Unofficial Guide to Mall of America," *Annals of the Association of American Geographers* 89, no. 1 (1999): 47.
59. Ibid., 64–65.

60. Ibid., 70.

61. See Hans Blumenberg, *The Legitimacy of the Modern Age*, trans. Robert M. Wallace (Cambridge, Mass.: MIT Press, 1983), 15.

62. Yuval Taylor and Jake Austen, *Darkest America: Black Minstrelsy from Slavery to Hip-Hop* (New York: Norton, 2012), 4.

63. Ibid., 12, 39.

64. I use the locution "white riot" because the word riot has been stereotyped as a black phenomenon at least since the 1960s uprisings in Detroit and Newark. There are two important points to be made about riots. So-called black riots occur almost exclusively within segregated black neighborhoods. Those who die are predominantly black. In contrast, white riots have explicitly been antiblack riots. They entail the invasion and destruction of black neighborhoods. They entail the murder of black people by both private citizens and the police powers of the state. The scale of destruction in both lives and property is greater. Unlike so-called black riots, white rioters are rarely assailed by the police powers of the state when they attack black people. Indeed, they are often abetted. The leading examples of white riots are the New York City Draft Riot (1864), the Wilmington, North Carolina, Riot (1898), the Tulsa, Oklahoma, Riot (1921), the Rosewood, Florida Riot (1923). See http://digital.library.okstate.edu/encyclopedia/entries/t/tuo13-.html; http://www.history.ncdcr.gov/1898-wrrc/report/report.htm; Sheila Smith McKoy, *When Whites Riot: Writing Race and Violence in American and South African Culture* (Madison: University of Wisconsin Press, 2001). One scholar puts the matter thus: "From individual lynchings to sustained violence against entire black communities, whites in both the North and South lashed out against black Americans in a ferocious and often calculated manner during the years 1917 to 1923. Aided by a federal government that refused to intervene to protect the life and property of black citizens, whites took whatever steps they felt were necessary to keep blacks in the place. From Chicago to Tulsa, to Omaha, East St. Louis, and many communities in between, and finally to Rosewood, Florida, white mobs, often in alliance with law enforcement officials, made clear their determination to deny blacks the rights and privileges accorded whites. Much, but certainly not all, of the violence in the South took the form of individual lynchings. By contrast, racial tensions in the North typically erupted into lawless outbursts by white mobs against entire black neighborhoods. Rosewood more closely paralleled the violence in the North." David R. Colburn, "Rosewood and America in the Early Twentieth Century," *Florida Historical Quarterly* 76, no. 2 (1997): 178.

65. Yuval and Austen, *Darkest America*, 8, 45, 66.

66. Ibid., 49.

67. Ibid., 6, 12, 27.

68. http://www.usatoday.com/story/sports/nfl/redskins/2013/05/09/washington-redskins-daniel-snyder/2148127.

69. Here I signify on the comments of the civil rights leader Charles Sherrod, a member of the SNCC during the Albany Movement in Georgia. Arriving in 1961, SNCC activists sought to organize the black community. "CHARLES SHERROD: I remember a statement that

Chief Pritchett made to me one time when he said, 'You know Sherrod, it's just a matter of mind over matter. I don't mind and you don't matter.'" http://www.pbs.org/wgbh/amex /eyesontheprize/about/pt_104.html.

70. As I do another round of editing for this article, I read a notice from the Office of the Dean of Students and the Office of Campus Activities and Programs at the University of North Carolina Greensboro: from October 16 to 23 students will be playing the game *Zombies Versus Humans.* According to the game's website, http://humansvszombies.org/, "Humans vs. Zombies is a game of tag played at schools, camps, neighborhoods, libraries, and conventions around the world. Human players must remain vigilant and defend themselves with socks and dart blasters to avoid being tagged by a growing zombie horde." This game underscores the argument I make. As the students frolic, there is an immense forgetfulness of the historical enslavement of people of African descent. But Haitians did not forget. Rather, they imagined slaveholder capitalism, colonialism, and white supremacy as a zombie-producing machine. No coloniality of power, no zombies.

71. Roxanne Dunbar-Ortiz, *An Indigenous People's History of the United States* (Boston: Beacon, 2014), 65.

# 8

# BINDING LANDSCAPES

## SECULARISM, RACE, AND THE SPATIAL MODERN

Willie James Jennings

**W**HERE IS secular space, and what are secular bodies? These questions angle at a peculiar relation, one that has not been sufficiently explored by intellectuals concerned with the question of secularity: the relation between space, race, and the secularizing operation.[1] The places I look to think through these questions are the sites where Christian thought and practice gave rise to colonial thought and practice and haunt modern thought and practice or, more precisely, where our thought and practice about space perform a secular modernity haunted by theology itself. This essay outlines the emergence of what I call the spatial modern, which is an aspect of secularity that remains concealed from most philosophical, theological, or historical treatments of secularism. I will outline this emergence not by offering a detailed history of its beginnings, growth, and expansion but rather by considering a Christian intellectual of the early colonial period whose writings expose the overturning of an indigenous world and the transformation of space and body. That transformation is precisely what is at issue because it constitutes an imperial enlightenment of sorts before the European Enlightenments and a Kantian-like rejection of transindividual authority long before the birth of Immanuel Kant. My point here is not to lodge an earlier enlightenment than conventional history or locate a pre-Kantian Kant; rather, I seek to expose the geographic dimensions of the secular, dimensions that are decisive for understanding secularism as a set of spatial and bodily practices formed inside a Christian theological architecture.

# THE COLONIAL AND CHRISTIAN CLAIM OF SPACE

I want to track a moment of discovery that is not the discovery of the new worlds by proto-European colonialists but a far more real and decisive discovery for them, the discovery of the demonic and of a new world that was in fact an old world, a fallen world. This was a world not simply with demonic influence but one in a fundamental way controlled by demons. The missionaries, merchants, and soldiers who came to the new worlds of the Americas shared a common narrative of the world beyond salvific closure, that is, beyond Christendom. Such a world awaited redemption in the form of deliverance from the evil one. As they entered the new worlds and confronted an overwhelming epistemological density of peoples, languages, animals, and the sheer power of these new landscapes, their deepest suspicion and greatest fear were realized. This was indeed the world signified by scripture, a world lost to demonic possession. What would be necessary in such a world was exorcism, eradication, and extirpation.

The work that lay ahead for the merchant, missionary, and soldier was to transition the new spaces from one reality of possession to another, from spirit possession to Christian possession. That transition marked a moment for the emergence of something we might call empty space, space in between the false gods of the New World and the Christian God now claiming that world. Along with this in-between space are bodies-in-between. These are bodies moving from spirit possession to being properly contained, even possessed, in a new, more lasting way. The conceptual groundwork for this lay in the emergence of a particular way of viewing the material world and a flexible new way of deploying a Christian doctrine of creation. We can see an example of this in the work of the Jesuit theologian José de Acosta, missionary to Peru in the 1570s. From him we gain the stark account of the providence of possession in his infamous *hija fea* (ugly daughter) analogy. But he also shows us something quite innovative. I quote at length here:

> The wisdom of God created metals for medicine and for defense and for adornment and as instruments of men's activities. We could easily give examples of all four of these uses, but the chief object of metals is the last of them; for human life requires not mere survival, like the life of beasts, but

must also be lived according to the capacity and reason bestowed on it by the Creator. And thus, just as man's intelligence extends to different arts and faculties, the Author of all things also provided it with materials of different kinds for man's investigation and for security and ornament and a great number of activities. Such is the diversity of metals that the creator enclosed in the storage places and hollows of the earth that all of them are useful for human life. . . . But above all these uses, which are simple and natural, communication among men resulted in the use of money . . . and although by its nature it is but one thing, actually it is all things, for money represents food and clothing and shelter, mounts to ride on, and everything of which men have need. And so all things obey money. . . . For this invention, that of making one thing serve for all things, men . . . chose the most durable and negotiable thing of all, which is metal. And among the metals they decided that those whose nature was most durable and incorruptible, namely silver and gold, must have primacy in the invention of money . . .

But it is a circumstance worthy of much consideration that the wisdom of our Eternal Lord has enriched the most remote parts of the world, inhabited by the most uncivilized people, and has placed there the greatest number of mines that ever existed, in order to invite men to seek out and possess those lands and coincidentally to communicate their religion and the worship of the true God to men who do not know it. Thus the prophesy of Isaiah has been fulfilled that the Church shall pass on to the right hand and the left which is as Saint Augustine declares, the way the Gospel must be propagated, not only by those who preach it sincerely and with charity but also by those who proclaim it through temporal and human aims and means. Hence we see that the lands of the Indies that are richest in mines and wealth have been those most advanced in the Christian religion in our time; and thus the Lord takes advantage of our desires to serve his sovereign ends. In this regard a wise man once said that what a man does to marry off an ugly daughter is give her a large dowry; this is what God has done with that rugged land, endowing it with great wealth in mines so that whoever wished could find it by this means. Hence there is great abundance of mines in the Indies, mines of every metal.[2]

Acosta theorized that we can see the hand of providence in the time of Spanish conquest. God had prepared this new land (in his case, Peru) and its people for intercourse with the Spanish by filling the land with abundance of every kind of metal in order to draw them to the work of possession, possession of land and people for Christ. This seduction by the divine is inside the more fundamental recognition for Acosta that the material world is first and foremost a resource. This is an Aristotelian-Thomist vision of the creation, in which the world should be seen in its potential, a potential that humanity has been ordained to draw out. The land of the New World in this vision is filled with metals placed there by God for the continuing cultivation of human civilization. Acosta offers us a powerful theological rationale for the symbolic logic of currency and, by direct implication, for the logic of a global extraction of the natural resources of peoples' lands.

Money is one (material) thing, but it actually is all things, Acosta argues. As he states, "All things obey money" ("*Y así obedece todo al dinero*").[3] Money holds an imperial position similar to God in facilitating growth and life by moving things from their potentiality to their actuality, that is, their full utilization in producing goods and services. Money is the invention that facilitates invention, and the inner logic of money is metal. God has placed metals, these crucial seeds of growth, in remote parts of the world in order to draw God's servants (in this case the Spanish) to places and peoples beyond their imagination—but not beyond their possession. The vision of the new world in Acosta's theology is one of commodity. The New World is a constellation of inert materials that exist in potential and that should be turned into something else, something useful.

On the one hand, such a vision is consistent with an ancient Christian trajectory of reading the world against idolatry. That way of reading the world resists any communicative character to nature other than a reflective character. Nature reflects the glory of God and the glorification of humanity in its proper uses. This trajectory demystifies land, landscape, and animals. They do not communicate with us in any substantive sense. Yet on the other hand, Acosta gives us something innovative. He deepens and expands the sense of distance between bodies and environment. Here the sense of remoteness of the New World from the Old World played inside his sense of native bodies moving on top of raw materials, neither close to the developed Spanish bodies or the built environment of Spain. Acosta did recognize some development and built environs in the New World, but these were beside the crucial point, which was that indigenes fundamentally misunderstood their proper relation to the material world and therefore were easily tricked by Satan into its worship, into idolatry. The demonic permeated the New World, in Acosta's view, because it was empty space and ripe for occupation by evil spirits.

Acosta understood that only through divine seduction could God bring about the holy deliverance of human creatures from Satan's grasp. Indeed, Acosta surmised the demonic in Andean societies first through the entrance of the devil himself into the New World, having been driven from the old by the power of the gospel and the presence of the church:

> And, employing the same tyranny, after the might of the Gospel defeated and disarmed him . . . he attacked the most remote and savage peoples, attempting to preserve among them the false and lying divinity that the Son of God had wrested from him in his church . . . once idolatry was rooted out of the best and noblest part of the world, the devil retired to the most remote places and reigned in that other part of the world, which, although it is very inferior in nobility, is not so in size and breadth.[4]

Knowing that the devil had traveled to the New World, the next task confronting the Christian colonizer was the discernment of the demonic precisely in the material arrangements of the new world. Acosta surmised that the demonic was at play in the performance of idolatry, that is, in the production and worship of false gods. He categorized idolatry into two types: those having to do with naturally occurring things in the world, such as lakes, mountains, and landscapes, and, second, those things "imagined or fabricated by human ingenuity."[5] Discernment of the demonic became a compelling heuristic through which to interpret Andean societies and the Amerindian body.

Acosta, like other theologians in the New World, deployed an Aristotelian-Thomist logic that would provide the modus operandi for the extirpation of idolatry. If the devil and the demonic were in full play and full power in the New World, how were they to be discerned? The answer to this question, as Sabine MacCormack noted in her groundbreaking work on these matters, was the use of the same reasoning that explained the Eucharist. "An object's accidents, its external appearance, could conceptually be separated from its substance, from what the object really was," and this insight illuminated precisely how "the demons and the devil were capable of playing havoc with human sense perception by deluding it with illusory images."[6] Intellection stood on such shaky ground, ground subject to deception, because just as "God could exploit this disjuncture between accidents and substance, appearance and reality, in the material universe, so could the devil."[7] Eucharistic logic in this moment resourced the optic for reading native life. More decisively, the confidence of divine presence in and with the Eucharistic elements fueled the confidence in reading the demonic at play in the Amerindian body and in the Andean world. MacCormack explains this reading strategy:

> Demonic power was recognizable in rituals not practiced by the Catholic Church, in authority not defined by canonical texts, and in experts lacking Catholic approval. However, the mode of describing and analyzing things divine and things demonic was one and the same. Because demons acted in the same human and natural universe as God, it followed that they obeyed the same psychological and physical laws. There was thus no need to devise a distinct vocabulary of otherness or difference with which to describe religious phenomena and experiences beyond or to one side of the Catholic Church in Spain.[8]

Acosta not only made powerful use of this discerning mode of the demonic but also launched what would become an innovation in theological anthropology. He gave an account of native being that would calibrate demonic influence to native intellectual and cultural maturity or immaturity, which in turn would be registered by analyses of native rituals, practice, behavior, language, governmental structure, and so forth.[9] Yet the discernment turned on how the indigenes understood land, landscape, animals, and the materials of the world. If they imagined them endowed with spiritual presence and spiritual power, or if they imagined themselves as inextricably bound in identity and existence to specific places, lands, or animals, this was clearly a sign of demonic influence mixed with sheer ignorance of the actual nature of the material world. This harbinger of the ethnographic gaze yielded sight of a clear coordination: the demonic in the people and the demonic in the land.

The answer to this coordination was simple: break the connection of the people to the land by breaking open their arrangements with space and animals as well as their built environs, thereby breaking open the connection of the people to the demonic. For Acosta, the land, the earth, was God's creation, but in its deepest sense the land was raw material, and because it was a divinely placed resource for the production of capital, the world read from the new site of the colonial space would yield a profoundly distorted Christian doctrine of creation. It would be stripped down to one primary angle of thought: possession. God created the world as possession for humanity, and it is a possession to be realized through the church. Possession is thus a redemptive work that pulls the New World from its chaos and disorder and draws it toward its proper meanings and uses.

What would be required in the New World is transformation, or as some Andeans would call it, *Pachacuti* (upheaval). This would be the transformation of the world that for intellectuals like Acosta would set the world on its proper course. The reordering of a fallen social order deeply influenced by the demonic required that any existing social form and its concomitant spatial arrangements be reorganized by tearing it down and rebuilding it toward salvific display. Thus for Acosta and so many others who would follow this kind of logic, it was the responsibility of the saved and the culturally advanced to show indigenes how best to use, develop, and make productive their lands, animals, and their own bodies. More decisively, the saved must teach the native to see the land as raw material: beautiful, pleasurable, but devoid of communicative density and disconnected from actual personal identity.

Andean peoples and many others like them found themselves being confronted with colonialists who could not and would not imagine the world with them. They would not join them in imagining a world of deep and abiding connectivity and relationality. As MacCormack captures so powerfully:

Andeans perceived the land differently than Spaniards. It was not merely that the majestic heights of the Andes and the far-flung plains of the lowlands sustained the presence of the living as much as that of the dead. It was also that these heights and plains, and the springs and lakes that demarcated them, were so many pointers to humankind's remote origin from and identity with that august environment.[10]

The gods, the land, and their identities were bound together. Like many other peoples, these natives interpreted their lives through the land; their ancestors walked the land, signified their existence through trees, mountains, rivers, rocks, animals, earth, and sky.[11] Thus the Spaniards brought the impossible: the necessity for New World peoples to conceive of their identities apart from specific orders of space—specific land, specific animals, trees, mountains, waters, and arrangements of days and nights. This separation of identity from land and place was part of the inner logic of demonic extirpation. Thus conquest logics were nurtured within the vision of the conquest of the devil in the New World.

This process of the transformation of land and identity meant that the earth, the ground, spaces, and places were removed as living organizers of identity and facilitators of identity. Moreover, this transformation constituted a very powerful denial that grows out of Christian theological sensibilities that deny any spiritual signification of land and animals and any deep processes of identification with such. The land becomes free and empty space through this denial just as people also become free and empty of the demonic. Both are ready now for true spiritual possession. Equally important, both people and land may now be set on a trajectory toward what was deemed authentic maturity. This work of displacement was inside the work of exorcism and extirpation, and that work would yield a secular possibility, that is, a godless space and godless bodies formerly occupied by the demonic but now on their way to being God-filled bodies. In my text, *The Christian Imagination*, I have noted the generative force of the reciprocal relation of racial formation and private-property formation in the alterations of indigenous worlds, yet one of the most devastating effects of this transformation was precisely in the way indigenous peoples were invited to map the demonic onto their worlds.

Here we have the emergence of a New World colonializing Christian subjectivity that performs a dual operation. On the one hand, it helps native peoples discern the demonic at work in them and in their land, and on the other hand it creates secular space (of land and bodies). That is, it posits bodies and lands no longer filled with spiritual (read as diabolical) presence or communicative reality but only as already possessed by God the creator witnessed through the church. Such new converted space could be seen not as secular space but Christian space. However, such Christian space is Christian by possession, that is, ownership not by presence. Indeed, spiritual presence among the indigenous peoples when discerned is always a sign of captivity to the devil as well as cultural and intellectual deficiency. Christian space is fundamentally empty space, space ready for capitalist cultivation. It is in this way fully secular. This empty space is space on the way to being converted, transformed, and made into something new. It is space that is Christian first by what it takes away, by what it extirpates and exorcizes, and then Christian second by what it imagines it will put in its place—Christian controls of space.

This way of approaching secularity focuses on absence as the natural state, that is, the proper (God-ordained) state of material reality devoid of communicative density or spiritual presence. Yet here we need to see the deep connection between the formation of a colonialized subjectivity and this kind of performance of secular space. A crucial text for helping us understand this connection and for illuminating the emergence of the spatial modern is the epic work *The First New Chronicle and Good Government*, by Felipe Guaman Poma de Ayala.[12] I cannot in the space of an essay do justice to the incredible power and significance of a text that is yet to receive the kind of philosophical, theological, and political analysis it deserves. I simply wish to tease out this element of the spatial modern and its concomitant work of performing a semiotics of Christian colonialized subjectivity. A Christian colonialized subjectivity in this regard is not simply the transformation of existing subjective states but also the creation and imposition of a subjective state through which to read space and body. Christian colonialized subjectivity has many aspects, but the aspect I draw attention to here is the transformation of indigenous ways of imagining bodies in space toward ways of seeing land and body as empty in their proper natural state. Such a state moves forward toward Christian possession (control) or backward toward demonic possession (occupation).

## GUAMAN POMA, SECULAR SPACE, AND MAPPING THE DEMONIC

In the year 1616, an elderly Peruvian man entered the city of Lima in Peru. It was the end of a long journey from his hometown of Huamanga. He had in his possession a manuscript now completed with his final additions. This man's name was Felipe Guaman Poma de Ayala, and the name he gave to the manuscript was *The First New Chronicle and Good Government.* We are not sure to whom he gave this manuscript once in Lima, perhaps a Franciscan friar by the name of Cordoba. But what we do know is that he wanted this manuscript (of 1,189 pages and 398 full-page drawings) and an accompanying letter to be given to the Spanish king, Philip III.

The manuscript did eventually arrive in Spain, but whether the king ever saw it is unknown. We do know that very few eyes encountered this manuscript until the 1930s, when it was rediscovered. What Guaman Poma gave to us was one of the most important witnesses to early colonial Peru and the transformation of the Andean world at the hand of the Spanish, and in so doing he gave us a profound theological text that exposes the troubled journey of modern Christian subjectivity. The Christian Guaman Poma writes from inside a Christian vision of the world, but one that reveals the cultural baroque, the mixture of Andean and Spanish visions of spatial existence.[13] Equally important, the text gives witness to the transition in the way the world will come to be perceived by many indigenous Christians. The world will become disenchanted. This is not to say that indigenous people or the Spanish settlers, for that matter, will come to reject the existence of a spiritual world that moves in and through the material world. Rather this disenchantment will be with the ground itself, with animal life, with mountain and landscape, lake and grassland.

They together will fall silent and speak no more of connection or relation. They become empty space, but that emptiness is calibrated to the bodies of the Spanish. Their presence banishes the demonic and restores proper perspective to earth and animal. Their presence draws earth and animal toward utility and away from communion. Equally important, Andean ancestors are banished from the land. They no longer speak to their descendents from the land and with the land. Yet even with the emerging transformation of space, Guaman Poma writes with a profound Andean sense of space.

The title page of Guaman Poma's masterwork shows his genius in how it instructs with both text and image. It brings together Andean and Spanish cultural logics in displaying what Serge Gruzinski called the Mestizo mind.[14] Most notable for our consideration is the spatial logic at work in this image, a logic that grows out of and mirrors what I call place-centered identity, identity that is constituted in and constitutive of life defined by and coordinated around specific lands, animals, plants, bodies of water, and objects created and situated in specific spaces.

In figure 8.1, the placement of figures communicates a message that situates the text that follows. As noted in the brilliant cartographical analysis of Guaman Poma's work by Rolena Adorno, the placement of image, icon, place, space, and people make intelligible the text that precedes or follows.[15] Guaman Poma's method of writing and depiction follow Andean spatial logics. As Adorno suggests, in order to grasp the multiple communicative levels of this text, we have to imagine the pictorial pages with a line through the middle and a line from top to bottom; we then have the basis for understanding an Andean spatial universe and Andean spatial culture. With the horizontal line through the middle reality is divided between upper (Hanan) and lower (Hurin), masculine and feminine, respectively. The line from top to bottom divides the right (viewer's left) as a position of superiority and the left (viewer's right) as a position of inferiority. The center is the position of ultimate authority and is coordinated with the upper-right position.

Thus the symbols of authority of church and state, both in Spain and in Peru, stand at the center. The pope as the head of the church is in the position of authority. Across from the pope is the kneeling king of Spain, and below the king of Spain is the author himself, Guaman Poma. Both he and the king kneel, but not in equality. There is a subtle but clear message here. Although the manuscript is sent to the king, as petition to him, Guaman Poma is also addressing the pope and beyond the pope addressing God. Indeed, the juxtaposition of a kneeling king above a kneeling Guaman Poma makes clear to whom the king must answer for his actions. These liturgical actions also gesture toward the pathos powerfully inscribed in the document: the salutatory kneeling king and Guaman Poma anticipate the tortured and suffering kneeling of the figures that are displayed in the text. These spatial placements would have been immediately intelligible to an Andean viewer even if the Spanish symbols remained not fully understood.

The brilliant Mestizo machinations of Guaman Poma expose the hybridity that will characterize an indigenous Christian thinking, a colonized Christian trying to make sense of his *world turned upside down*, as Guaman Poma put it

FIGURE 8.1 "The First New Chronicle and Good Government Composed by Don Felipe Guaman Poma de Ayala, Lord and Noble. His Holiness, His Royal Catholic Majesty, F.G.P. de Ayala, Prince, His Royal Catholic Majesty, the Kingdom of the Indies."

*Source:* The Royal Library, Copenhagen, GKS 2232 4°: Guaman Poma, *Nueva corónica y buen gobierno* (1615), title page.

so eloquently.[16] In this regard, the text is a profound witness of resistance to Spanish colonial rule. Yet it also reveals the transformation of life inside the new discursive regime of Christianity and with it a new way to see the world.

Guaman Poma lived in the world that José de Acosta helped change. Born in 1550 in the southern Peruvian province of Huamanga, Guaman Poma, was a native speaker of Quechua, the language of the Incas, and he was fluent in Castilian. He was born of the local Andean ruling class, the *mitmaqkuna*, and witnessed, firsthand, the absolute transformation of his world at the hands of the Spanish. Guaman Poma's beginnings are a matter of some historical debate because it is clear that he exaggerated the royal status of his lineage. He claims to be the child of an Indian mother of Incan royalty and an Indian father who was second in command in the Incan government, both serious Christians. The reason for such exaggeration is clear: only someone of high status may dare write to the king of Spain.

Guaman Poma's account of how he learned the faith is even more significant. He said he learned the faith from his brother, a child not of his mother and father but of his mother and a Spanish conquistador. This child, Martin de Ayala, becomes a holy hermit, a Mestizo of virtue and holiness. Yet what is implied here is fairly obvious. His brother is the result of the rape of his mother. What does it mean that his knowledge of the faith originates from such troubled beginnings? Indeed, the rape of Indian women is a crucial theme that runs through this work. Such troubled beginnings express a contingency and instability of existence that Guaman Poma wrestles with throughout the text, that is, the presence of mixture, of unanticipated difference born of violence done to women's bodies.

What we do know of Guaman Poma's actual Christian formation clarifies many of the themes that run through his text. He began his career as an assistant to the priest Cristobal de Albornoz, who traveled the country as an extirpator of idolatries among the Indians. Albornoz sought detailed knowledge of Andean ways in order to rid them of demonic influence more precisely. Guaman Poma then served as an assistant to another cleric by the name of Martin de Murua, who wanted to write a chronicle of Inca history. Guaman Poma seems to have been a crucial collaborator with Murua in this project. Finally, Guaman Poma served as an interpreter for a Spanish judge in charge of adjudicating land titles.

These collaborations gave him a strategic position from which to understand the colonial operation. They also shaped his theological sensibilities, giving him the tortured vision that constituted this New World Christianity. It is important, however, not to read Guaman Poma's work as simply a reflex of the colonial operation. His work offers the most penetrating theological critique of Spanish colonial Christianity of his time. Moreover, Guaman Poma exposes to us the complexity of Amerindian Christian life trying to make sense of itself between an earlier Incan invasion and the current Spanish conquest. Living between and in these different worlds, he registers in image and text Spanish atrocities.

Figures 8.1 through 8.7 offer only a small portion of the poignant textual and pictorial account that Guaman Poma gives of the ways Spanish conquest and oppression were woven into the quotidian realities of Amerindian life. The various agents of conquest come into sharp view throughout his masterwork. The *encomenderos* were those granted lands and control of the particular inhabitants who lived there, and they received such bounty usually as a result of exemplary service to the Spanish crown as, for example, a conquistador or because of significant political influence in the Old World. Normally the wealthiest and most powerful of the settler class during the early imperial decades, the *encomenderos* promised not only to cultivate the land for Spain but also to see to the spiritual cultivation of the people by helping establish the conditions for the church to come and thrive. The *corregidores de indios* or *corregidores* were bureaucrats who worked on behalf of the Spanish crown in general and often in concert with the *encomenderos* in particular and managed the villages into which the indigenes were concentrated and housed. The *caciques* were "the nobles who were in power when the Spanish arrived, and they maintained it under Spanish hegemony. They were the go-betweens, translating Spanish economic and cultural interests into native modalities and interpreting native realities to their Spanish overseers."[17] The *doctrina* were the parishes for the Indians where catechetical instruction and socialization into the new political and economic order were woven together to form docile indigenous bodies. The *doctrina padres* were the priests and friars given absolute control of the *doctrinas* to instruct, discipline, and punish the Andeans. Finally, the *tambos* had been inns established under Inca rule for travelers;

FIGURE 8.2 "Don Francisco Pizarro Burns Capac Apo Waman Chawa in a House, demanding gold." The words superimposed on the stones read, "The noble lords, walled in to be burnt." The words coming from the mouth of Pizarro read, "Give me gold and silver, Indians." The words at the bottom of the image read, "In Cusco."

*Source*: The Royal Library, Copenhagen, GKS 2232 4°: Guaman Poma, *Nueva corónica y buen gobierno* (1615), page 398, drawing 159.

MALACONFICIONO

que haze los padres y curas de las dotrinas apurrea a las yn-
preñadas y a las bi ejos ya yñs y a las ahas solteras no las qui ere cõ-
fezar de dad de bey te anos no se cõ fiesa ni ay remedio de ellas-

dotrina                                         con fiesa

**FIGURE 8.3** "Bad confession: a priest abuses his pregnant parishioner during confession." The words at the bottom of the image read, "In the doctrina."

*Source*: The Royal Library, Copenhagen, GKS 2232 4°: Guaman Poma, *Nueva corónica y buen gobierno* (1615), page 590, drawing 231.

**FIGURE 8.4** "The encomendero has the cacique hanged; the corregidor orders it to please the encomendero." The words at the bottom read, "In Cusco."

*Source*: The Royal Library, Copenhagen, GKS 2232 4°: Guaman Poma, *Nueva corónica y buen gobierno* (1615), page 571, drawing 225.

**FIGURE 8.5** "Indian parents defend their daughter from the lascivious Spaniard." The words at the bottom read, "pride and lust."

*Source*: The Royal Library, Copenhagen, GKS 2232 4°: Guaman Poma, *Nueva corónica y buen gobierno* (1615), page 882, drawing 325.

FIGURE 8.6 "Mercedarian Friar Murúa. They are so fierce and exacting; they mistreat the Indians and beat them to make them work in the doctrinas of this kingdom. There is no remedy." The words at the bottom read, "In the doctrina."

*Source*: The Royal Library, Copenhagen, GKS 2232 4°: Guaman Poma, *Nueva corónica y buen gobierno* (1615), page 661, drawing 258.

FIGURE 8.7 "Six Ravenous Animals Feared by the Poor Indians in This Kingdom."
Counterclockwise from left to right: "Serpent—Corregidor, Lion—
Encomendero, Mouse—noble cacique, Cat—notary, Fox—doctrina padre, Tiger—
Spaniards of the tambos." The bottom section reads, "Don't all of you strip me
naked, for the love of God. These animals, which have no fear of God, skin the poor
Indians in this kingdom. There is no remedy. The poor of Jesus Christ."

*Source*: The Royal Library, Copenhagen, GKS 2232 4º: Guaman Poma, *Nueva corónica y buen gobierno*
(1615), page 708, drawing 272.

under Spanish rule they became sites where the Spanish conquerors and their agents traveled to and stole, raped, murdered, and enslaved indigenous people.

Together colonial agents and their servants constituted an ecology of suppression and death for Amerindians that led Guaman Poma to state repeatedly and hauntingly in his text, "and there is no remedy":

The Indians fear the *corregidores* because they are worse than serpents. They eat people, because they eat their livelihoods and their entrails and take away their property like fierce animals . . . the Indians fear the *encomendero* because he is the lion. When he grabs his prey he never lets go . . . he never pardons the poor man and never feels grateful to him . . . The Indians fear the *doctrina* priests because they are wily foxes . . . who know more than foxes about hunting the Indians, catching them, and stealing their estates, their women, and their daughters . . . The Indians fear the notary because he is a hunting cat. He stalks . . . the poor Indians' estates until he grabs them and once he grabs them, he does not allow them to wriggle . . . The Indians fear the Spaniards of the *tambos*, travelers who fear neither God nor justice . . . [The Spaniards at the *tambos*] . . . beat . . . [the Indian] . . . badly, and take everything he has and walk off with it, the same in the pueblos as in the countryside . . . The poor Indians fear the noble *caciques* . . . They steal from Indians' estates by day and by night; without anyone noticing it, they steal and rob. Thus, between the serpent, the lion, the tiger, the fox, the cat, and the mouse these six animals who eat the poor Indian leave him no room to move; between them all, they skin him, and he cannot move. Among these thieves, they help one another and protect each other.[18]

However, even as he offered us these images along with his brilliant account of colonial operations, he also constantly performed a spatial logic in his work. Recall that the right position (the reader's left) is a position of authority, which is coordinated with a second position of power, which is the center of the picture. In the figures in this chapter, the oppressed Indian is in the position of (moral) authority even as they are being killed (figures 8.2 and 8.4), being beaten (figures 8.3 and 8.6), and even during attempted abduction and rape (figure 8.5). Thus although the actions of the Spaniards execute imperial power, they are done from a position of moral weakness. Indeed, in figure 8.7 the woman simulates the position of the suffering Jesus: Guaman Poma gives the image the title "the poor of Jesus Christ." This is a purposeful identification that he establishes for the reader; it denotes that as Christ suffered at the hands of his enemies, so too do his poor Indians follow his via dolorosa. Additionally, Guaman Poma notes at the bottom of the pictorial pages the locations of these events, signaling not only the precision of his witness but his spatial frame of reference. The notification of locations is sometimes juxtaposed with notifications of the kind of sin being enacted in the picture; thus in figure 8.5 he notes this as a place of pride and lust, and in figure 8.7, a particular place is not specified, but a condition is—one that covers the entire realm as a site of no remedy.

As powerful as his account of the horror of conquest, the question I pose is: where are the demons? Where is the demonic to be found? Surely, the demonic must be registered in the rape, murder, torture, theft, and abuse committed by the Spanish. However, both in his account and his iconic presentation, Guaman Poma does not present the demonic among the Spanish but primarily among the Indian, at work in indigenous cultural realities. To be sure, he marks idolatry to have been introduced to the Indians by the Incas. Furthermore, he describes the actions of the Spanish to be evil, born of disobedience and faithlessness. But almost always moving in close proximity to Indian bodies and interpenetrating their ways is the demonic, influencing, guiding, and directing them. In figure 8.8, Guaman Poma depicts the Incan Festival of the Sun, where the ceremonial drink *chicha* was poured in libation to the Sun; here he imagines a demon delivering the *chicha* to the Sun. The man is in the position of authority over the woman in this image.

In figure 8.9, as Sabine MacCormack notes, we see "the demonization of Andean religion [involving reverence for the Sun, Moon, and Stars]. Two Andean priests supervise a sacrificial ritual, the beneficiary of which is the devil. Both priests are depicted as elderly, for, as missionaries regularly complained, it was the elderly who maintained the ancient religion of the Andes most devotedly."[19] The demon is in the central position of authority, and the most visible priest is in the inferior subservient position.

Figure 8.10 depicts an Andean drunk during a harvest festival, and here Guaman Poma inscribes, as Rolena Adorno notes, a world in disorder. The woman is in the position of authority, the man is in the position of

**FIGURE 8.8** "... drinks with the Sun during the Festival of the Sun—poured into the ushnu [a pit for sacrificial offering] in Haucaypata."

*Source*: The Royal Library, Copenhagen, GKS 2232 4°: Guaman Poma, *Nueva corónica y buen gobierno* (1615), page 248, drawing 95.

FIGURE 8.9 "High priests, walla wisa, layqha, umu, sorcerer."

*Source*: The Royal Library, Copenhagen, GKS 2232 4°: Guaman Poma, *Nueva corónica y buen gobierno* (1615), page 279, drawing 108.

**FIGURE 8.10** "Indians speak with the devil while practicing a traditional Andean drinking ritual."

*Source*: The Royal Library, Copenhagen, GKS 2232 4°: Guaman Poma, *Nueva corónica y buen gobierno* (1615), page 876, drawing 323.

subordination, and the sign of this disorder is not only his drunken state but the demon on his back inhabiting his body.[20]

These depictions of demonic influence and activity on Andean bodies and on the land must be juxtaposed with the way Guaman Poma depicts Spanish oppression of and atrocities against Amerindians. His depictions in this regard are powerful and comprehensive, yet the missing element of demonic influence upon the Spanish is extraordinary. Like Acosta, Guaman Poma binds demonic influence with Indian inferiority or, at the least, Indian cultural immaturity. Here indigenous life is unstable, that is, subject to demonic penetration; indeed, it is already permeated with demonic possibility. The immoral and the demonic among the Andeans are joined together. Figure 8.11 shows us a man dressed as an Indian noble saying to the devil, "Here is a hundred pesos." And the devil replies, "You'll be a good thief. I'll help you." Here in the space of Amerindian and animal, the devil is alive, active, and speaking.

The demonic and the immoral are not joined in the presence of Spanish bodies because their bodies constitute a Christian space, a redeemed space that has been emptied of the realities that penetrate indigenous bodies. Yet why would this suggest a secularity, even a spatial secularity? The Christianity presented to colonial subjects tied together evil practices and destructive acts toward God's creation with demonic activity. They existed in the same space as they existed in the same bodies. As Acosta showed us, this belief, fundamental to the work of exorcism of the demonic from the body and extirpation of demonic spatial strongholds from the land, was woven inside the Christian pedagogy offered up to the Amerindians.[21] Guaman Poma himself testified he learned from Albornoz the operation of the demonic on Indian and land:

> The sorcerers who were like priests served in the *wamanies* [provinces], at the *apachitas* [sacred piles of stone], and the common *wacas* [idols, gods], of which there were many in the kingdom. They served as confessor-priests. They tricked men, telling them that the *wacas* [idols] ate and drank and talked when they did not. Thus all across the kingdom people kept *wacas* [idols] and those who did not keep them were immediately ordered to be killed. I know about all that I have written on the pontiffs because I used to serve Cristóbal de Albornoz, the inspector general of the Holy Catholic Church, who burned all the *wacas* [idols] and sorceries in the kingdom. He was a Christian judge.[22]

**FIGURE 8.11** "The Lives of Thieves" (title); "Thief—Suwa" (bottom).

*Source*: The Royal Library, Copenhagen, GKS 2232 4°: Guaman Poma, *Nueva corónica y buen gobierno* (1615), page 942, drawing 338.

The activity of the demonic was always a false copy of the activity of God, so Guaman Poma saw the native healers, that is, sorcerers, as false confessor-priests and their activities as a demonic copy of the work of the church, even if that work was to heal people.[23] In figure 8.12 Guaman Poma recounts yet another demonic operation active both during the time of the Incas and his time. Below we see illness-sucking sorcerers who, working with demons, claim to heal people, but they are charlatans. Guaman Poma states:

> Other sorcerers speak with the demons and claim to suck out the illnesses from people's bodies, claiming to suck out silver, pebbles, twigs, worms, toads, straw, or corn from the bodies of men and women. These men are false sorcerers; they fool the Indians, with the sole aim of tricking them out of their estates and teaching the Indians to be idolaters . . . all these are idolatrous sorceries of the Inca, who taught them to the sorcerers.[24]

The sorcerer at the bottom of figure 8.12 is pictured with a demon on or in him working in concert with his efforts to heal the sick, efforts that for Guaman Poma encapsulate this practice as both ineffectual and bound up in evil.

Spanish bodies, however, presented the reconfiguration of space that had banished or at least rerouted spiritual presence and penetration. The colonial landscape created a new space that circulated life around white bodies as preferred and cleaned space. Even if those bodies commit sin, do evil, and destroy life, they are not penetrated by the demonic.

This transformation is no small achievement, and, in fact, it presents a profound theological innovation constituted on the colonial theater. Just as indigenes are invited to reject native imaginaries of communicative density with nature, seeing them as so much demonic influence and therefore false, so too they are formed to envision a colonial world that is expanding demon-free space even as acts are being committed in the constitution and emerging ecology of that world that should signal demonic possession.

Guaman Poma did imagine divine intervention and angelic presence, but even here he did not imagine that intervention or presence as mitigating or preventing Spanish oppression and atrocities. Spanish bodies, that is, white bodies, created a new space freed from spiritual interference because it was also space that had already denied any communicative density with land

FIGURE 8.12 "Dream Sorcerers" (top to bottom), "Lying layqas and umus" (words by the demonic image at the top of the drawing), "Dream sorcerer" (words at mid-level), "Fire sorcerer" (words near the bottom), "Illness sucking sorcerer" (words at the bottom of the picture), "False sorcerers" (words under the picture).

*Source*: The Royal Library, Copenhagen, GKS 2232 4°: Guaman Poma, *Nueva corónica y buen gobierno* (1615), page 281, drawing 109.

FIGURE 8.13 "Padres: Forcing the Indian Women to Weave Cloth by Accusing Them of Having Lovers—They Beat Them and Do Not Pay." The bottom of the page reads, "[in the] doctrina."

*Source*: The Royal Library, Copenhagen, GKS 2232 4º: Guaman Poma, *Nueva corónica y buen gobierno* (1615), page 578, drawing 227.

and animals. Those bodies represented the world as inert, silent ground and animals as enclosed in utility. From this operation comes the deepest architectonics of development and the grand achievement of seeing the world as nothing but that which is ready to be possessed. Moreover, the body emerges in this operation as insular, as a mobile entity moving on top of the earth, and as what must be freed from demonic influence and intellectual and cultural deficiencies. That body must be changed, prepared for redemption and civilization by being emptied—by being made secular.

# NOTES

1. Charles Taylor, *A Secular Age* (Cambridge, Mass.: Belknap Press of Harvard University Press, 2007); John Lardas Modern, *Secularism in Antebellum America* (Chicago: University of Chicago Press, 2011).

2. José de Acosta, *Natural and Moral History of the Indies* (Durham, N.C.: Duke University Press, 2002), 162–164.

3. Acosta, *Natural and Moral History of the Indies*, 163; *Historia natural y moral de las indias*, Kindle ed. (2011), loc. 2327. Acosta is here drawing from scripture—Ecclesiastes 10:19 in the Septuagint: "Men prepare a meal for enjoyment, and wine makes life merry, and money is the answer to everything."

4. Acosta, *Natural and Moral History of the Indies*, 254.

5. Ibid., 255.

6. Sabine MacCormack, *Religion in the Andes: Vision and Imagination in Early Colonial Peru* (Princeton, N.J.: Princeton University Press, 1991), 34.

7. Ibid., 28.

8. Sabine MacCormack, "Demons, Imagination, and the Incas," in *New World Encounters*, ed. Stephen Greenblatt (Berkeley: University of California Press, 1993), 107.

9. Willie James Jennings, *The Christian Imagination: Theology and the Origins of Race* (New Haven, Conn.: Yale University Press, 2010), 102–103.

10. MacCormack, "Demons, Imagination, and the Incas," 113.

11. Ibid., 114. MacCormack states, "The relationship Andeans perceived between life and death, and between humankind and the natural environment, were thus profoundly different from Spanish and Christian equivalents. The land surrounding one told the story of one's first ancestors as much as it told one's own story and the story of those yet to come. It was right that the familiar dead were seen walking through the fields they had once cultivated, thus sharing them with both the living and with the original ancestors who had raised the first crops in the very same fields. Death was thus the great leveler not because, as in Christian thought, it reduced all human beings to equality in relation to each other and before God. Rather, death was a leveler because by means of it humans were reintegrated into a network of parents and offspring that embraced the entire natural order" (114).

12. The work of Felipe Guaman Poma de Ayala is located at the National Library of Denmark and Copenhagen University Library, http://www.kb.dk/en/nb/tema/poma. In Latin American studies this is a notoriously difficult text because it combines multiple semiotic systems: Christian, Spanish, and Quechen. In this essay, I have leaned heavily on the work of scholars such as Sabine MacCormack, Rolena Adorno, Arturo Escobar, Walter Mignolo, and many others. Yet the overarching Christian logic of the text is powerful and deserves study and constitutes my central interest.

13. Timothy J. Reiss, "American Baroque Histories and Geographies from Siqüenza y Góngora and Balbuena to Balboa, Carpentier, and Lezama," in *Baroque New Worlds: Representation, Transculturation, Counterconquest*, ed. Lois Parkinson Zamora and Monika Kaup (Durham, N.C.: Duke University Press, 2010). Also see Sabine MacCormack, *On the Wings of Time: Rome, the Incas, Spain, and Peru* (Princeton, N.J.: Princeton University Press, 2007), 56–65.

14. Serge Gruzinski, *The Mestizo Mind: The Intellectual Dynamics of Colonization and Globalization* (New York: Routledge, 2002), 53–68. Gruzinski also notes the censuring of the metaphysical in relation to the land. He states, "surveys conducted by Spanish missionaries, bureaucrats, and doctors placed an interpretative grid on the indigenous environment, reducing it to the level of desanctified nature, to a 'flora' and 'fauna' devoid of any Amerindian pagan presence. With only a few exceptions, the 'metaphysical' dimensions attributed by Amerindians to their environment were censured, ignored, or scorned by Europeans. Indigenous informants, for that matter, adopted the habit of understating or overlooking such aspects in an effort to deflect the invasive curiosity of their powerful questioners" (46).

15. I am drawing heavily on the work of Rolena Adorno, the premier scholar in the world on Guaman Poma and his writings: *Guaman Poma: Writing and Resistance in Colonial Peru* (Austin: University of Texas Press, 1986); Rolena Adorno, "The Depiction of Self and Other in Colonial Peru," *Art Journal* 49, no. 2, "Depictions of the Dispossessed" (Summer 1990):110–118; Rolena Adorno, "Racial Scorn and Critical Contempt: Review of *Nueva cornica y buen gobierno* by Guaman Poma de Ayala," *Diacritics* 4, no. 4 (Winter 1974): 2–7; Rolena Adorno, *Guaman Poma and His Illustrated Chronicle from Colonial Peru: From a Century of Scholarship to a New Era of Reading* (Copenhagen: Museum Tusculanum Press, University of Copenhagen & the Royal Library, 2001).

16. Felipe Guaman Poma de Ayala, *The First New Chronicle and Good Government*, trans. David Frye (Indianapolis, Ind.: Hackett, 2006), 135.

17. Jennings, *Christian Imagination*, 75.

18. De Ayala, *First New Chronicle and Good Government*, 149, 227.

19. MacCormack, *Religion in the Andes*, 256.

20. Rolena Adorno, ed., *From Oral to Written Expression: Native Andean Chronicles of the Early Colonial Period* (Syracuse, N.Y.: Maxwell School of Citizenship and Public Affairs, Syracuse University, 1982), 155.

21. Acosta, *Natural and Moral History of the Indies*, 327–328.

22. De Ayala, *First New Chronicle and Good Government*, 88.

23. Acosta, *Natural and Moral History of the Indies*, 275–276.

24. De Ayala, *First New Chronicle and Good Government*, 87–88.

# CONCLUSION

## JAMES BALDWIN AND A THEOLOGY
## OF JUSTICE IN A SECULAR AGE

Jonathon Kahn

T HE SOURCE of my reflections is a scene from James Baldwin's *The Fire Next Time*. Some of you know the scene. The young Baldwin is taken by his friend to meet Mother Horn, the dynamic pastor of the sanctified church he ends up joining. Before she learns Baldwin's name, Mother Horn interrupts any formal introduction and preemptively asks: "Whose little boy are you?" Baldwin has heard the question before—the pimps and the racketeers of the "Avenue" try to claim him with the exact same phrase. Faced with the terrors and temptations of the Avenue—the "heat" and "odor" of what Baldwin calls "carnal knowledge"[1]—Baldwin, in effect, leaps into Mother Horn's arms, choosing to be "spiritually seduced" by what he thinks is the safer and higher ground of church: "For when the pastor asked me, with that marvelous smile, 'Whose little boy are you?' my heart replied, at once, 'Why yours.'"[2]

This scene has haunted, troubled, and compelled me since I first read it. I find myself returning inexorably to this scene. The question "Whose little boy are you?" stays with me. My sense was that there was something about this moment in Baldwin—where he presents what seems like a clear distinction between the secular street and the sacred church as, in effect, a question about the ethics of belonging—that might be helpful thinking through the neglected relationship between race and secularism. My feeling was that Baldwin sets up this dichotomy, where a choice seems to be made between an infantile religious past and a modern secular present, as a false one. Yet Baldwin presents it because it is all too prevalent when it comes to framing the meaning and status of African American religion: with religion, black America has roots but remains stuck in a mythic past, and without religion—well—there's the base terms of the ghetto. My sense was that the work that Baldwin does in *The Fire Next Time* was, first, toward revealing these as false terms. In effect, I hear Baldwin saying that the terms of secular modernity are profoundly distorting of black American subjectivities. And second, I began to hear Baldwin as beginning to craft a different set of terms—terms that have taken into account race—for religious subjectivity in this modern secular age.

This reading of Baldwin requires a thicker frame. It requires a fuller account of how these become the terms—the church or the street—that Baldwin finds himself facing. Thus over the first half of this essay I provide a larger and broader narrative of race and secularity—one that has been informed by the essays of this volume. That narrative shows how the dominant accounts of the secular—both the "secularization thesis" that prevailed during the twentieth century and the now-current attempts to correct its errors—essentially ignore the experience and conditions of African Americans as racialized subjects. And, again, with the help of the essays of this volume, I begin to sketch some constructive repairs to the damage done by the dominant frames. It is only with this frame sketched that I turn in the second half of the essay back to Baldwin, when we can get a better sense of Baldwin's response to the depredations of the secular age.

\\\\\\\\\\\\\\\\\\\\\\\\\\\\\\\\\\\\\\\\\\\\\\\\\\\\\\\\\\

Since the dawn of the twentieth century, two broad narratives dominate accounts of the American secular. The predominate is the "secularization-thesis narrative." Spun over the course of the twentieth century from modern giants such as Weber, Durkheim, Comte, and Spencer, the secularization thesis anticipated what Owen Chadwick described as the "growing tendency in mankind to do without religion."[3] This tendency is a complex story in which the pressures of Enlightenment thought along with the desire for political and material power arranged to reduce religion to historical curiosity, public irrelevance, or both.[4] This is the first broad narrative.

The second broad narrative begins with Mary Douglas's 1982 essay "The Effects of Modernization on Religious Change," in which Douglas, acting as a canary in a coal mine, writes: "Events have taken religious studies by surprise. . . . According to an extensive literature, religious change in modern times happens in only two ways—the falling off of worship in traditional Christian churches, and the appearance of new cults, not expected to endure. No one credited the traditional religions with enough vitality to inspire large-scale political revolt."[5] But in 1982 it was all too obvious that religion—from Belfast to Beirut, from Tehran to Gdansk, from Johannesburg to Lynchburg, Virginia—was as ever relevant to the world's ways, particularly its political ways. By the 1990s, the secularization thesis was in fast retreat. When Peter Berger, whose 1960s text *The Sacred Canopy* personified the spirit of the secularization thesis, writes at the start of the twenty-first century that "a whole body of literature by historians and social scientists loosely labeled 'secularization theory' is essentially mistaken," a new day had arrived for the study of the secular.[6]

Ever since, correctives to the failures of the secularization thesis have come fast and furious. From the ashes of the secularization thesis, the secular—what I like to call the "new secular"—has been born anew. (*The king is dead! Long live the king!*) That the demise of the secularization thesis should lead to an intense and prolific rebirth of interest in the very idea of the secular should not be surprising. Because what critics such as Jeffrey Stout, Charles Taylor, Talal Asad, Saba Mahmood, Janet Jakobsen, and Ann Pellegrini (to name only a few) have done is present a decidedly different story of the secular, a vastly complicated story in which the secular is no longer flatly taken to mean "the absence of religion."[7] Instead, these recent contributions at the intersection of ethics, religion, and political theory claim that there are no distinct and separable realms of the secular and the religious.[8] Instead, the secular is now theorized to include religion as variously and multiply imbricated and implicated in the development of modern imaginaries, publics, and subjectivities. The secular has become inseparable from and, at times, indistinguishable from the emergence and nature of the religious in modernity. Where there is the secular, there is religion, and vice versa. These recent accounts of the secular have insisted that we grow more comfortable in thinking about these two categories simultaneously, as neither banishing the other, as each needing the other for its own formation. Ambiguity between the two categories, and the will to not resolve but live with this ambiguity, is the name of the game.

Following Stout, the new secular has emerged as a discursive and ethical condition that allows religious citizens to express their commitments fully and freely.[9] At the same time, secular citizens must also balance the right to their expression of conviction in whatever terms they hold them against the awareness that these same prized commitments are not held by other citizens and can at times act as a bludgeon against them.[10] Stout tries to reinforce this newly revalued notion of the secular by making a semantic distinction between "secular" and "secularist," between "secularity" and "secularism." Notions of *secularism* and *secularist* entail policing religious commitments from the public square. Notions of the *secular* and *secularity* imply a complex ethics of public engagement where citizens endlessly work to find appropriate expression of their religious commitments. That is, the secular are not secularists, and secularization is not secularism.[11] Where secularism represents an ideological commitment to denying religious reasons public purchase and scrubbing the pubic sphere of religious residue, secularity is a discourse of exchange between religious and nonreligious citizens who are acutely aware that their own convictions are contestable.[12]

Whether these efforts to make what amount to radical distinctions between secularity and secularism are rhetorically successful—indeed, the distinction between the secular and secularism may be simply too fine to resonate—they have helpfully contributed to reimagining and retheorizing the relationship between religion and modernity. They have introduced a new openness to a variety of social and political imaginaries. Charles Taylor's "immanent frame" and his conception of "fullness" in the secular age represent a crucial attempt to spur an important conversation "between a host of different positions, religious, nonreligious, antireligious, humanistic, antihumanistic and so on, in which we eschew mutual caricature and try to understand what 'fullness' means for the other."[13] Under this new dispensation, the secular is no longer a fantasy of liberal tolerance where conversation and political procedure follow a set of pellucid rules.[14] Instead, new narratives about the secular have revealed the nation-state as applying theological pressure and, in turn, have revealed the ways citizens have pressured back in theological kind. Instead of being about the presence or absence of religion, the new secular names a much broader set of political tropes, techniques, and actions that do the work of doing and undoing, legitimizing or delegitimizing visions of justice and fairness.[15] In other words, when the secular is no longer about rational procedures for controlling religion, the secular is instead revealed as a deeply contested language of justice: a variety of rhetorics used by the nation-state, by the legal system, by political actors, and by you and me to denote, as George Shulman says, "in visceral ways who and what people count as real"—as deserving of attention, recognition, resources, and recompense.[16] That religious discourse does this work within the secular is obvious, and thus, under this new secular moon, it is not just possible but crucial to speak of religion as critical to figuring out how people are varyingly rendered socially and politically visible and invisible.

It is thus surprising and even shocking to consider that race—in particular accounts of race that are rooted in the African slave trade and the experience of black people in the Americas—has not been a critical part of recent narratives of the secular. These same corrective responses—responses ostensibly radically open to a variety of social and political imaginaries—have essentially overlooked and neglected the concerns of race. Charles Taylor's *The Secular Age*—the Ur-text for contemporary secularity studies—is eight hundred pages long, but never does it take up the question of how patterns of enslavement and colonization in the Americas shape Enlightenment and post-Enlightenment conceptions of the secular. Taylor's text prompted the creation of the Social Scientific Research Council's (SSRC) website "The Immanent Frame," which publishes some of the best work rethinking the secular. Go there, however, and you will find very little discussion of the intersection of race, religion, and the secular.[17] I find myself wanting to ask a version of Buggin' Out's immortal question from Spike Lee's *Do the Right Thing*: "How come you ain't got no brothers up on the wall?" That is, where are the accounts and considerations of race in this new and burgeoning conversation about the secular? What would it mean and sound like to include race in theory, historiography, and anthropology of the new secular?

This question grows even more poignant when we consider that this is now the second time that narratives about the secular have omitted and been downright hostile to black religion and considerations of race. The first time, of course, is obvious. The long arc of the twentieth century's secularization thesis, with its claims that religion is irrational, on the wane, and inappropriate for political work in the public square, should be called for what it is: a version of whiteness, if not white supremacy, that served to question the right of political place of African American citizens. Thus, both of the narratives of the secular that I have outlined—first, the secularization thesis, and second, recent correctives to the secularization thesis—have failed to consider the conditions and fullness of racialized subjectivities. One cannot help but wonder whether there is something dramatically limited about the way the category of the secular, even newly construed, is being conceived. Why historically have accounts of the secular—from the twentieth century's secularization thesis to its modern correctives—struggled to include race? Does contemporary theory on the secular continue to struggle to address race, and blackness in particular, because contemporary theory is, however unwittingly, using the same conventions, the same rhetorical strategies, that discussions of the secular have long used? That is, though contemporary corrections to the secularization thesis reject the content of its claims, do they nevertheless continue to hew reflexively to its conceptual categories?

*Race and Secularism in America* is the first self-conscious scholarly attempt to address these questions adequately and consider the conditions and fullness of racialized America, black America in particular. As a whole, the essays of this volume bring attention to what amounts to a historical set of hostilities toward race in the study of the secular over the last hundred years. The essays reveal the way the secularization-thesis narrative—where religion is thought to be an atavism in decline—represents nothing less than shots across the bow of black religion. For what these essays make clear is that historically African American religion resists the secularization thesis's social, political, and epistemological demands. Following Hart, Shulman, and Jennings, if the secular represents a colonial discourse, then the pressures of secularization, insofar as they shape and discipline the very notion of what it was to participate in the citizenry, represent the pressures of whiteness and even white supremacy. Why is this the case? Because the secular, insofar as it comes to function as a deranged discourse of injustice, functions to deny the crucial means by which black Americans, from David Walker to King, were able to recognize themselves as citizens: as God's children. And because the secular, when it functions to eliminate religious subjectivity, effectively eliminates black political subjectivity, the secular stands as yet another way to question the very right of political place of African American citizens.

The essays of this collection, however, do not simply make a case for the secularization thesis as a form of whiteness. They also do the crucial constructive work of introducing the terms of race into contemporary conversations of the secular. How do they make this introduction? What is their critique? Collectively the essays of *Race and Secularism in America* say something like the following: Clearly contemporary theorizing about the secular has been productive. The secularization thesis has rightly been replaced by the new secular. Yet the new secular, even in introducing a productive ambiguity about the place of religion in public, leaves intact the notion that the secular is at heart about the status and place of religion: more religion is allowed in than before, but the reconstructed secular remains stubbornly wedded to a project of naming and identifying the religion as a distinct entity. We can see this, for example, in the way the "buffered self" emerges famously as the key form of modern subjectivity in Taylor's work.[18] This self, as Taylor presents it, is modern because it is now faced with a choice of whether to be religious; premodern "porous selves" were as a matter of course interpenetrated with religiosity. What remains the same, however, is religion, or religiousness, as a discrete category of selfhood; one has it, or one does not.

The essays of this volume, through the introduction of race, push back against this framing. For through the lens of race, the secular is revealed to be not only about the status of religion, religious expression, or religious freedom but also crucially about the nature of justice—about who counts and who does not, who is seen as fully human and who is not, and how rights and material goods are apportioned in this light. This, ultimately, is the terrain of Harriss's understanding of Ralph Ellison's theology of invisibility. And it is equally the terrain of Blum's essay, in which he points out the absurdity of Taylor's notion of a buffered self for nineteenth-century black Americans. What Blum shows is that the question of the secular, translated into Henry Box Brown's terms, is decidedly not about whether the self is vulnerable or invulnerable to revelatory incursions or how it "can see itself as invulnerable, as a master of the meanings of things for it."[19] Instead, the "religious self" of Box Brown is devoted to figuring out how to achieve freedom and dignity. In other words, when inflected through concerns of race, the secular age is not about the choice that the buffered self affords to the expression of one's religious self in public. Instead, the secular is much more centrally about the way sets of rhetoric, beliefs, and actions—often involving concepts of religion—work to deny or establish people of color recognition and place within the workings of the state. Here are the deep terms of the racialized secular. The story of this secular is a story about justice.

When framed in this way, it is clear why stories of race are deeply critical to accounts of the secular, for the language of race is nothing if not a complicated language of in/justice. As the essays in this volume make clear, that language is rich and about complicated considerations of identity, recognition, belonging, and community. These considerations are multidirectional: they take the form of outward appeals to the nation in order to name and denounce the injustice practiced in the nation's name. They take the form of appeals inward to raced communities about ways and modes not only to survive but also to achieve excellence while living under unjust conditions. And they also take the form of complex changes in those appeals as living conditions change. Edwards's, Dubler and Blecher's, and Sorrett's essays give accounts of these complexities, of the way black religions are necessarily engaged in tension-filled dialectical struggles with the terms of the secular modern. And what these diverse struggles seem to have in common—from the nature of charisma post-King, to Salafi subjectivity, to Long's attempt to expand the category of black religion—is the ways in which they contest the very framing of the secular age around the idea of the buffered self. The religious selves in this volume (if ramified in decidedly diverse ways) are more directly concerned with the nature and expression of dignity and justice under contemporary conditions and less concerned with their vulnerability to God.

As a whole, *Race and Secularism in America* changes in important ways what we talk about when we talk about the secular, pointing us toward a more productive conversation. Instead of talking solely about religion, we will start to talk about the public histories and the stories we want to recognize as central to those who have been seen as real and as fully human in this nation. We will examine whether our publics honor those stories adequately. And when we find that our publics do not, as they surely do not, then we will talk about ways—some small and some dramatic—to move us to address this. Indeed, in this vein, it does not escape us that *Race and Secularism in America* is limited by the ways it explicates race in terms that largely hew to a black-white binary and that also largely neglect the ways gender and sexuality are also interpolated in racialized terms. Other communities—Arab, Latino, Asian, and Native American voices—will provide yet further nuance to our understanding of the way race intersects the secular. Our wish is that *Race and Secularism in America* stands as an invitation and call to action.

\\\\\\\\\\\\\\\\\\\\\\\\\\\\\\\\\\\\\\\\\\\\\\\\\\\\\\\\\\\\\\\\\\\\\\\\\\\\

James Baldwin, as we might imagine, has something to tell us about inflecting race into the unsteady categories of the religious and the secular. Better said, Baldwin, long before it was fashionable, used race to unsteady the secular, to critique profoundly the reign of the secularization thesis among his intellectual contemporaries. Baldwin's work prefigures so much of the work today that has helpfully revealed the mutually reinforcing embrace of the secular and the religious. More, I think we can look to Baldwin's dramatic expositions of blackness and whiteness as ways that reveal justice—accounts of who counts and how—as the terrain of the secular. We may, however, find ourselves challenged by the nature of justice that emerges out of his wrestling.

As I said at the start of the essay, I'd like to begin with that crucial scene when Baldwin poses what is for him the central question of identity: Whose little boy are you? And at that time in his life, Baldwin decides to be the boy of Mother Horn and the church. In the phrase "Whose little boy are you?" I hear the echoes of Ella Baker's "Now, who are your people?"[20] Already we can begin to hear the way Baldwin shifts the framing of the secular: Baldwin's choice is less about whether to be religious than it is about what it means to align himself differently with different communities. That religion can and would play a role in Baldwin's conception and construction of his people is, actually, neither the question nor the issue. Baldwin's secular—I want to suggest—is not calibrated either to tracking amounts of religion or to religion as a question of agentic assent.

Yet I have to admit that this reading is not there on the surface. For on the surface it would seem that Baldwin is actually setting up a stark choice between the church and the avenue—the sacred versus the secular. That is, this scene would suggest that the larger story that Baldwin tells in *The Fire Next Time* about religion, in fact, fits a potted twentieth-century account of secularization: Nothing more than another "racket" like those of the iniquities of the street—"Some went on wine or whisky or the needle, and are still on it. And others, like me, fled into the church"[21]—religion rests on fundamentally flawed grounds. Throughout *Fire*, religion can appear to be the province of the fearful, the aggressive, the delusional, and the politically irresponsible. Thus, with Freud, Baldwin explains religion as a set of obsessive practices to quell sexual fears: "I myself had also become a source of fire and temptation."[22] And with Nietzsche, Baldwin claims that all theology is "designed for the same purpose: namely, the sanctification of power."[23] White Christianity, the Nation of Islam, and black Christianity all come under review. In particular, *Fire* is unsparing of what he calls the "shameful" effect of Christianity on black America.[24] For example, on the nature of devotion in his own holiness tradition, Baldwin writes: "And the passion with which we loved the Lord was a measure of how deeply we feared and distrusted and, in the end, hated almost all strangers, always, and avoided and despised ourselves."[25] The "price of this ticket"—of becoming Christian—has been severe.

So, on this secularist reading, Baldwin recounts and repeats the line "whose little boy are you" by way of renouncing or expressing shame at the very question and his own need to have it fulfilled. In other words, to need to belong, in this sense, is to admit, as Baldwin does, to being "so frightened, and at the mercy of many conundrums, that inevitably, that summer, *someone* would have taken me over."[26] In this moment, Baldwin would seem to indulge a secularist wind that reinforces or reduces religion to an immature allegiance wherein the wages of belonging are pure, absolute, and subsuming. The problem of religion, from this perspective, is the problem of desiring to be somebody's little boy.[27]

It is something of this spirit that leads Clarence Hardy to conclude that for Baldwin religion "serves as a refuge for the meek from the combustible and secular world pulsing with danger."[28] Hardy's intent in his work is to treat Baldwin's "ultimate rejection of the Christian god seriously enough" while also rendering "Baldwin's ambiguous posture toward black holiness culture."[29] Thus, Hardy suggests that while Baldwin certainly is able to appreciate the historical value of black religion as a cultural system—Baldwin sounds wistful notes for certain aspects such as communal song, and he continues to draw on the rhetoric and rhythms of holiness culture—Baldwin nevertheless comes to feel that the social, political, and cultural costs of being a black Christian, or for that matter a black Muslim, have been far too great:

> So, despite Baldwin's consistent portrayal of a black holiness culture full of energy and passionate life, there is an implicit criticism throughout his work that understands the principal backdrop to black people's conversion to Christianity in the United States to be shame and not hope . . . its redemptive value ultimately fails to overcome the extent to which Christianity has contributed to African disfigurement.[30]

These are tough words. Hardy's intent is not, I think, to give a secularist reading that reifies religion and the secular as diametrically opposed. He wants to reveal Baldwin as painfully ambivalent about religion, as subject to a set of intense and deep religious memories that haunt and whisper to him but that he can no longer afford to remain attached to. Yet to capture that dynamic, Hardy resorts to a stark contrast: "Although Baldwin seems continually caught throughout his career between intensely religious and secular worlds, he squarely faces the secular—he always faces the city."[31] By constructing the secular and the religious in opposition, Hardy necessarily imposes limits on how much work the rhetoric, vocabulary, and practices of holiness culture can do for Baldwin—for if they were to do too much Baldwin would no longer be squarely secular. Note that this version of what I think of as secularist ideology does not flatly dismiss religion. Hardy appreciates religious resonances. Still, because the secular and the religious are understood in opposition, his reading has to track—and keep a wary eye on—the religious qua religious in his midst. And at some point, the secularist, in order to remain secular, has to repel religion, even attach shame to religion, and pay allegiance to something—an epistemology, a set of values, an account of authority—that is distinguished as secular over and against the religious. Thus Baldwin decisively faces the secular city.

Yet as *Fire* unfolds, it becomes clear that the stakes of this one scene—the relationship between the religious and the nonreligious and what it means to belong—are enormous. In the fullness of the text, Baldwin does not try to dismiss these. He is trying to worry them—to resist a stark dichotomy between the sacred and the secular, to mark the ethics of what it means to become somebody's little boy as perilous but also deeply necessary for survival. What Baldwin makes beautifully and tragically clear in *Fire* is that the stakes of all belonging—the terror, vulnerability, and suffering that grips us all—are precisely the ones that the question "whose little boy are you" bring to the surface. These stakes—the "totems, crosses, blood sacrifices, steeples, mosques, races, armies, flags, nations" (339) from which we all derive—cannot be renounced or sloughed off. What I am calling the ethics of belonging is another way of describing what Shulman describes as Baldwin's practice of "acknowledgment": "Baldwin depicts the fatality of bonds we cannot really repudiate," thus forcing us to face "that identificatory bonds are inescapable in human life, at once costly [and] valuable."[32]

On these terms, the question "whose little boy are you?" is in fact the most important question about identity that there is. It should be seen as a way of honoring Baker's question of peoplehood. It is only by facing the primal energies of these bonds that Baldwin thinks we can begin to trace our frailties and fragilities, our knotted sources of anger, and our passions and prejudices that continue to deform and misshape: "I knew the tension in me between love and power, between pain and rage, and the curious, the grinding way I remained extended between these poles."[33] Knowing this tension is the only way, on Baldwin's account, of knowing what, if any, possible versions of justice are still available for America.

What sort of belonging is Baldwin after? Who are his people? And how is this question of belonging helpfully illuminated by engaging religion—religion not as a concept essentially opposed to the secular but as fully imbricated in the secular? J. Kameron Carter's work *Race: A Theological Account* is of help here. Carter's central claim is that modern notions of race are rooted in the theological problem of the status of Christ's flesh and spirit. Carter's view is that Christianity never fully rejected the Gnostic view and thus historically struggled against the idea of Christ's flesh as necessarily impure, as already and always embodied in historically constituted communities. In turn, Christianity became practiced at denigrating the flesh—often actual Jewish flesh—in the name of an ahistorical, idealized Christianity of abstract, unembodied, and essentialized spiritual ideals. And ultimately, these theological patterns, when fired by colonial expansionism, gave rise to a discourse of whiteness that allowed for conquering and overcoming actual embodied communities of darker flesh.[34]

In contrast, Carter characterizes the tradition of "New World Afro-Christian" faith as a "countertheology" of blackness: "early Afro-Christians understood their bodies as reinscribed in Christ's body and that this reinscription was the locus of a theologically secured freedom."[35] In other words, black theology fashioned itself in opposition to the Gnostic tendencies of orthodox Christianity. The case that Carter makes is that African American Christians in the New World realized from the start that what is at stake in becoming and being Christian is the status, position, and meaning of their bodies. Black theology pushed back against Gnostic tendencies and sought to recapture the Irenaean emphasis on the "impurity" of Jesus's socially and politically embodied Jewish flesh. Black theology "redirected the discourse of race as it had come to inhere in their bodies precisely by redirecting Christian identity itself and thereby redirecting Christian theology as a discourse."[36] That redirection was always focused on social and material realities. It was focused on communities, black communities with particular histories and stories. In other words, black theology names a tradition of socially active wrestling with being subject irrefragably to both earthly and heavenly economies. It is a theological discourse of impurity. The "impurity" of black theology is in its clarity about the ways in which shards of the theological spin their way into political consciousness and material form.

How does Carter's account of black theology speak to my reading of Baldwin? What I think Carter's work does is give a framework for understanding Baldwin as part of this tradition of black theology. While Carter does not deal with Baldwin in his work, he very well could have. Baldwin himself long understood race to be at root a theological problem about the nature of black flesh: about white anxieties about purity and about black consciousness of sacred flesh as material and real: "There is a sense in which it can be said that black flesh is the flesh that St. Paul wants to have mortified. There is a sense in which it can be said that very long ago, for a complex of reasons, but among them power, the Christian personality split itself in two, split itself into dark and light, in fact, and it is now bewildered, at war with itself."[37] On Baldwin's view, whiteness, which on these terms might simply be called white theology, is a "particular true faith . . . more deeply concerned about the soul than it is the body, to which fact the flesh (and corpses) of countless infidels bear witness."[38] This faith represents an adolescent and violent refusal of complex and difficult admixtures, symbolized by that "*blasphemous* tasteless foam rubber" that Americans call bread.[39] The blasphemy of white bread speaks directly to Baldwin's critique of Saint Paul: it is based on the degradation of blackness and brownness as impurities. As such, American white bread represents the refusal to take the sacramental host. Elsewhere, Baldwin speaks of white Americans' need to "preserve their innocence," and it is not too much to say that this need to deny American complexities of the flesh represents the refusal to take the sacramental host, as well.[40]

The sanctity of brown bread, of the host, is as an amalgamated and adulterated composite. Baldwin's efforts—the critical intervention he is trying to affect—stands in dramatic contrast to the pursuit of purity. As such, *Fire* represents an attempt to expose and come to terms with the necessary conditions of impurity. Thus it was "down there at the foot of the cross" that Baldwin learned not purity of faith or univocal devotion to God but instead a carnal account of belonging, of love for his people, one forged as he says "in spite of—or, not inconceivably, because of the shabbiness of my motives." In these moments, his Pentecostal church taught him not the purity of his spirit or his soul but a sense of attachment based in communal "anguish and rejoicing," "speaking from the depths of a visible, tangible continuing despair of the goodness of the Lord."[41] And these conditions of impurity must be revealed because impurity is going to be the only term by which he can find a way to belong to America and by which America has a chance to save itself. This is precisely the sense in which for Shulman Baldwin "queers prophecy by abandoning the purity entailed in the logic of fidelity to God."[42] What Carter helps us see is that this abandonment of purity is not antitheological or atheological but, in fact, *theological* in the black tradition. Shulman is exactly right in seeing Baldwin as embracing "a worldview stained by carnal embodiment, willfull particularity, and moral ambiguity."[43] But where Shulman or Hardy insist on describing Baldwin as a secular prophet, Carter would have us understand this very same "stained carnal embodiment" as the black theological tradition whose faith is in recognizing and working through the human stain. With its paradoxical tensions between the tangible and the divine, Baldwin shows how this theological frame fuels a type of agonistic belonging: Baldwin's own attachment to something that he knows to be ultimately flawed.

This is a theological frame that Baldwin never outgrows. He is a practitioner of this black theology throughout his life, beyond his childhood in the church. Later in *Fire*, when he is older and attempting to craft the terms by which he can fashion this country, he relies on the same theological frame. Love is needed but only a love that realizes "the torment and the necessity of love."[44] The races "deeply need each other here if we are to achieve our identity,"[45] but if and only if the races accept themselves as adulterated composites rife with hatreds and rages, if and only if they come up with actions and practices that reflect an understanding of their own dispensations, borne differently but also interconnectedly, to love and murder.

When seeing Baldwin through this theological lens, ironically the terms religious and secular resemble gossamer and dissolve into thread and film. It is of no great importance or interest to determine whether Baldwin is secular or religious in the sense that being one or the other implies having, or not, something identifiably religious within. Like Henry Box Brown, Baldwin does not possess a buffered self. The self that seeks out its connections to love and murder is porous, necessarily in contact and conflict with other intersecting selves. On this view, to call Baldwin theological is not to start a conversation about whether Baldwin is religious or secular, but instead it is to instruct a conversation about Baldwin's vision of justice, a theological vision that extols a rollicking and plangent discourse of impurity, one that allows him to produce accounts of "*all that beauty*" in those "many thousands gone"[46] of black Americans. That beauty is "nothing less than the perpetual achievement of the impossible."[47] The impossible is not perfect; it is, in fact, imperfect and does not accord to normative standards of beauty. The impossible is in the way accounts of that type of beauty—of generations "raising their children, eating their greens, crying their curses, weeping their tears, singing their songs, making their love, as the sun rose, as the sun set"[48]—decisively illuminates the sight of who is counted as fully human and real. *Fire* is nothing if not a (re)writing of the reality of America through a black theological lens in an attempt to get us all—from whatever positions we inhabit—to honor impurity. The "fire next time" burns on the denial of impurity. The theology here is not concerned with the right mix of the religious and the nonreligious but instead with dispelling illusions of innocence.

And here are the stakes of this contemporary moment, this age of high theory and conversation about the secular. Do these conversations feed those fires that occlude the real and reinforce discourses of purity, or do they help us see anew who is being denied the status of the real—as deserving of attention, recognition, resources, and recompense. Until today's secular age comes to understand and wrestle with its own commitments to a politics of innocence, until it comes up with actions and practices that reflect an understanding of its own dispensation to love and murder, I fear our age will only skirt the central questions of the secular. This is the intervention of *Race and Secularism in America:* interrogating and disrupting the organizing power contained in the secular, loosening its grip to allow our collective impurities to flourish.

## NOTES

1. James Baldwin, *The Fire Next Time*, in *Collected Essays*, ed. Toni Morrison (New York: Library of America, 1998), 297, 303.
2. Ibid., 303.
3. Chadwick is quoted in Jonathan Sheehan, "Enlightenment, Religion, and the Enigma of Secularization: A Review Essay," *American Historical Review* 108, no. 4 (October 2003): 1071.
4. Sigmund Freud's work, of course, is foundational to this tradition of thought. Christian Smith provides a masterful account of the way higher education contributed to this tendency. See Christian Smith, ed., *The Secular Revolution: Power, Interests, and Conflict in the Secularization of American Public Life* (Berkeley: University of California Press, 2003). Jose Casanova's classic *Public Religions in the Modern World* (Chicago: University of Chicago Press, 1994) gives a good sociological account of this tendency. Robert Audi's work seeks to diminish the role that religious reasons should play in public discourse. See Robert Audi and Nicholas Wolterstorff, *Religion in the Public Square: The Place of Religious Convictions in Political Debate* (Lanham, Md.: Rowman and Littlefield, 1997). Steven Bruce's current works extend this tradition. See Steven Bruce, *God Is Dead: Secularization in the West* (Malden, Mass.: Wiley-Blackwell, 2002); and Steven Bruce, *Secularization: In Defense of an Unfashionable Theory* (New York: Oxford University Press, 2013).
5. Mary Douglas, "The Effects of Modernization on Religious Change," *Daedalus* 111, no. 1 (Winter 1982): 1.
6. Peter L. Berger, "The Desecularization of the World: A Global Overview," in *The Desecularization of the World: Resurgent Religion and World Politics* (Washington, D.C.: Ethics and Public Policy Center, 1999), 2.
7. Charles Taylor's epic *A Secular Age* alone is responsible for an entire oeuvre of writings. The Social Science Research Council (SSRC) launched the website "The Immanent Frame: Secularism, Religion, and the Public Sphere" to discuss Taylor's work. Multiple sets of essays have emerged from these efforts including Craig Calhoun et al., eds., *Rethink-*

*ing Secularism* (New York: Oxford University Press 2011); Philip Gorski et al., eds., *The Post-Secular in Question* (New York: NYU Press 2012); Michael Warner et al., eds., *Varieties of Secularism in a Secular Age* (Cambridge, Mass.: Harvard University Press, 2010); and Judith Butler et al., *The Power of Religion in the Public Sphere* (New York: Columbia University Press, 2011).

8. This literature is now vast. In addition to the work by the authors named above, other good examples include John Lardas Modern, *Secularism in Antebellum America* (Chicago: University of Chicago Press, 2011); Winnifred F. Sullivan, *The Impossibility of Religious Freedom* (Princeton, N.J.: Princeton University Press, 2007); and William Connolly, *Capitalism and Christianity, American Style* (Durham, N.C.: Duke University Press, 2008).

9. Freedom—particularly increased religious expression—often becomes a discourse that defines the "new secular."

10. Jeffrey Stout's *Democracy and Tradition* (Princeton, N.J.: Princeton University Press, 2004) makes the most important case for the epistemological and political legitimacy of religious expression in public discourse. The account here is deeply influenced by his work.

11. "Secular, Not Secularist" was the title of the keynote address Jeffrey Stout gave at the conference "The Varieties of Secular Experience," Vassar College, November 13, 2008.

12. On the importance of acknowledging the "contestable" nature of cherished commitments, see William Connolly, *Why I Am Not a Secularist* (Minneapolis: University of Minnesota Press, 1999), 7, 39.

13. Charles Taylor, "Afterword: *Apologia pro Libro suo*," in *Varieties of Secularism in a Secular Age*, ed. Michael Warner et al (Cambridge, Mass.: Harvard University Press, 2010), 318.

14. Wendy Brown, *Regulating Aversion: Tolerance in the Age of Identity and Empire* (Princeton, N.J.: Princeton University Press, 2008).

15. I'm thinking here of George Shulman's account of prophecy in his magisterial work, *American Prophecy: Race and Redemption in American Political Culture* (Minneapolis: University of Minnesota Press, 2008).

16. Shulman, *American Prophecy*, 235.

17. For example, take the four volumes I mentioned above published in conjunction with the SSRC. Three of them—*Varieties of Secularism in a Secular Age, Rethinking Secularism,* and *The Post-Secular in Question*—do not contain a single essay on race or African American religion. *The Power of Religion in the Public Sphere* includes comments and conversations with Cornel West, yet even in these I am struck by how infrequently race is distinctly theorized within these conversations about the secular.

18. Charles Taylor, *A Secular Age* (Cambridge, Mass.: Belknap Press of Harvard University Press, 2007), 3–42.

19. Ibid., 38.

20. See Barbara Ransby, *Ella Baker and the Black Freedom Movement: A Radical Democratic Vision* (Chapel Hill: University of North Carolina Press, 2003), 13.

21. Baldwin, *The Fire Next Time*, 299.

22. Ibid., 301.

23. Ibid., 315.

24. Baldwin, "Many Thousands Gone," in *Notes of a Native Son*, in *Collected Essays*, 23. Speaking with the voice of "an American" about black identity, Baldwin writes: "As he accepted the alabaster Christ and the bloody cross—in the bearing of which he would find his redemption, as, indeed, to our outraged astonishment, he sometimes did—he must, henceforth, accept that image we then gave him of himself; having no other and standing, moreover, in danger of death should he fail to accept the dazzling light thus brought into such darkness" (23).

25. Baldwin, *The Fire Next Time*, 310.

26. Ibid., 303, emphasis original.

27. His later meeting with Elijah Muhmammed is but a repetition of this primal scene.

28. Clarence E. Hardy III, *James Baldwin's God: Sex, Hope, and Crisis in Black Holiness Culture* (Knoxville, TN: The University of Tennessee Press, 2009): 6.

29. Ibid., 110.

30. Ibid., xi.

31. Ibid., 7.

32. Shulman, *American Prophecy*, 158.

33. Baldwin, *The Fire Next Time*, 321.

34. J. Kameron Carter, *Race: A Theological Account* (New York: Oxford University Press, 2008), especially 11–121.

35. Ibid., 343–4.

36. Ibid., 344.

37. Baldwin, "White Racism or World Community?" in *Collected Essays*, 754.

38. Baldwin, *The Fire Next Time*, 313.

39. Ibid., 311, emphasis mine.

40. Baldwin, "Preservation of Innocence," in *Collected Essays*, 594–600. Shulman makes a similar point in his essay in this volume.

41. Baldwin, *The Fire Next Time*, 306.

42. Shulman, *American Prophecy*, 163.

43. Ibid., 146.

44. Baldwin, *The Fire Next Time*, 335.

45. Ibid., 342.

46. Ibid., 346, emphasis original; Baldwin, "Many Thousands Gone," in *Notes of a Native Son*, in *Collected Essays*, 19–34.

47. Baldwin, *The Fire Next Time*, 346.

48. Ibid., 344.

# AFTERWORD:
# CRITICAL INTERSECTIONS:
# RACE, SECULARISM, GENDER

Tracy Fessenden

N 2008, the African-born Ayaan Hirsi Ali, a former Dutch parliamentarian and newly appointed fellow of the American Enterprise Institute, was recognized with an impressive slate of international awards. These included the inaugural Prix Simone de Beauvoir pour la liberté des femmes, established by the feminist philosopher Julia Kristeva for the advancement of gender equality and human rights; the Richard Dawkins Prize, awarded by the Atheist Alliance International, a "positive global voice for atheism and secularism"; and the Anisfield-Wolf Book Award for "recent books that have made important contributions to our understanding of racism and appreciation of the rich diversity of human culture," a prize whose past recipients include Zora Neale Hurston, Ralph Ellison, Toni Morrison, and Martin Luther King Jr. The honors followed the publication in English of Hirsi Ali's books *The Caged Virgin* (2006) and *Infidel: My Life* (2007), both international bestsellers. In them Hirsi Ali tells of her early years in Somalia, the arranged marriage she escaped by emigrating and the childhood genital cutting she did not, her renunciation of her Muslim faith in favor of atheism in 1992, and her post-9/11 activism on behalf of women who suffer violence in the name of religion. The latter includes her work on the short film *Submission* with the filmmaker Theo van Gogh, who was assassinated by a gunman with Islamist ties shortly after the film opened. Since 2006 Hirsi Ali has lived and worked in the United States, where she has shaped her writing and advocacy to the vision of the conservative Washington policy institute (the AEI) that sponsors her.

Taken together, the Dawkins Prize, Prix de Beauvoir, and Anisfield-Wolf Award, all conferred on Hirsi Ali in the year of Barack Obama's election to the presidency, would suggest that the commitments they respectively honor—to secularization, to women's freedom, and to racial equality—proceed apace as companion projects. Hirsi Ali's books and commentary likewise tend to frame secularization, feminism, and racial justice as neatly meshing gears in the advancement of human progress. The subtitle of *The Caged Virgin*, offered as a how-to guide for Muslim women to free themselves from religious oppression through the application of Enlightenment principles, is *An Emancipation Proclamation for Women and Islam*. Her spin on the well-established critique of racial privilege in the U.S. women's movement is to take U.S. feminists to task for their blindness to women's *religious* oppression beyond the West. The problem with Western feminism, Hirsi Ali asserts, is that it "still defines the white man as the oppressor"; Obama's presidency, she noted in a 2009 interview, might instead signal to the world that "we have taught the white man that bigotry is bad and he has given it up, at least most of it" and so set the stage for recognition of "bigotry . . . committed in the name of the black man, the brown man, the yellow man, whatever color" against women in the name of religion. When women's human rights are at last successfully wrested from religious control, she predicted, gender equality will come into being as inevitably as "the eradication of apartheid."[1]

The present volume tells a more troubled story of secularization, race, and progress. Hirsi Ali's example, in turn, invites us to think about the place of feminism among the terms—secularism, race, progress—whose vexed relations the volume calls into view.

The essays in this book tell a story of invisibility and erasure. In their accounts of black literary and political struggles "with the terms of the secular modern," in their stories of escaped slaves and colonial maps, post-MLK freedom marches and Salafi subjectivities, contributors take stock of a "surprising, even shocking" neglect of race in the reigning narratives of secularization in the American academy and public life. As the editor Jonathon Kahn charges, neither the standard secularization thesis that prevailed in the twentieth century nor much of its reconsideration in the twenty-first—a project that includes Charles Taylor's massive *A Secular Age*—has sought to engage the experiences of African Americans as racialized subjects or the "question of how patterns of enslavement and colonization in the Americas shape Enlightenment and post-Enlightenment conceptions of the secular."

Cumulatively, these essays' identification of a startling lacuna gives way to suspicion that the omission of race is, in fact, necessary to the operations of secularization itself. As Vincent Lloyd observes in the introduction to this volume, the unspoken corollary to the disappearance of religion in accounts of the secular is the disappearance of race. This is so insofar as the secularization story remains grounded in what Anibal Quijano, invoked here in William Hart's contribution, calls modernity's "two principal founding myths: first, the idea of the History of human civilization as a trajectory that departed from a state of nature and culminated in Europe; second, a view of the differences between Europe and non-Europe as natural (racial) differences and not consequences of a history of power." To this view, secularization is its own driver, actuated by the irresistible logic of its own inevitability, and therefore it happens in a space swept clean of its own relations of power—swept clean, that is, of alternative modes of being in the world and the record of their vanquishing. The absence of race from accounts of the secular is a function of that sweeping clean.

Worse, the story secularism has learned to tell about itself, a narrative of modernity from which race and racism alike have been scrubbed, is a story of freedom. Secularism's "moral narrative of modernity," as Webb Keane parses it, "is a story about human emancipation and self-mastery," of "human liberation from a host of false beliefs and fetishisms that undermined freedom in the past." This is the path along which reliance on religious authority ostensibly gives way to the freedom of conscience that makes democratic agency possible. To this view, those who persist in religious identification or observance, "displacing their own agency," as Keane puts it, onto "rules, traditions, or fetishes (including sacred texts)," are a puzzle and a problem, perhaps even a threat to democratic politics as such.[2] Or as Jonathon Kahn pointedly contends, "The long arc of the twentieth century's secularization thesis, with its claims that religion is irrational, on the wane, and inappropriate for political work in the public square, should be called for what it is: a version of whiteness, if not white supremacy, that served to question the right of political place of African American citizens."

Not only race but also gender and sexuality have largely been absent from the telling and the retelling of the story of the secular.[3] And in this case, too, the omission appears to be structural: the opposition between public and private, so basic to the relation between secular and religious domains, is also what organizes gender and sexuality in modernity. Are the "points of intersection between the American disciplining of religion and the American disciplining of race," as Vincent Lloyd identifies them here, also places where gender and sexuality are disciplined by secular rule? In a word, yes—but not in ways that allow for any simple overlay or retrieval of secularism's occluded terms. Gender adds its own troublesome strand to what Lloyd aptly calls the "secularist-racializing knot."

In the United States, the intertwining of religion with race and gender has been and remains instrumental for projects of secular governance, white supremacy, and the control of women, even as it likewise plays a role in the advancement of, variously, religious freedom, racial equality, and women's flourishing—none of which is necessarily pursued in service to the others and all of which come in for management by the secular state. To see how the disciplining of religion, race, and gender intersect in the United States it is helpful to tack back and forth between history and policy specific to the United States and the larger arc of secular governance in the West.

The ascendency of secular governance in the Enlightenment implicitly cast religion as anterior to the rational, secular state. By domesticating religion as a matter of opinion or belief—"It does me no injury for my neighbor to say that there are twenty gods or no God," as Jefferson famously glossed the different orders of religion and government in the United States[4]—secular governance renders religion subordinate to the state and its institutions, henceforth identified with the deliberative mechanisms of a shared rationality for which private, potentially idiosyncratic belief must stand aside. As Gauri Viswanathan observes, such a move lays bare "the uneven development of colonizing and colonized societies," for it "permit[s] religion to be more 'naturally' identified as a necessary prior stage in the progression toward nationhood."[5] When "religion came to be identified as such—that is, more or less in the same sense that we think of it today," writes Tomoko Masuzawa, "it came to be recognized above all as something that, in the opinions of many self-consciously modern Europeans, was in the process of disappearing from their midst or, if not altogether disappearing, becoming circumscribed in such a way that it was finally discernible as a distinct, and limited, phenomenon."[6]

In this sense, the positing of the bounded phenomenon "religion," understood even in terms of the private convictions of deist statesmen and their neighbors, belongs crucially to the colonial enterprise and its attendant project of racialization. As Josef Sorett explains in this volume, the "category of 'religion' emerged as central to a necessarily comparative, missionary enterprise that posited (for the West) secular reason as the present of a Christian past and attributed (to the rest) a notion of 'religion' as grounded in a past governed by outmoded ways of being in the world."

In this sense, the category of religion in modernity is not only implicitly racialized but also feminized in being counterposed to the public sphere as the domain of reason. In the United States, the feminization of religion has been most visible and accessible to historians in the form of the ideology of woman's domestic sphere, which emerges in the early nineteenth century as capitalism's salvific counterpart. In its usual iterations, the ideology of separate spheres assigns the work of religious and familial nurture to women, freeing the public sphere from networks of obligation that would hamper the virile exercise of market competition. Increasingly removed from economic productivity and other aspects of worldliness, women, in this model, devoted themselves to the home as a haven of tranquility and spiritual value and became avid consumers of the magazines, advice literature, sermons, and novels that trained them in their new, primary role as selfless and pious guardians of the Christian family state.

As Aída Hurtado and others have pointed out, however, the separate-spheres model that assigns women to the home and men to the public world of politics and commerce, whatever its enormous and enduring cultural power, "is relevant only for the white middle and upper classes since historically the American state has intervened constantly" in the private and familial lives of outsiders to this sector, for whom there has been no private sphere "except that which they manage to create and protect in an otherwise hostile environment."[7] So contextualized within the matrices of race and class, "woman's sphere" emerges as the site of multiple and conflicting hierarchies, in which "woman" means differently for the different women thus organized, even if gender and religion are the primary categories through which their subjection, under the broader conditions of patriarchy, is maintained.

The feminization of religion in America follows on its founding move of privatizing religion in the cause of secular governance. What Mark Lilla extols as the "great separation" of religion from politics that marks the transition to modernity promises both to free a space of rational deliberation for the exercise of democracy, unbeholden to dogma and fiat, and at the same time to protect religious belief from coercive intervention from the state.[8] Cordoned off from politics, however, the newly private and domesticated domain of the religious is secured not only as the space of personal belief, to which all in a secular democracy are entitled. It is also the space of sexuality and, pending their recent, uneven, and incomplete political enfranchisement, the space of women. Secularism leaves religion to find its strongest articulations in this private domain, the domain not only of legally protected belief but also of the regulation of gender and sexuality in the service of religious conviction.

*Pace* Ayaan Hirsi Ali, then, secularism is less a remedy for the religious control of women than its structuring condition. The gendering of religion in modernity is not simply a peaceable settlement that assigns the private sphere to women, religion, and the family and the public sphere to men, rationality, and citizenship. Insofar as "religious authority becomes marginal to the conduct of civic and political affairs," Saba Mahmood suggests, "it simultaneously comes to acquire a privileged place in the regulation of the private sphere (to which the family, religion, and sexuality are relegated)."[9] To invoke Vincent Lloyd's formulation, secularism circumscribes "a religious domain that is managed by [nonreligious] power"; likewise "racial-minority communities are managed by power and circumscribed by nonminority, that is, white, forces." So too the assignment of women and sexuality, together with religion, to the private sphere enlists women and religion alike in forms of management that would make each commensurate with public norms. The marginalization of religion under the reign of secularism and the religious control of women and the family in matters of sexuality, marriage, and reproduction are the two sides of one coin.

At the same time—to pull on the secularist-gendering-racializing knot—the implicit link between religion and women's oppression could also be made a pretext of empire in the name of women's rescue. The view of religion that Hirsi Ali has come to represent—in Azza Karam's gloss, "that religion is oppressive, subordinating and marginalizing of women in general and an obstacle to women's rights movements, let alone gender equality," in short, that "religion = women's (sexual, political, economic and sociocultural) subordination"[10]—was and remains a staple of the triumphal narratives of modernization that undergird the West's imperial projects, from the British Raj to the conquest of the Philippines to the invasion of Afghanistan and Iraq. Far from being anti-Christian, however, these discourses typically set Western Christianity ahead of other religious cultures as belonging to a later, more enlightened stage of development on the path of civilization. Undergirding such projects are implicit assumptions about modernity, religion, and progress: some societies are manifestly more advanced than others, and the treatment of women indexes who is ahead and who behind on the path that moves religion into the modern, secular world.

Here is where religion in association with women and religion in association with colonial subjects come to occupy distinct but related terrains. In secularism's founding separations, both women and colonialism's primitive others are made to bear the fleshly limitations from which white men are ostensibly emancipated, by reason, for the work of secular governance. George Shulman's contribution to this volume helps us see that the Enlightenment separation of politics from religion maps at once onto the "Cartesian/Enlightenment separation of mind/reason from body/animal" and onto what J. Kameron Carter identifies as European Christianity's "denigrat[ions of] the flesh" in service to "abstract, unembodied, and essentialized spiritual ideals." Both patterns, Carter suggests, fueled a colonial "discourse of whiteness that allowed for conquering and overcoming actual embodied communities of darker flesh." Against Charles Taylor's account of secularization as disembodiment, in this volume Ed Blum insists that African Americans "did not live 'less embodied' lives. Their selves were not buffered, and the law made sure of that." Blum's reading of the narrative of Henry "Box" Brown, a slave who mailed himself to freedom nailed inside a wooden crate, points instead to the way that African Americans were made to bear a surplus embodiment, the residue of secularization as disembodiment and abstraction.

Within the colonial schema, those who resist the "secular terms of the liberal state," Judith Butler observes, are pegged as laggards whose notions of religion *and* sexuality are "invariably considered childish, fanatic, or structured according to ostensibly irrational and primitive taboos."[11] But domestic ideology provided the American woman, ensconced within her private sphere, a way forward on the path of freedom from embodied limitation to which both secular governance and Christianity's spiritual disciplining of the flesh laid claim. The job of these women was to teach the nation, and the world, to behave. And for many, the elevating path of Christian regeneration was also the path of politics.

According to Catharine Beecher's *Treatise on Domestic Economy*, it was the task of American women to "exhibit to the world the beneficent influences of Christianity, when carried into every social, civil, and political institution."[12] Beecher's *Domestic Economy* belongs to an outpouring of antebellum cultural production that elaborated at length on the duties of women to their homes and families and attributed a spiritual authority to the well-managed home and the woman enclosed within it. A revised and expanded version of Beecher's treatise published with her sister Harriet Beecher Stowe as *The American Woman's Home* asks: What "is the end designed by the family state which Jesus Christ came into the world to secure?" It is, they answer, "to provide for the training of our race to the highest possible intelligence, virtue, and happiness . . . with chief reference to a future immortal existence."[13] And since a "state is but an association of families," Stowe wrote in another work on domestic management, "there is no reason why sister, wife, and mother should be more powerless in the state than in the home."[14]

If the racializing of religion marks religion's otherness to the secular state, the gendering of religion in the ideology of woman's domestic sphere specifies religion's potential for *partnership* with the secular state in, among other projects, the management of race. As Amy Kaplan observes, the domestic sphere, associated with women, is typically opposed at once to two registers: the public and the foreign. When the domestic sphere is opposed to the public sphere, Kaplan contends, women and men occupy separate terrains, but when the domestic is opposed to the foreign, men and women occupy a shared terrain. The work of nineteenth-century domesticity, then, was not only to provide a spiritual, feminine haven from the corruptions of masculine politics and industry but also to unite white men and women in a national, familial domain and "to generate notions of the foreign against which the nation can be imagined as home."[15] Thus a key function of Christian nurture in *The American Woman's Home* is to enable "Christian families" to gather about them "Christian neighborhoods . . . [so that] ere long colonies from these prosperous and Christian communities [may] . . . go forth to shine as 'lights of the world' in all the now darkened nations."[16]

So organized, the nation could be imagined as a white, Protestant family that nevertheless harbored darkened nations within it, much as domestic ideology set white mothers over the children and variously nonwhite, non-Protestant servants who required her tutelage to be acculturated, as far as possible, to Protestant middle-class norms. The racializing of religion in the colonial enterprise, meanwhile, carried with it the assumption that the more distant a culture from those Protestant norms, the more damaging to women and the more in need of colonial or missionary reform.

Feminization and racialization in this way track a split between "good" and "bad" religion, jointly producing what Winnifred Fallers Sullivan identifies as the "curiously Janus-faced quality" of religion in modernity. Religion's one face, Sullivan observes, is "regarded as a primary source of ethical reflection and behavior and is thought by some to be the only source." Its other face "is associated with the irrational, the savage, and the 'other' in a profoundly constitutive way. That face is to be feared and kept separate"[17]—made subject to what Willie Jennings describes in this volume as the desires at once of whiteness and of secularism "to abstract, isolate, delimit, and sequester." So isolated and delimited, racialized religion is rendered no religion, or false religion, or as too literal, too ritualistic, too embodied. Feminized religion, on the other hand, could be improving and expansive, a path of spiritual promotion amounting, if not to disembodiment, then to the possibility of agency that extended beyond even national borders.

For women who found their compulsory, if elevating, identification with "good" religion oppressive, the feminization of religion could eventually also be freeing insofar as it illuminated the path of secularism as the path of liberation.[18] The view that religion—particularly "bad" religion—was what emancipated women were emancipated *from* continues to resonate strongly in projects that pit the secular West, as champion and guardian of gender equality, against the recalcitrant rest, most especially the Muslim world.[19] Evidence of the particular backwardness of Muslim societies today is often adduced in the persistence of sharia (religious law) in the governance of families, including laws pertaining to the rights of women. As Saba Mahmood suggests, the place of sharia in modern Islamic family law is conventionally seen as the result of the laxity or forbearance of colonial powers, "who supposedly refrained from interfering in the religious affairs of colonized peoples, thereby leaving their family laws intact as the space of native culture and autonomy" and as the enduring marker of the failure of Muslim societies to enter the modern, secular world. Mahmood argues instead for seeing the entrenchment of religion-based family law, which prevails among nearly all religious cultures in postcolonial societies, not as a disquieting relic of a premodern past but rather as a product of the modern state's "simultaneous relegation of religion and sexuality to the private sphere." Under the auspices of the modern state, she suggests, religion-based family law persists less as an expression of the colonial power's benign or naïve tolerance of native culture than as a crucial feature of colonial rule itself.[20] That is to say, the commonsense assertion that religiosity registers primarily in sexual attitudes, whether elevating or oppressive to women, is both an invention and an instrument of modernity. What was "tolerated" and fostered by colonial powers in the Muslim world was the close association of religion with gender and sexuality already operative, and formative, in modern states.

In this sense, the ready assumption that secularization is liberating for women is both racist and spurious. It's racist insofar as its displacement of gender and sexual inequality onto "backward" religious cultures makes the continuing subordination of the raced, colonial subject the marker, if not the necessary condition, of secular women's emancipation. And it's spurious insofar as the exceptional status of religion-based sexual governance is already deeply embedded in secular law. Secular remedies have proven so largely unavailing in the face of religious claims to special, opt-out status vis-à-vis legal protections for women's freedoms because the legal separation of religious and secular domains is precisely what *grounds* these claims. As the U.S. Supreme Court recently decided in *Hobby Lobby*, the sufficient basis on which for-profit corporations may legally deny the full scope of federally mandated medical coverage to their female employees is the avowed sincerity of their officers' religious opinion about contraception. Even as it remains a necessary, structural feature of the narrative of women's emancipation from religious constraint under the reign of liberalism, the special relationship between religion and sexuality in secular law reliably empowers voices that move to restrict women's freedoms on religious grounds. The power of secular law to advance women's freedom, in other words, is curtailed by the secular dispensation itself.

When religion is permitted to speak to and within the secular, what is it permitted to speak *for*? A dispiriting corollary to *Hobby Lobby* may be the "Reigniting the Legacy" campaign analyzed in this volume by Erica Edwards, which aimed to move black voices "back into the conversation of the nation" by enlisting them in defending the patriarchal family from the incursions of gender and sexual equality. As Edwards shows, orchestrations of black opposition to marriage equality have worked by reframing the spiritual and political legacy of Martin Luther King Jr. as the project of recuperating "the black family through the recovery of the black male head of the household." The call of the Reigniting campaign to "Stop the Silence" of those who would purge outsiders to the patriarchal family from its vision of the Kingdom of God on earth, Edwards notes, was explicitly cast as a black religious coming-out narrative.

Again under the banner of "freedom," visibility in one or more of secularism's occluded registers comes at the expense of justice in the others. These are the terms of the secularist-gendering-racializing knot. Nothing in the contemporary discourse of secularism as the dawning of religious option, the possibility of being religious or not as the condition of our secular present, permits us to cut through it.

This volume's editors call boldly on the disruptive potential of the theological to open a way of imagining otherwise. Vincent Lloyd reminds us that "the exclusion or management of religion prompts us to remember the potency of what is excluded or managed." Theology, Lloyd urges, might yet speak as that potent, unmanaged religious. Jonathon Kahn calls in particular for a theology amounting to "a rollicking and plangent discourse of impurity" to counter secularism's clean lines that delimit and sequester, conferring and withholding the "status of the real." But impurity, like purity, is something of a shell game: we do well to recall that the manifest blurring of Christian and secular powers in the West, now a fashionable object of academic theorizing, is rather more blandly assumed in triumphal narratives like Bernard Lewis's "The Roots of Muslim Rage," which coined the term "clash of civilizations" as "that perhaps irrational but surely historic reaction of an ancient rival against our Judeo-Christian heritage, our secular present, and the world-wide expansion of both."[21]

Ayaan Hirsi Ali's third book, *Nomad: Islam to America* (2010), is subtitled *A Personal Journey Through the Clash of Civilizations.* It was less widely praised than its predecessors, perhaps for its transparency to the policy aims of her supporters on the right. In the spring of 2014, Brandeis University publicly rescinded its earlier offer of an honorary degree to Hirsi Ali in view of "certain of her past statements that are inconsistent with Brandeis University's core values."[22] The decision followed a letter signed by eighty-three Brandeis faculty who praised Hirsi Ali's commitment to ending violence against women but who condemned "her virulently anti-Muslim public statements" and "triumphalist narrative of western civilization, rooted in a core belief of the cultural backwardness of non-western peoples."[23] The debate played out in the blogosphere and mainstream media largely as a referendum on Islam, with Hirsi Ali and her defenders faulted for overlooking crucial differences between Muslim extremists and more palatable moderates, and Brandeis criticized for its unwillingness to confront hard truths about Islam. Some outraged by the Brandeis decision condemned it as racist and sexist and wondered, plausibly, whether a Sam Harris or Richard Dawkins would have fared differently. What went missing in the uproar was any critique of secularism as a remedy for inequality: namely, a recognition that secularism has not brought freedom and justice for women or racial minorities and cannot uproot "the triumphalist narrative of western civilization" that structures inequalities in the United States and abroad.[24]

The "'impurity' of black theology," writes Jonathon Kahn, "is in its clarity about the ways in which shards of the theological spin their way into political consciousness and material form." The worldwide expansion of a Christian/secular present, posited as given or imperative, is one way the theopolitical spins. But "impurity" resides also in the impossibility of knowing in advance what political forms the shards of the theological might take. To consider the secularist-gendering-racializing knot in the context of that impurity, to "stare blankly," as Vincent Lloyd enjoins, at what now seems most intractable or illegible in the "networks of ideas, practices, and relationships" that constitute our secular present might yet point to "something powerful, something potentially transformative" in that present—a something, let us hope, that sustains the practice of freedom and dignity under conditions of secularism and not simply their much-touted promise.

## NOTES

1. Ayaan Hirsi Ali, interviewed by Patt Morrison, "Feminism's Freedom Fighter," *Los Angeles Times* (October 19, 2009), http://articles.latimes.com/2009/oct/17/opinion/oe-morrison17.
2. Webb Keane, "Christian Moderns," *Immanent Frame* (November 11, 2009), http://blogs .ssrc.org/tif/2009/11/19/christian-moderns/; Webb Keane, "What Is Religious Freedom Supposed to Free?" *Immanent Frame* (April 3, 2012) http://blogs.ssrc.org/tif/2012/04/03 /what-is-religious-freedom-supposed-to-free/. See also Webb Keane, *Christian Moderns: Freedom and Fetish in the Mission Encounter* (Berkeley: University of California Press, 2007).
3. A growing list of exceptions to this record of neglect includes Judith Butler, "Sexual Politics, Torture, and Secular Time," *British Journal of Sociology* 59, no. 1 (2008): 1–23; Janet R. Jakobsen and Ann Pellegrini, *Love the Sin: Sexual Regulation and the Limits of Toleration* (New York: New York University Press, 2003); Saba Mahmood, *The Politics of Piety: The Islamic Revival and the Feminist Subject* (Princeton, N.J.: Princeton University Press, 2005); and Joan Scott, *The Politics of the Veil* (Princeton, N.J.: Princeton University Press, 2007). See also Linell E. Cady and Tracy Fessenden, eds., *Religion, the Secular, and the Politics of Sexual Difference* (New York: Columbia University Press, 2013).
4. Thomas Jefferson, *Notes on the State of Virginia*, Query 17, 157–161 (1784), in *The Founders Constitution*, Web ed., ed. Philip B. Kurland and Ralph Lerner, http://press-pubs.uchicago .edu/founders/print_documents/amendI_religions40.html.
5. Gauri Viswanathan, *Outside the Fold: Conversion, Modernity, and Belief* (Princeton, N.J.: Princeton University Press, 1998), 16.
6. Tomoko Masuzawa, *The Invention of World Religions* (Chicago: University of Chicago Press, 2005), 19.
7. Aída Hurtado, "Relating to Privilege: Seduction and Rejection in the Subordination of White Women and Women of Color," *Signs* 14, no. 4 (1989): 849.
8. Mark Lilla, *The Stillborn God: Religion, Politics, and the Modern West* (New York: Knopf, 2007), 3–13.
9. Saba Mahmood, "Sexuality and Secularism," in *Religion, the Secular, and the Politics of Sexual Difference*, ed. Linell E. Cady and Tracy Fessenden (New York: Columbia University Press, 2013), 54.

10. Azza Karam, "Must It Be Either Secular or Religious? Reflections on the Contemporary Journeys of Women's Rights Activists in Egypt," in *Religion, the Secular, and the Politics of Sexual Difference*, ed. Linell E. Cady and Tracy Fessenden (New York: Columbia University Press, 2013), 60.

11. Butler, "Sexual Politics, Torture, and Secular Time," 14.

12. Catharine E. Beecher, *A Treatise on Domestic Economy* (Boston: Marsh, Capen, Lyon, and Webb, 1841), 12. The antebellum literature of domesticity is vast; I focus on Stowe's and Beecher's contributions to underscore its centrality to American religion and culture.

13. Catharine E. Beecher and Harriet Beecher Stowe, *The American Woman's Home*, ed. Nicole Tonkovich (1869; Piscataway, N.J.: Rutgers University Press, 2002), 15.

14. Harriet Beecher Stowe, *House and Home Papers* (Boston: Ticknor and Fields, 1865), 99.

15. Amy Kaplan, "Manifest Domesticity," *American Literature* 70, no. 3 (September 1998): 582.

16. Beecher and Stowe, *American Woman's Home*, 337. Despite Stowe's occasional nods to the piety of Irish Catholic servants, "Christian" in her writings and the writings of her Beecher family stands implicitly for varieties of New England Protestantism. For a fuller discussion, see my "From Romanism to Race: Anglo-American Liberties in *Uncle Tom's Cabin*," *Prospects* 25 (2000): 229–268.

17. Winnifred Fallers Sullivan, *The Impossibility of Religious Freedom* (Princeton, N.J.: Princeton University Press, 2005), 154.

18. For a fuller discussion, see my "Disappearances: Race, Religion, and the Progress Narrative of U.S. Feminism," in *Secularisms*, ed. Janet R. Jakobsen and Ann Pellegrini (Durham, N.C.: Duke University Press, 2008), 139–161.

19. See, in addition to Hirsi Ali's oeuvre, Susan Moller Okin, *Is Multiculturalism Bad for Women?*, ed. Joshua Cohen, Matthew Howard, and Martha C. Nussbaum (Princeton, N.J.: Princeton University Press, 1999); Ronald Inglehart and Pippa Norris, "The True Clash of Civilizations," *Foreign Policy*, no. 135 (March–April 2003): 62–70.

20. Mahmood, "Sexuality and Secularism," 51–53.

21. Bernard Lewis, "The Roots of Muslim Rage," *The Atlantic* (September 1, 1990), http://www.theatlantic.com/magazine/archive/1990/09/the-roots-of-muslim-rage/304643/.

22. Statement from Brandeis University (April 8, 2014), http://www.brandeis.edu/now/2014/april/commencementupdate.html.

23. "To President Lawrence Concerning Hirsi Ali" (April 6, 2014), https://docs.google.com/document/d/1MoAvrWuc3VonMFqRDRTkLGpAN7leSZfxo3y1msEyEJM/edit.

24. The 2013 recipient of the Prix de Simone de Beauvoir, awarded to Hirsi Ali in 2008, was the teenaged Malala Yousafzai, who subsequently won the Nobel Peace Prize for her advocacy for Muslim women and girls. Yousafzai makes an interesting counterpoint to Hirsi Ali: her own, amply arresting personal narrative is not a story of renouncing Islam but rather of finding resources for change within religious community, theology, and practice.

# CONTRIBUTORS

**JOEL BLECHER** is assistant professor of religion at Washington and Lee University. His research explores the intersection of exegesis and sociocultural history in medieval and modern Islamic contexts. He has published on the interpretation of prophetic traditions (*hadith*) in medieval Cairo.

**EDWARD J. BLUM** is professor of history at San Diego State University. He is the coauthor of *The Color of Christ: The Son of God and the Saga of Race in America* and the author of *W. E. B. Du Bois: American Prophet*. He coedited *The Columbia Guide to Religion in American History*.

**JOSHUA DUBLER** is assistant professor of religion at the University of Rochester. He is the author of *Down in the Chapel: Religious Life in an American Prison*. His research focuses on Muslims and Christians in prison using ethnographic and cultural studies methods.

**ERICA R. EDWARDS** is associate professor of English at the University of California, Riverside. She is the author of *Charisma and the Fictions of Black Leadership*. Her specializations are African American literature, gender and sexuality, and black political culture.

**TRACY FESSENDEN** is professor of religious studies at Arizona State University. She is the author of *Culture and Redemption: Religion, the Secular, and American Literature* and the coeditor of *Religion, the Secular, and the Politics of Sexual Difference*.

**M. COOPER HARRISS** is assistant professor of religious studies at Indiana University. He is the author of *Things Not Seen: Race, Religion, and Ralph Ellison's Invisible Theology*. His research centers on intersections of American and African American religion, literature, and culture.

**WILLIAM D. HART** is Margaret W. Harmon Professor of Religious Studies at the University of North Carolina, Greensboro. His publications include *Afro-Eccentricity: Beyond the Standard Narrative of Black Religion* and *Black Religion: Malcolm X, Julius Lester, and Jan Willis*.

**WILLIE JAMES JENNINGS** is associate professor of theology and black church studies at Duke Divinity School. He is the author of *The Christian Imagination: Theology and the Origins of Race*. His research explores the intersection of cultural studies, systematic theology, and black religion.

**JONATHON KAHN** is associate professor of religion at Vassar College. He is the author of *Divine Discontent: The Religious Imagination of W. E. B. Du Bois*. His research focuses on philosophy of religion, race, and American pragmatism.

**VINCENT LLOYD** is assistant professor of religion at Syracuse University. His publications include *The Problem with Grace: Reconfiguring Political Theology* and an edited collection, *Race and Political Theology*. He edits the journal *Political Theology*.

**GEORGE SHULMAN** is a professor at New York University's Gallatin School of Individualized Study, where he studies political thought and American studies. He is the author, most recently, of *American Prophecy: Race and Redemption in American Political Culture*.

**JOSEF SORETT** is assistant professor of religion and African American studies at Columbia University. He is the author of the forthcoming book *Spirit in the Dark: A Religious History of Racial Aesthetics*, and he is editing *The Sexual Politics of Black Churches*.

# INDEX

AAR. *See* American Academy of Religion

activism: civil rights, 13; Islamist political, 130; post-9/11, 257; role of everyday, 106. *See also* black religion

Adib, Dawud, 125–28

African Americans: as racialized subjects, 240, 259; incapable of salvation, 53; inclusion in the military, 9; religious communities, 10, 244–45; religious worldview of, 61; thought, 16; tropes of, 199

Africana religion, 179; tropes of, 179; as primitive, 180

Albani, Nasir al-Din al-, 130

Ali, Ayaan Hirsi, 257, 268

American Academy of Religion, 44

American studies, as a discipline, 8

American Tract Society, 81, 84

Arrested Development (band), 106–7

antisecularism, 12–13; and blackness, 52

antislavery activists, 84; deployment of the visual, 84–85

Arendt, Hannah, 27, 32, 35

Asad, Talal, 24, 241

ATS. *See* American Tract Society

Baldwin, James, 18, 29, 32–33, 40, 135, 142, 239, 247, 249, 251, 253

belonging: Baldwin's notions of, 250- 252; ethics of, 239, 248, 250; and religion 248, 250

Black Church, 45; centrality of, 65. *See also* liberalism

black critics, 30; of white supremacy, 31–32

black insurgency, 16; and black agency, 38; and prophecy, 32; and the political, 28; as political theology, 25, 33

Black Methodists, 82

black nationalists, 11, 61, 127, 137, 144

black noise, 37–38

black popular culture: and charisma, 104; and patriarchy, 113; and religiosity, 34; and the past, 103; as criteria grammar, 35; Martin Luther King Jr. and, 104

black religion: and activism, 100; and Christianity, 45–46, 248–49, 251; and entanglement, 63; and flesh 250–52; and homophobia, 62; and theories of secularization, 44. 244–45; and secular modern, 246; and thought, 100; as bad religion, 50; as New World formation, 251;